Michael Riedel

Poster–Painting–Presentation

Michael Riedel
Poster—Painting—Presentation

David Zwirner Books

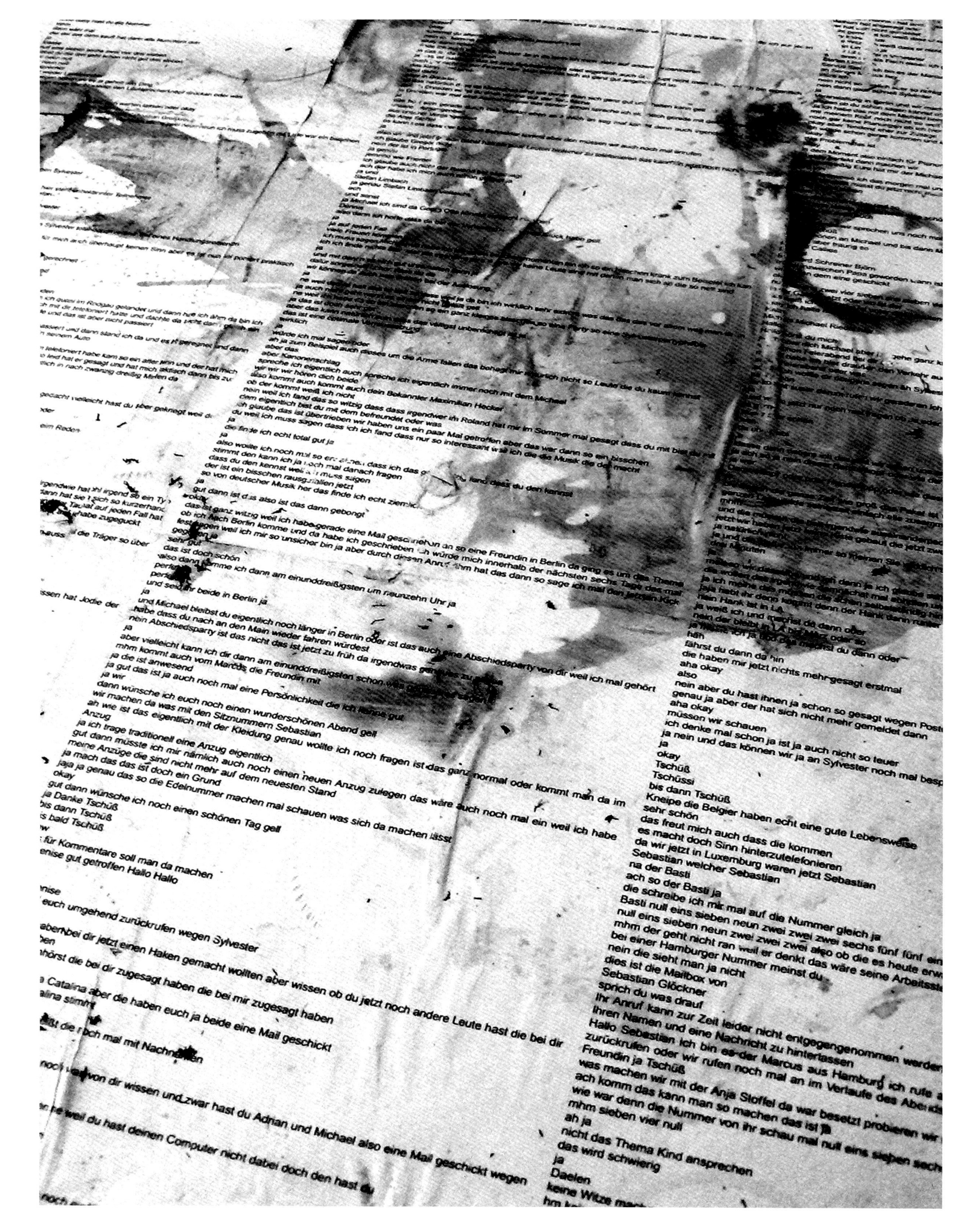

und seid ihr beide in Berlin ja
ja
und Michael bleibst du eigentlich noch länger in Berlin oder ist das auch eine Abschiedsparty von dir weil ich mal gehört
habe dass du nach an den Main wieder fahren würdest
nein Abschiedsparty ist das nicht das ist jetzt zu früh da irgendwas
ja
aber vielleicht kann ich dir dann am einunddreißigsten schon
mhm kommt auch vom Marcus die Freundin mit
ja die ist anwesend
ja gut das ist ja auch noch mal eine Persönlichkeit die ich kenne gut
ja wir
dann wünsche ich euch noch einen wunderschönen Abend gell
wir machen da was mit den Sitznummern Sebastian
ah wie ist das eigentlich mit der Kleidung genau wollte ich noch fragen ist das ganz normal oder kommt man da im
Anzug
ja ich trage traditionell eine Anzug eigentlich
gut dann müsste ich mir nämlich auch noch einen neuen Anzug zulegen das wäre auch noch mal ein weil ich habe
meine Anzüge die sind nicht mehr auf dem neuesten Stand
ja mach das das ist doch ein Grund
jaja ja genau das so die Edelnummer machen mal schauen was sich da machen lässt
okay
gut dann wünsche ich noch einen schönen Tag gell
ja Danke Tschüß
bis dann Tschüß
bis bald Tschüß
für Kommentare soll man da machen
euch umgehend zurückrufen wegen Sylvester
hörst die bei dir zugesagt haben die bei mir zugesagt haben
fährst du dann da hin
die haben mir jetzt nichts mehr gesagt erstmal
aha okay
also
nein aber du hast ihnen ja schon so gesagt wegen
genau ja aber der hat sich nicht mehr gemeldet dann
aha okay
müssen wir schauen
ich denke mal schon ja ist ja auch nicht so teuer
ja nein und das können wir ja an Sylvester noch mal
ja
okay
Tschüß
Tschüssi
bis dann Tschüß
Kneipe die Belgier haben echt eine gute
sehr schön
das freut mich auch dass die kommen
es macht doch Sinn hinterzutelefonieren
da wir jetzt in Luxemburg waren jetzt Sebastian
Sebastian welcher Sebastian
na der Basti
ach so der Basti ja
die schreibe ich mir mal auf die Nummer gleich ja
Basti null eins sieben neun zwei zwei zwei sechs fünf
null eins sieben neun zwei zwei zwei also ob die es heute
mhm der geht nicht ran weil er denkt das wäre seine
bei einer Hamburger Nummer meinst du
nein die sieht man ja nicht
dies ist die Mailbox von
Sebastian Glöckner
sprich du was drauf
Ihr Anruf kann zur Zeit leider nicht entgegengenommen
Ihren Namen und eine Nachricht zu hinterlassen
Hallo Sebastian ich bin es der Marcus aus Hamburg ich rufe
zurückrufen oder wir rufen noch mal an im Verlaufe des
Freundin ja Tschüß
was machen wir mit der Anja Stoffel da war besetzt probieren wir
ach komm das kann man so machen das ist ja
wie war denn die Nummer von ihr schau mal null eins sieben
mhm sieben vier null
ah ja
nicht das Thema Kind ansprechen
das wird schwierig
ja
Daelen

Fade Through Black

by TINA KUKIELSKI

Poster

Every month for the last several months, a big cardboard box of books arrives at my Manhattan apartment. With each delivery, I puncture the corners of the neatly wrapped package with my X-Acto knife, but recently, when unloading the contents onto my shrinking desk, I get déjà vu. I think, I *already* have this book. My mind immediately rushes to the urgent question: Where can I put it? My bookshelves are full. I get annoyed and drop the book on the stack of its copies. I ask myself: is this a trick?

Each book cover is marked with black text on a white field, and most measure at a size of 10 1/2 x 10 1/2 inches (26.7 x 26.7 cm)—what I promptly recognize as the trim size of *Artforum* magazine. From there, traits diverge: some have barcodes, some do not, some carry fragments of coding, some have geometric or graphical markings, and one has the only sign of an "image" on its cover, an especially famous self-portrait of Andy Warhol that last sold at auction for $17 million. When I turn over this particularly hefty book, I notice the jacket is a facsimile of yet *another* undoubtedly slimmer and trimmer book whose blurb indicates it's a biography of Warhol classified as "fiction" and issued in a new, updated edition. This is representation of representation of representation, or representation twice removed. Without even opening the book I already count three authors: Warhol, his contested biographer Victor Bockris, and then across the spine, cover, and flap, it reads Oskar-von-Miller Strasse 16. The Warhol cover was used, it turns out, because the book *a: A Novel* made it easy to write "Osk(a)r" around the original letter "a."

The books are the result of an ongoing exchange between me and the artist Michael Riedel, initiated by a loyal and steadfast group of supporters at David Zwirner. A few months before they began arriving, I borrowed a painting by Riedel for a group exhibition about information processing I had curated a few blocks away from the Zwirner gallery's expanding environs in Chelsea. When I first met Michael at lunch over Thai food more recently, we fumbled through a conversation about cybernetics vis-à-vis the theories of Niklas Luhmann. Luhmann was a German sociologist who believed society could be described best as a series of communication systems. According to Luhmann, social systems are in fact communication systems demonstrated most notably in the accepted set of rules by which society agrees to play. Explaining Luhmann's theories in his own terms, Riedel tells me, over a thin ceramic bowl brimming with vermicelli noodles, that "each system needs a good container."

Riedel began discovering and shaping the contours of this container in the 2000s when he collaborated with some friends and fellow artists on an art space in an abandoned apartment building at Oskar-von-Miller Strasse 16 in Frankfurt. His practice of self-perpetuating processes began at that now legendary location, where he and his small group of artist-friends would mount exhibitions and one-night-only events that were often replicas of what was happening elsewhere in Frankfurt. Oskar operated as a "gigantic replication device" and reiterated the language of Frankfurt's cultural offerings, often without a full understanding of what was being repeated, but always with an acute aesthetic interest in the mistakes made during transmission and transference. The arbitrariness of determining which event to mimic, and the relative marginality of these events in the broad system of art, were key. The people (all handsome and mostly young), the barely decipherable activity or event, the free booze, and the good times were documented almost obsessively, first with photographs and then frequently with voice recordings. The Oskar days launched Riedel's earliest explorations into errors of reproduction and transmission—and the resulting differences between original and copy—as the most essential means for art's production.

Moreover, documentation of these events became the raw material that fueled Riedel's ongoing interest in poster design—an undercurrent of this book and his work in general. As one of the most simple, agreed-upon containers for information in the art world, the poster was an easy vehicle for reaching more people than could possibly have visited the show. The posters from those early days were sometimes—like the events themselves—facsimiles of other advertisements professionally designed to announce the event that the Oskar crew decided to record and play back. Its copy would subtly, amateurishly, and awkwardly change, but as the documentation and the number of Oskar events and author-contributors grew, the original source dislodged from its now hard-to-trace iterative copy. In these posters—part copy, part documentation, part artwork—black-and-white imagery elides with text, cut and pasted as a sea of rectangular icons. In the catalogue *Kunste zur Text* (which translates as Art on Writing, a riff on the German art magazine *Texte zur Kunst*, or Writing on Art), produced for Schirn Kunsthalle Frankfurt in 2012, the index of Riedel's poster designs can be perplexing: one can never be quite certain where one poster ends and the other picks up again. Although, the posters themselves serve as a kind of index, the closest comprehensible record of what may (or may not) have occurred at Oskar. Yet, the constant self-referentiality functions more like a mise en abyme, eroding at any use value to the point of effacement. On the one hand, you had to be there. On the other hand, the strategies for mass dissemination taking place after the fact were as much part of the art experience.

Painting

In the years following the closing of Oskar, Riedel continued to design posters and announcement cards for his various exhibitions around Germany and abroad. In 2009, in preparation for a presentation of his books in an exhibition of his work at Kunstverein Hamburg the following year, Riedel made a poster that became the conceptual foundation of what are presently called the *Poster Paintings*. The crackling, fragmented, and diminutive text running like broken code across the poster page resembles ASCII art (American Standard Code for International Information), subject to some glitch in its printing. Except unlike ASCII, the text does not build into any comprehensible image as it rhythmically dances across the page justified left and right. This is not design alone; rather, Riedel's work is built on information—fractured, yet still legible.

The dominant characteristics of Riedel's designs for his *Poster Paintings* emerge here. At first glance, the text appears to be a stand-in for a symbolic or graphical system, yet the wording is always carefully selected for its content. With few exceptions, the extracts derive from websites that carry information on Riedel and his work—sometimes original criticism and sometimes simple, banal exhibition listings or announcements. Around 2009 was the first time Riedel copied a complete website into one of his posters. The text became the foundation of his posters, with words highlighted throughout. Riedel's design strategies were already led by a cut-and-paste aesthetic inclined to build content like an algorithmic machine; in this way, he found a better way to accumulate material exponentially and so began to feed more directly from information available for free on the Internet. As the Internet developed, more and more material could be sourced from the web via Riedel's select all>copy>open new file>paste>print strategies. New paintings provoked new reviews and announcements online, creating material that could be used by Riedel for future *Poster Paintings* in a kind of infinite feedback loop. Using web-based content was easier and faster than scanning recordings, uploading photographs, or processing and hoarding other kinds of data to be used in later productions. In the thirty-four finished posters, Riedel employs the most digital, most primal of modern sources: HTML code.

Riedel's HTML posters swap in to become the palette for his paintings; thirty-four different designs offer the raw material for the many compositional possibilities or combinations of the paintings. But importantly, the number is not infinite: the thirty-four posters, which can be arranged in any orientation, set the limit for the number of possible recombinations. The canvas thus becomes the container for the system that generates Riedel's paintings. In 2010, when Riedel first made a group of paintings from the posters for an exhibition whose title was also an English-language pangram *The quick brown fox jumps over the lazy dog* at Kunstverein Hamburg, he used real posters wheat-pasted onto canvas. Riedel brushed the paste onto the canvas, gluing the posters into place by literally painting them on, a subversive nod to the status of the works as paintings. A year later at David Zwirner in New York, Riedel exhibited another show of *Poster Paintings* but made the paintings more permanent by silkscreen printing them onto canvas, which is how they typically continue to be produced.

Concurrently, Riedel arrived at an iconographic antidote to the appropriated sea of code he was amassing. It was a single symbol that captured the density, the capacity, and at the same time approximated what we might call the "digital drag" existent in a copious and information-rich place like the World Wide Web: the color wheel. The circle persists throughout the *Poster Paintings* series as a sly reference to the rotating pinwheel familiar to any Apple user awaiting processing completion, otherwise affectionately known as "the spinning wheel of death." It recurs in many forms, configurations, and colors in Riedel's paintings, formed by an arrangement of posters, each of which contains part of the circle. The wheel-as-image functions as a distinct design layer in Riedel's work, attracting the eye with the sensorial charge of its pie-chart colors. As a signal of information overload, it is also the rhythmic punctum or heartbeat in Riedel's installations where the paintings line one to the next, telling a story of our times akin to that in a classical frieze.

In reference to a developing and evolving system of production, Riedel also inserts symbols of analog text production into his exhibitions. For instance, one painting called *Untitled (Correctable film ribbon for AX10/20/30)* is a digital print of an image in negative of a sinewy typewriter spool laid out on a scanner bed. Resembling a brushstroke, this piece of analog text production—the typewriter ribbon—signals an immediate visual link between language and painting. What defines the *Poster Paintings* is the tendency to put a great deal of information into a small format, not unlike the way text production manifests in books or other printed material.

Mass production provides Riedel his guide, and yet content is still chosen. He doesn't pick at random—he chooses *which* websites to copy—even if the portion that makes it into a poster, and thus a painting, is randomly copied. Another of Riedel's artistic choices is his controlled design strategy: the zeroing in on and choosing a single vocabulary word that is then highlighted in larger text wherever it appears across the page. Examples include: method, slideshow, return, print, scroll, link, type, width, update, form, drop, display, alt, background, click, doubleclick, poster, color, visible, clear. The word refers to aspects of the poster's default technological production—the moments that make the technical process transparent.

Presentation

Alongside his interest in dominant distribution channels such as the web, Riedel began to look to other default information processors. One especially prevalent tool that Riedel, and artists like him, employs is Microsoft PowerPoint. In participating in the systems of art and thereby performing public lectures on his work, Riedel began to play with the transition effects available in PowerPoint display toolbox (an earlier version of the program was called Presenter, reflecting the work as something new to be presented and creating another ongoing system of production through presentation). As images of his work moved from one slide to the next, a different transition effect was applied to the presentation. Stopping or freezing on the movement midstream became another way to marvel at the errors in transmission, the skips and hiccups that playback caused, drawing attention to the gaps between two existing works, which, in turn, produced new gaps. From there a whole new group of paintings emerged, referred to as *PowerPoint Paintings*—screenshots of transitions taking place, with a similarly enormous number of possible outcomes, each built on a different default transition: Checkerboard, Checkerboard Across, Cover Left-Down, Cover Left-Up, Box In, Box Out, Cut Through Black, Strips Left-Down, Strips Left-Up, Uncover Up, Uncover Down, and my personal favorite, Fade Through Black.

Riedel had previously been interested in other automated software programs such as speech recognition software and had regurgitated a vast amount of transcribed data from one such program into many bodies of work. Yet to think that the work exists as a simple manifestation of the mystery of automated technological tools would be missing the point. Riedel's art is designed as an autopoietic system, a system that harks back to Luhmann's beliefs about communication systems. An autopoietic system is one that reproduces itself through its connections to the various component parts of the environment in which it operates. In Riedel's case this means art's relationship to the art world: its publicity, its audiences, its collectors, its gallerists, its curators, its criticism, and its market. An autopoietic system is autonomous and as Riedel prefers it, operationally closed. Within that system, there are sufficient continuous processes, or processes that can be set in motion, to maintain the whole. It is these processes that shape and define Riedel's container, and one of the challenges of writing about his work is that the feedback systems cannot be separated from the forces that manipulate them. Riedel's art is based in text and its production, not its reading and interpretation. And despite my best assumption that the system must and will collapse, it self-perpetuates. At an artist talk at The Kitchen in New York, Riedel recently stated: "In this case I am overwriting myself. In other words, I'm not just the artist making art but also the artist watching himself making art and perceiving this process as art. This also shifts the position of the viewer, who watches the artist watching himself making art."

This is Michael Riedel's eighty-third book, each one overwriting the last with a new set of information. Yet knowing now what we know about Riedel's approach, the books—like the posters—might be better seen as sketchbooks rather than real books. They carry information but never close off as a set. This book, like his other books—and for that matter most of his other work—seeks to double the real space of the exhibition at the same time that it doubles the information level of the real space. Riedel sounds tautological when he says it this way at the beginning of his book *Oskar*: "We're talking about a space full of possibilities, though none of the possibilities are as interesting as the space itself, which contains these possibilities." Yet what he is getting at is the question of how work is presented, itself a means for dissemination and consumption as powerful as the poster. Riedel believes there is an ideal cycle of time between one gallery exhibition and the next, or one book project and the next: two years. Why? Because the characteristics of modern communication systems deal not only in what is generated, but equally so in what is lost due to transferences, compressions, and the occasional system failure. The mind is not that different; memory fades and our thoughts move onto other subjects. Riedel's container signals the effects of data overload as much as it attaches to the loss of that data throughout the process. The experience is like that feeling of déjà vu, both euphoric and confounding.

Poster

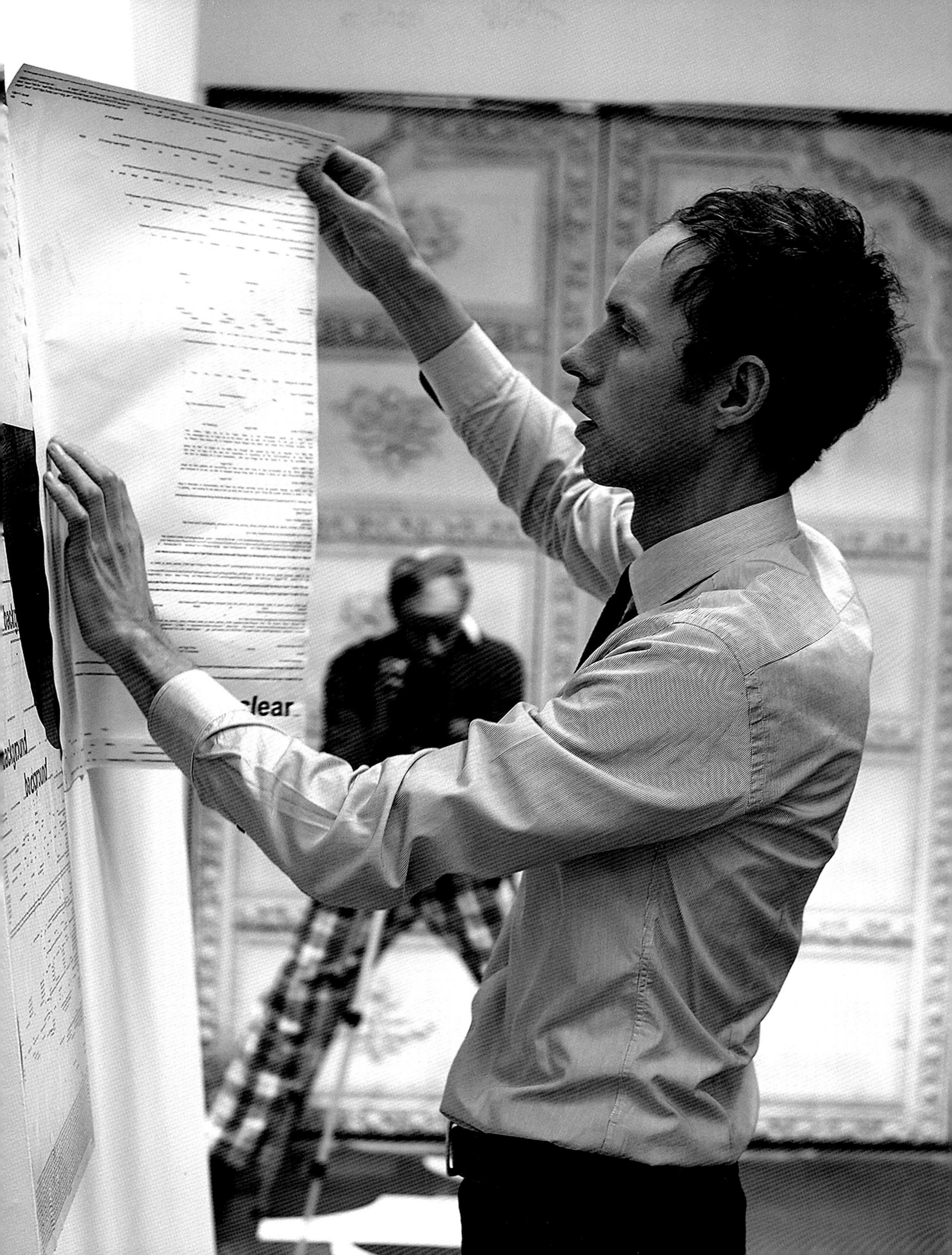
clear

http://www.artfacts.net/index.php/pageType/artistInfo/artist/38183/lang/1/

```
<!DOCTYPE HTML PUBLIC "-//W3C//DTD HTML 4.01 Transitional//EN">
< h t m l >
< h e a d >
<title>Michael Riedel - Biography</title>
<meta http-equiv="content-type" content="text/html; charset=iso-8859-1" >
name="author" content="Artfacts.Net Ltd. , London" >
name="publisher" content="Artfacts.Net Ltd. , London" >
name="copyright" content="Artfacts.Net Ltd. , London" >
name="verify-v1" content="JlpOm6dG2DGYonXMvgjbgqdMNSx38Yb+GF/bMGSQ4a8=" >
type="application/rss+xml" title="Artfacts.Net - News" href="http://feeds.feedburner.com/ArtFactsNetNews" >
type="application/rss+xml" title="Artfacts.Net - Exhibitions" href="http://feeds.feedburner.com/ArtFactsNetExhibitions" >
content="Michael Riedel - Biography" >
Biography, Artworks, Artist Ranking, Public exhibitions, Solo shows, Group shows, Dealer Directory, Public collections, Catalogs, Auction results" >
http-equiv="language" content="en" >
http-equiv="content-language" content="en" >
name="language" content="en" >
="audience" content="all" >
ts" content="index,follow" >
type="text/css" href="/parts/tabs.css" media="screen" >
text/css" href="/afn_elements/css/afn_styles.css" media="screen" >
IE]>
href="/afn_elements/css/afn_styles_ie.css" media="screen" >
d i f ] - - >
type="text/javascript">
muestratab1() {
= ‚visible';
= ‚hidden';
= ‚hidden';
muestratab2() {
= ‚hidden';
= ‚visible';
= ‚hidden';
uestratab3() {
= ‚hidden';
= ‚hidden';
= ‚visible';
src='http://partner.googleadservices.com/gampad/google_service.js'></script>
type="text/javascript">
e ( ‚ c a - p u b - 2 0 3 4 4 7 0 2 4 6 3 9 3 7 6 0 ' ) ;
e A l l S e r v i c e s ( ) ;
r i p t >
type="text/javascript">
‚AFN_Side_Block_01_Banner_01');
‚AFN_Side_Block_01_Banner_02');
‚AFN_Side_Block_01_Banner_03');
‚AFN_Side_Block_01_Banner_04');
‚AFN_Side_Block_02_Banner_01');
‚AFN_Side_Block_02_Banner_02');
‚AFN_Side_Block_02_Banner_03');
‚AFN_Side_Block_02_Banner_04');
‚AFN_Side_Block_03_Banner_01');
‚AFN_Side_Block_03_Banner_02');
‚AFN_Side_Block_03_Banner_03');
‚AFN_Side_Block_03_Banner_04');
‚AFN_Side_Medium_Block_01');
‚AFN_Side_Medium_Block_02');
i p t >
type='text/javascript'>
t c h A d s ( ) ;
i p t >
src="/afn_elements/js/prototype.js"></script>
src="/afn_elements/js/scriptaculous.js?load=effects,builder"></script>
src="/afn_elements/lightbox/js/afn_lightbox.js"></script>
= 1;
= ‚Artwork';
i p t >
type="text/css" media="screen" >
IE]>
/css/afn_lightbox_ie.css" media="screen" >
f ] - - >
type="image/x-icon" >
type="image/x-icon" >
src="/afn_elements/js/afn_scripts_for_parts_wwwroot.js"></script></head>
id="afn_sitewrapper">
id="afn_content">
id="afn_head">
id="afn_logo">
```

rm

```
ation for your benefit. We love Art." width="260" height="75"></a>
i v >
id="afn_langlogin">
login selector start</span></div>
id="afn_langlogin_center">
id="afn_language">
id="afn_langselect">
class="aural">Language</dt>
href="/index.php/pageType/artistInfo/artist/38183/lang/2/">Deutsch</a></dd>
class="active"><span>English</span></dd>
href="/index.php/pageType/artistInfo/artist/38183/lang/3/">Espa&ntilde;ol</a></dd>
href="/index.php/pageType/artistInfo/artist/38183/lang/6/">Italiano</a></dd>
d l >
i v >
id="afn_login">
id="afn_member_links">
e s t < / d t >
more</a></dd>
href="https://www.artfacts.net/index.php/pageType/login/proc_rqst/login/lang/1">Login</a></dd>
d l >
i v >
i v >
and login selector end</span></div>
i v >
id="afn_shortlinks">
id="afn_aboutlinks">
s="aural">Artfacts Shortlinks:</dt>
s_new/?Company,Introduction">About us</a></dd>
href="/marketing_new/?Services,Membership">Products/Services</a></dd>
href="/newsletteren">Newsletter</a></dd> -->
href="/about_us_new/?Contact">Contact</a></dd>
d l >
i v >
id="afn_mainlinkbar">
id="afn_mainlinks">
Main Links:</dt>
ndex.html">Exhibitions</a></dd><dd><a href="/en/institutions/index.html">Institutions</a></dd> < / d l >
="afn_search" name="mainsearch" action="/index.php" method="post">
type="hidden" name="pageType" value="search">
type="hidden" name="lang" value="1">
e l d > < / l s e g e n d >
class="aural" for="searchkeyword">Search</label>
="searchkeyword" type="text" name="search" value="Search" title="Please enter search keyword" onfocus="if (this.value == ‚Search') this.value=''" onblur="if (this.value == ‚') this.value='Search'">
for="sarea"><img src="/afn_elements/css/images/afn_arrowlink.png" alt="Search"></label>
id="sarea" name="sarea" class="searcharea" size="1">
value="a" selected="selected">Artists</option>
value="e">Exhibitions</option>
tion value="i">Institutions</option>
<option value="n">News</option>
/ s e l e c t >
<input class="searchbutton" type="submit" name="searchsubmit" value="Search">
< / f i e l d s e t >
```

f o r m

```
< / >
< / d i v >
```

input

http://frieze-magazin.de/archiv/features/digital-dandy/?lang=en
(Accessed December 3, 2015)

```
<input value="Search" type="submit">
          </div>
        </fieldset>
      </form>
    </div>

  </div> <!-- // #header -->

  <ul class="nav_h" id="navigation_pri">
    <li>
      <a href="/">Home</a>
    </li>
    <li>
      <a href="/aktuelle-ausgabe/">Current issue</a>
    </li>
    <li class="cur">
      <a href="/archiv/">Archive</a>
    </li>
    <li>
      <a href="http://blog.frieze-magazin.de">Blog</a>
    </li>
    <li>
      <a href="/abonnieren/">Subscribe</a>
    </li>
  </ul> <!-- // #navigation_pri -->

  <ul class="nav_h" id="navigation_pri_sub">
    <li>
      <a href="/uber/">About</a>
    </li>
    <li>
      <a href="/kontakt/">Contact</a>
    </li>
    <li>
      <a href="/anzeigen/">Advertise</a>
    </li>
    <li>
      <a href="http://www.frieze.com/classifieds/">Bulletin</a>
    </li>
  </ul> <!-- // #navigation_pri_sub -->

  <ul class="nav_h" id="navigation_pri_account">
    <li>
      <a href="/shop/basket/">Basket (0)</a>
    </li>
    <li>
      <a href="/shop/help/">Shop help</a>
    </li>
        <li>
      <a href="/account/register/">Register</a>
    </li>
    <li class="login">
      <a href="/account/login/">Login</a>
      <div id="quick_login">
        <div id="quick_login_inner">
          <form name="login_form" method="post" action="http://frieze-magazin.de/">
<div class="hiddenFields">
<input name="XID" value="a61fdeac529cf68a73f01f0cabc0aaf3b4ce4382" type="hidden">
<input name="ACT" value="55" type="hidden">
<input name="RET" value="/archiv/features/digital-dandy/" type="hidden">
<input name="site_id" value="1" type="hidden">
</div>

              <div>
                <label for="login_email">Your email</label>
```

Untitled (form), 2011
Offset print
23 x 16 1/2 inches
(58.4 x 41.9 cm)

```
        <input id="login_email" name="username" size="30" type="text">
      </div>
      <div>
        <label for="login_password">Your password</label>
        <input id="login_password" name="password" size="30" type="password">
        <p class="helper"><a href="/account/forgotten-password/">Forgotten your password?</a></p>
      </div>
      <div class="submit">
        <input name="auto_login" value="1" type="hidden">
        <input value="Login" type="submit">
      </div>
    </form>
  </div><!-- //#quick_login_inner -->
 </div><!-- //#quick_login -->
</li>

</ul> <!-- // #navigation_pri_account -->

<div id="content_wrapper">

 <div id="content_pri">

  <div class="content_pri_sub1a">

   <div class="header">
    <h1>Digital Dandy</h1>
    <h4 class="alt">Essay</h4>
   </div><!-- //.header -->

   <div class="article">

    <p class="standfirst">Michael Riedel records, copies and repeats whatever he can get his hands on and combines the material to
create austere and ironic works</p>



          <div class="media_row">
     <img alt="" src="/uploads/images/resizer_cache/4fb0ad72391d6d1e6f2d5b7aa580370002fab712.jpg" height="339"
width="500">
                 <p>Installation view of David Zwirner booth, The Armory Show, New York, 2012</p>
          </div>


     <p>In the introduction to his book <em>Art After Appropriation</em> (2001), John C. Welchman discusses Georges Bataille's
essay on the Marquis de Sade – <em>The Use Value of D.A.F. de Sade (An Open Letter to My Current Comrades)</em> from 1930.
Here, Welchman notes, Bataille correlates appropriation with bodies; Bataille identifies 'two polarized human impulses: excretion and appro-
priation', which result from 'the division of social facts into religious facts [...] on the one hand and profane facts [...] on the other'. Excretion
is associated with the heterogeneous expulsion of foreign bodies: with 'sexual activity [...] heedless expenditure [...] certain fanciful uses of
money' and 'religious ecstasy'. Appropriation, by contrast, finds its 'elementary form' in 'oral consumption'; its process 'is thus characterised
by a homogeneity (static equilibrium) of the author of the appropriation, and of objects as a final result'. Appropriative experience may begin
with the ordering of foreign bodies through digestive incorporation, but it extends to analogous forms of additive material: 'clothes, furniture,
dwellings, and instruments of production [...]'. 'Such appropriations', Bataille continues, 'take place by means of a more or less conventional
homogeneity (identity) established between the possessor and the object possessed'. But in Bataille's opinion, there is no binary separation,
because 'production can be seen as the excretory phase of a process of appropriation'1. Appropriation is not separated from production but
rather one of its possible manifestations.</p>


        <div class="media_row">
                 <img alt="" src="/uploads/images/general/A-61076_JS.jpg" height="699" width="500">
                                  <p>Kunstrichtungen von 1800 bis heute,
1998, Photocopies</p>
               </div>


    <p>The work of Michael Riedel (born in 1972) is rooted in the long history of appropriation strategies in art. Throughout a career
spanning almost 15 years, Riedel has adopted different modalities of appropriation (recording, quoting, copying, doubling, inverting) and used
a wide range of media (works on canvas and fabric, films, videos, audio recordings, artist books, posters, installations, events). Historically,
appropriation strategies – from Marcel Duchamp to the Pictures Generation – have been linked to questions regarding originality, authorship
and authority. Yet Riedel has also devoted his attention to the process of producing, labelling, branding and distributing since his studies at
Frankfurt's Städelschule (1997–2000). In a very early work that took the form of a lecture <em>Signetismus</em> (1997), he wrote his name
on a paper bag, adding an 'S.' between his first and last name. At the end of the lecture, he pulled the bag over his head and said: 'I'm Mi-
chael Riedel'. By labelling himself as a brand with a slight alteration (Michael S. Riedel), he stressed the economic and commercial character
of his role as an artist.2</p>
```

<p>As a result, Riedel soon adopted entrepreneurial and business-like activities as part of his creative strategies. In 2000, he and fellow artist Dennis Loesch launched a collaborative project called <em>Oskar-von-Miller-Straße 16</em>. The space, named after the Frankfurt address where it was located, hosted different events with the common strategy of re-staging and re-producing already existing ones. Readings, film screenings, art exhibitions and music concerts were sometimes presented shortly after the actual event had taken place elsewhere in the city. These imperfect copies – with multiple omissions and mistakes – eventually created a curious delay effect in the perception of reality.</p>

<div class="media_row">
<img alt="" src="/uploads/images/general/EDEU0530_JS.jpg" height="329" width="500">
<p><span class="caps">NOSNHO</span>.-
......(<span class="caps">ROBERT</span> <span class="caps">JOHNSON</span>), 2004, from the series Club(b)ed Club</p>
</div>

<p><em>Clu(b)bed Club</em> (2001–7) is another example of the 'copy and paste' attitude. This series of events held at <em>Oskar-von-Miller Straße 16</em> consisted of audio-recordings (another favourite tool in Riedel's passion for appropriation) which documented the nights that Riedel and Loesch spent at different clubs. Dance music, ambient noises and conversations were diffused in their Frankfurt space, while parts of the architecture of the original clubs were occasionally borrowed or specifically made as replicas, thus creating the false and cheap illusion of being part of a cool and entertaining experience which actually took place somewhere else. </p>

<p>Early on, Riedel used appropriative strategies in the art world with both deadpan humour and a renewed institutional critique. In 2001, he and fellow artist Achim Lengerer entered Galerie Michael Neff in Frankfurt during a Jeppe Hein exhibition, which featured two large white moving walls, activated by motion sensors. Hiding inside two cardboard boxes poorly painted white, the two artists mimicked the movements of Hein's walls in a humorous way which added a more human, even pathetic, gesture to the Danish artist's mechanical apparatus. In a meta-discursive moment, Riedel involved Hein in a sort of repartee on issues of Institutional Critique while using an absolutely non-technological tool.</p>

<p>Neo Rauch's 2005 exhibition at David Zwirner gallery in New York became a bigger target of Riedel's irony. For his own first solo exhibition at the same gallery a few months later, Riedel photographed and reprinted Rauch's works. The printouts were subsequently cut into multiple sections and mounted on <span class="caps">MDF</span> panels, so that each image could be re-arranged in different configurations, somewhat like a puzzle. By calling his show <em>Neo</em> ('new' in Latin), Riedel once more played with the expectations of the market for new products and with his own desire to produce the minimum possible amount of new information and images.</p>

<p>Repeating and copying does not necessarily involve iconic moments of art or high-brow cultural production. Riedel seems attracted by the banal, marginal and in-between: background noises and chit-chat have a prominent position in his world as a black and white replica of the world around him. Banal conversations overheard between art installers in a gallery or among crowds at an opening are recorded, transcribed and printed; they turn into books and posters which function as art works and as an imprecise kind of documentation. Here, language is treated more as a visual material than as a carrier of meaningful messages. Words – at times barely readable, cut and pasted, blanked out, shifted from one context to another – become a sort of verbal white noise, a form of visual poetry for the digital age, a monument to the constant twittering in our media-scape.3 As Michel Foucault – citing Samuel Beckett – asked in his famous lecture on the author, Riedel seems to be asking (but probably with more pessimism): 'What difference does it make who is speaking?' 4 While Roland Barthes predicted the death of the author in favour of the birth of the reader, Riedel appears to follow a more nihilist and disillusioned path. Barthes's emancipated 'reader' becomes an inattentive 'hearer' in Riedel's work and in today's technological scenarios.</p>

<p>It should be clear from these examples that neither romantic drives nor humanistic hopes are at play in Riedel's idea of art and creative labour. His practice seems to follow a well-established German tradition whereby the artist's gestures closely resemble the impersonality, repetitiveness and cold detachment of the machine, albeit with a touch of irony. Take the Pop-Minimalism of Peter Roehr or Thomas Bayrle and the dialogue they established with industrial production's modes of reproduction and repetition. In music, consider the pivotal example of Kraftwerk with the robot-like look, repetitive electronic sounds and lyrics focused on technological and media landscape. While these examples refer to the industrial forms of production proper to Taylorism and Fordism, Riedel belongs to a generation of artists who became familiar with the Internet in the mid-1990s along with the digitization of the production, distribution and consumption of images and sounds. In the German culture of the early 1960s, the detachment of Pop and Minimal art represented an antidote to romantic and existential forms of expression and could be seen as a manifestation of a new confidence in progress and welfare after the moral and material destruction of <span class="caps">WWII</span>. Riedel's motivations are different. His withdrawal from most intentional decisions in the art-making process – his productive modalities, where personal and expressive choices are reduced to a minimum or based on a set of pre-defined rules – can be seen as the latest product in a long tradition of Minimal and Conceptual gestures. But the targets of his interventions are the conditions of production, diffusion and distribution in the digital era. As the artist himself said, the <em>Oskar-von-Miller</em> project and others must be 'read as a process, not as a product'. 5 In our current media-scape – saturated with an increasing number of new images and products, more and more easily produced, transmitted and dispersed – Riedel's impersonal attitude, his Bartleby-like 'I would prefer not to' approach to reality, can be read as a critical form of resistance which produces new images, forms and sounds, but in the smallest possible amount. </p>

<p>At the same time, his compulsive attitude to repetition could be interpreted as a new form of dandyism. Detachment from personal and intimate forms of expression, a repetitive set of creative gestures, recurring codes in the appearance of the art works (totally black and white until 2007 with a rare use of colour afterwards), abstention from physical labour, a refusal to produce something 'new' – these are perhaps the tools used by today's 'digital dandy' to express his discomfort and critical stance towards reality.6 </p>

<div class="media_row">
<img alt="" src="/uploads/images/general/Riedel_Senn_2011_2.jpg" height="333" width="500">
<p>The quick brown fox jumps over the lazy dog, 2011</p>
</div

<p>This attitude goes with a subtle, two-fold form of narcissism, evident in a recent series of works. For his solo exhibition in 2011 at Zwirner <em>The quick brown fox jumps over the lazy dog</em>, Riedel presented so-called 'poster paintings' and 'Power-Point paintings'.

Once again, he uses pre-determined rules and quasi-mechanical actions which detach the final result from any possible expressivity, even if the content of these works is the artist, his public persona. To create backgrounds for these works, the artist searched for his name online, used the 'select-all' function and then copied and pasted the material onto the canvases. Divorced from a graphically-designed layout, the words appear in a linear, yet nonsensical, order and include algorithmic commands, search keywords and links. Any reference to a personal position is obliterated in an undifferentiated verbal white noise; any residual desire of self-expression is reduced to graphic motives which recall economic charts and statistics. </p>

<p>For his show at Frankfurt's Schirn Kunsthalle from June to September 2012, Riedel applies his appropriative strategies to the exhibition's title <em>Kunste zur Text</em> (Arts on Text, a pun on the magazine <em>Texte zur Kunst</em>) as well as to the Schirn's previous show <em>Edvard Munch. The Modern Eye</em>. The walls from the Munch blockbuster will lean on the walls of Riedel's exhibition space and be decorated with wallpaper which bears a pattern made with the source code of the Schirn website announcing Riedel's show. While this gesture reflects on the artworld and the representation of himself in it, the anticipation of the show becomes part of its form, merging expectations with reality. Once again, Riedel demonstrates the fluidity and continuity of production, distribution and consumption. Our digital world recalls exchange in an oral culture of storytelling: any form of production can go through many transformations; any product is a temporary expression of a chain of incarnations which are almost indifferent to hierarchies. Bataille linked appropriation to oral consumption, but production in today's technological-social scenario is getting closer to the excretory phase of orality. </p>

<ul>
<li>The opening paragraph and footnote corrected from the original version, amended 14 April 2014.</li>
</ul>

<p><cite>—by Luca Cerizza</cite></p>

<div class="author_bios">

<p>Luca Cerizza is a curator, writer and art historian based in Berlin.</p>

</div>

<div class="block footnote">
<p>Subscribe to frieze d/e <a href="http://frieze-magazin.de/shop/subscriptions/subscribe-to-frieze-d-e/?lang=en">here</a> and have it delivered to your door</p>
</div>

</div> <!-- //.article -->

</div> <!-- //.content_pri_sub1a -->

<div class="content_pri_sub2">

<div class="block about">

<h5>About this feature</h5>

<p class="right">
<img class="right" alt="" src="/uploads/images/resizer_cache/a2207ede11e4401b70a21a79220f4c8343c2f987.png" height="91" width="70">
</p>
<p>First published in <a href="/archiv/ausgaben/ausgabe-5">Issue 5</a>, Summer 2012</p>
<p><em>by Luca Cerizza</em></p>

</div> <!-- //.block.about -->

<ul class="sublisting actions">
<li class="print"><a href="javascript:window.print()">Print this article</a></li>

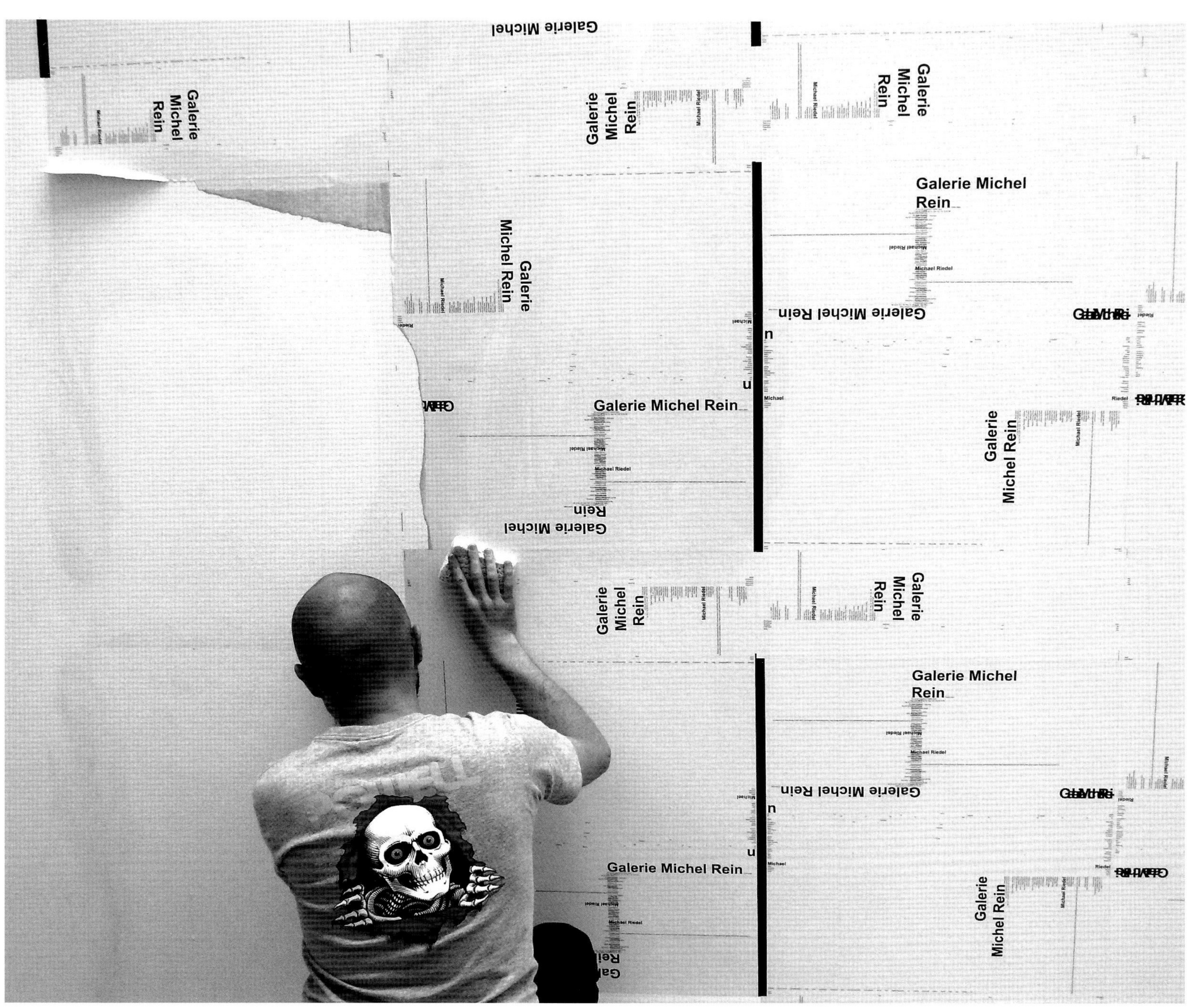

Deinstallation, *Michael Riedel*
Galerie Michel Rein, Paris, 2010

```
        <div class=”block”>
          <h3>Publications</h3>
          <a href=”http://www.frieze.com/publications”>
            <img class=”right” alt=”” src=”/uploads/images/resizer_cache/f96f7714fa128e86447a738d670b037c1be9d7f2.jpg” height=”134”
width=”110”>
          </a>
          <p>Buy the new Frieze Art Fair New York Catalogue 2012-13</p>
          <p><strong>£24.95</strong></p>
          <p class=”cta_button”><a href=”http://www.frieze.com/publications”>Purchase</a></p>

        </div>

        <div id=”stay_updated”>

          <h3>Stay updated</h3>

          <ul id=”social_big”>
            <li class=”twitter”><a href=”http://twitter.com/#!/frieze_de”>Frieze on Twitter</a></li>
            <li class=”facebook”><a href=”http://www.facebook.com/pages/frieze-de/117300325031496”>Frieze on Facebook</a></li>
          </ul>

          <form action=”http://www.frieze.com/newsletter/” method=”post” id=”newsletter_subscribe”>
            <fieldset>
              <p>Sign up to our newsletter</p>
              <div>
                <label for=”nl_name”>Name</label>
                <input name=”name” id=”nl_name” value=”” type=”text”>
              </div>
              <div>
                <label for=”nl_email”>Email</label>
                <input name=”email” id=”nl_email” value=”” type=”text”>
              </div>
              <div class=”submit”>
                <input name=”list” value=”8840” type=”hidden”>
                <input value=”Sign up” name=”SubscribeButton” type=”submit”>
              </div>
            </fieldset>
          </form>

        </div>

      </div> <!-- // #footer_pri -->

      <div id=”footer_sec”>


        <p class=”copyright”>Frieze d/e, Zehdenickerstr. 28, 10119 Berlin, Deutschland, +49 (0) 30 23626506</p>




        <p class=”credit”>Site by <a href=”http://erskinedesign.com/”>Erskine Design</a></p>

      </div>

    </div> <!-- // #footer -->

</div> <!-- // #page -->

<!-- JAVASCRIPT -->
<script src=”http://ajax.googleapis.com/ajax/libs/jquery/1.5.1/jquery.min.js”></script>
<script src=”http://frieze-magazin.de/static/js/jquery-ui-1.8.11.custom.min.js” type=”text/javascript” charset=”utf-8”></script>
<script src=”http://frieze-magazin.de/static/js/jquery.cookie.min.js”></script>
<script src=”http://frieze-magazin.de/static/js/jquery.slideshows.js”></script>
<script src=”http://frieze-magazin.de/static/js/onload.js”></script>
<!--[if IE 6]>
  <script src=”http://frieze-magazin.de/static/js/ie6/DD_belatedPNG_0.0.8a.js”></script>
  <script src=”http://frieze-magazin.de/static/js/ie6/ie6.js”></script>
<![endif]-->




</body></html>
```

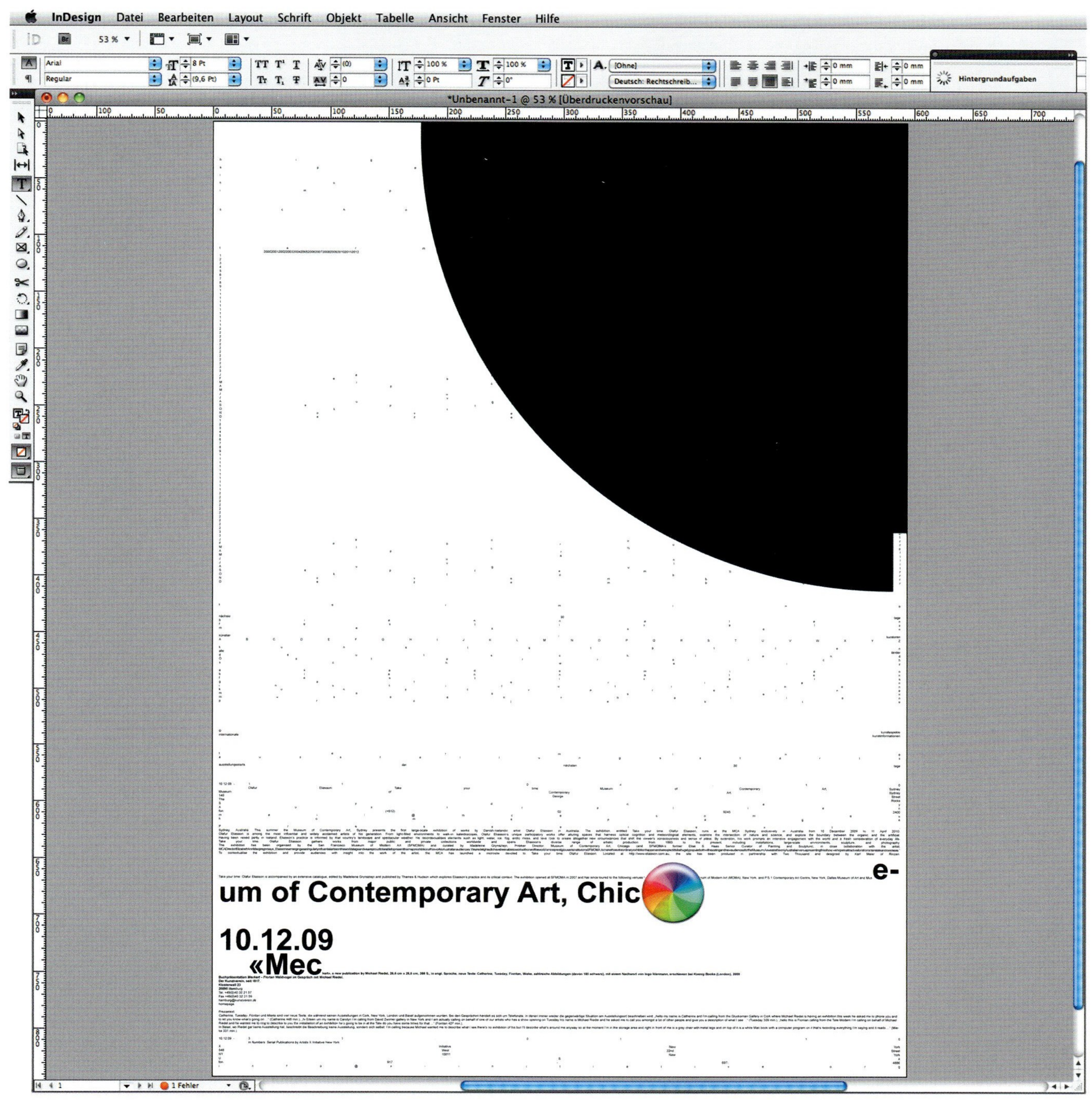

Screenshot of color wheel

A color wheel or spinning wait cursor indicates that the application is temporarily busy, a state from which the application may recover; however, it may also indicate that the application has entered an unrecoverable state or an infinite loop.

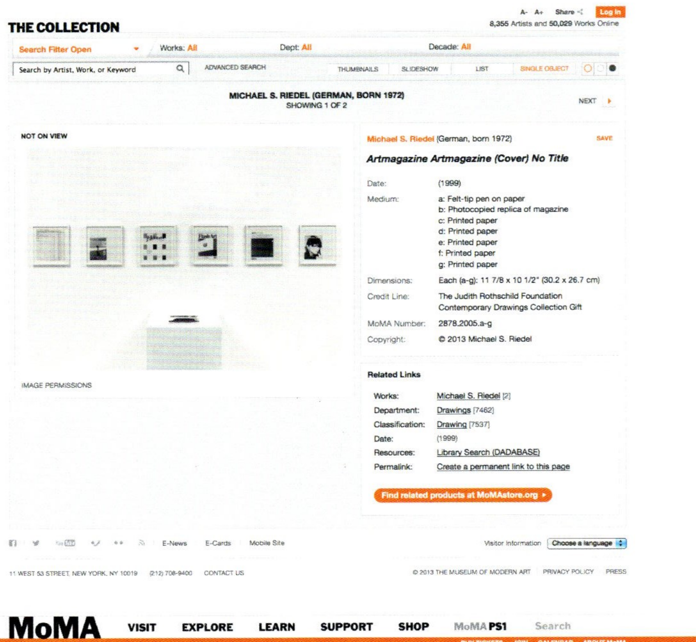

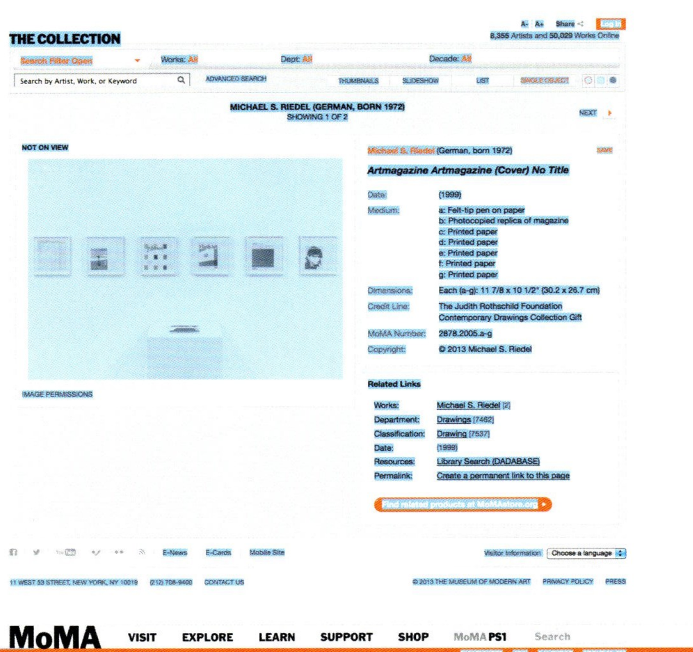

Screenshot of Riedel's artist page on MOMA's website, http://www.moma.org/collection/works/97162?locale=de

Screenshot of Riedel's artist page on MOMA's website with everything marked (>select all)

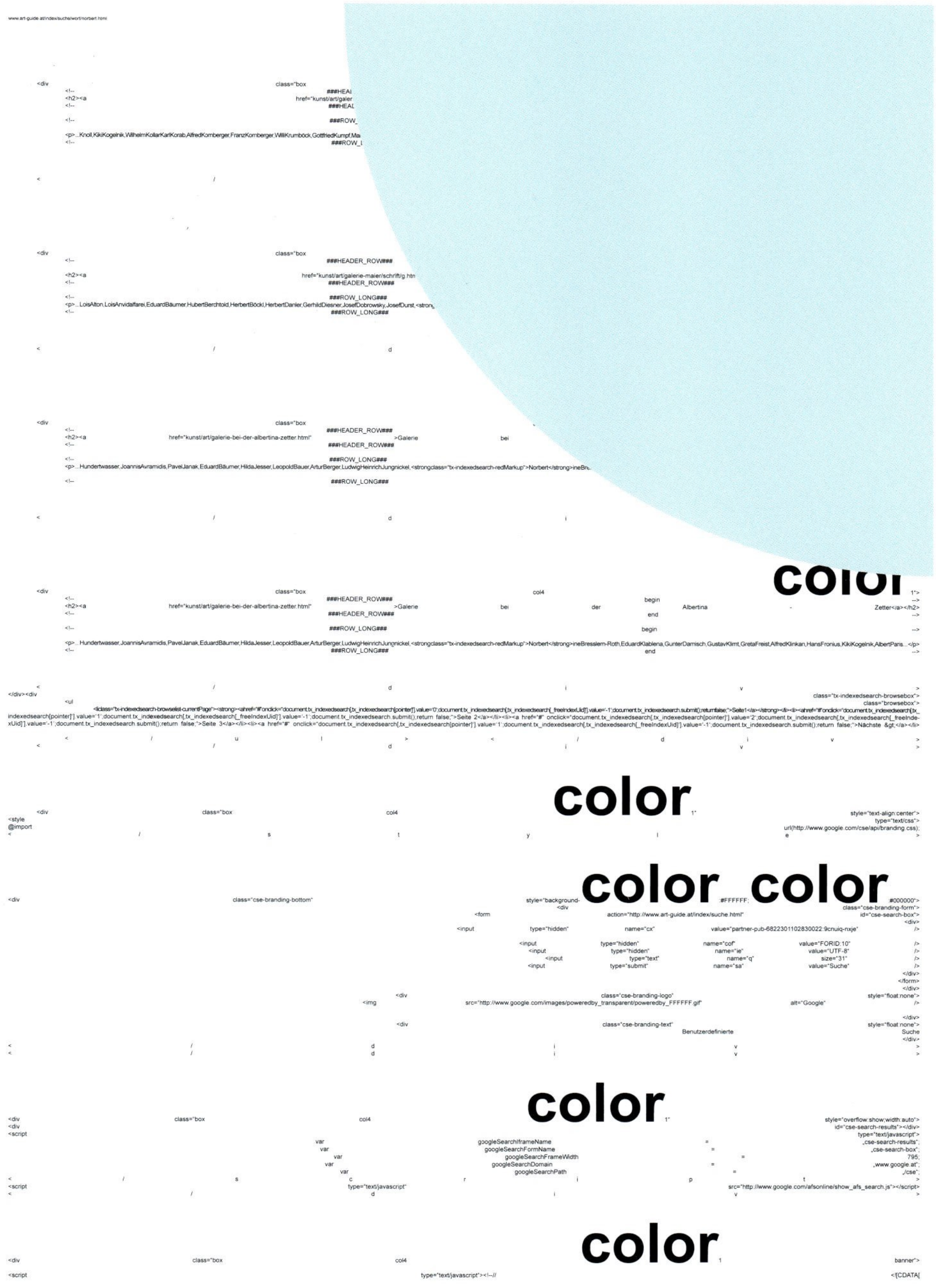

color

color

color color

color

color

Untitled (color, light blue), 2011
Offset print
23 x 16 1/2 inches
(58.4 x 41.9 cm)

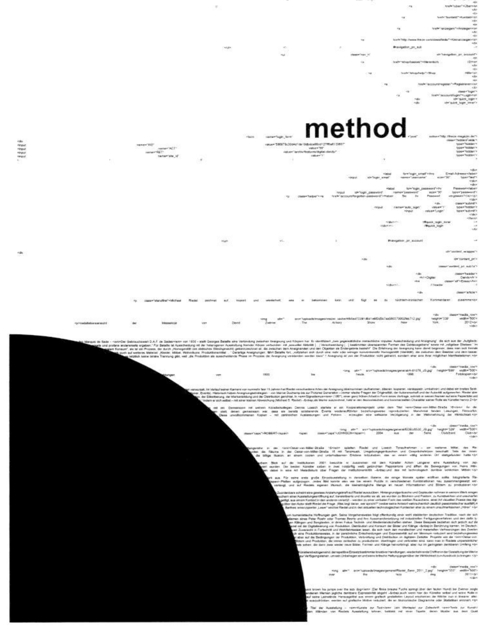

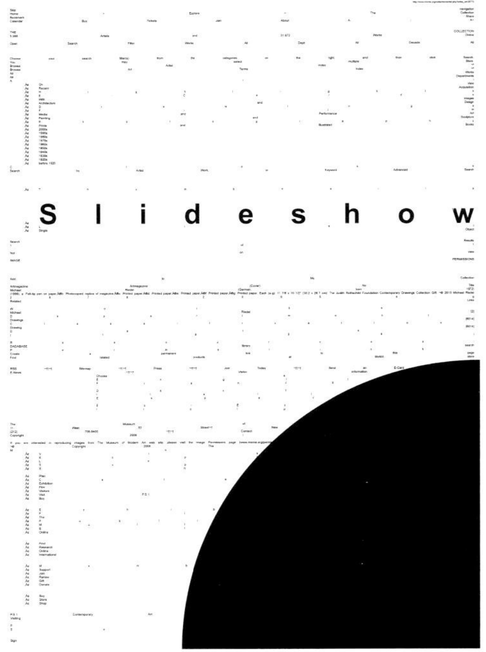

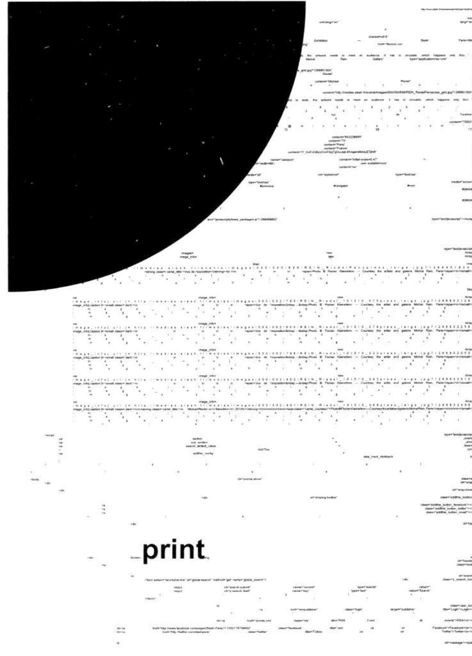

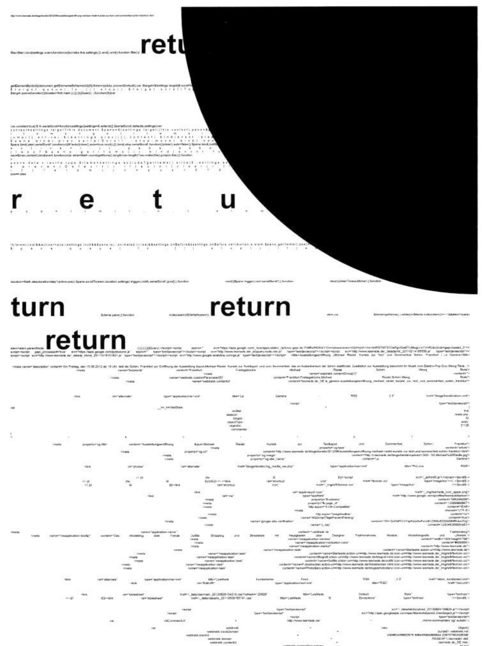

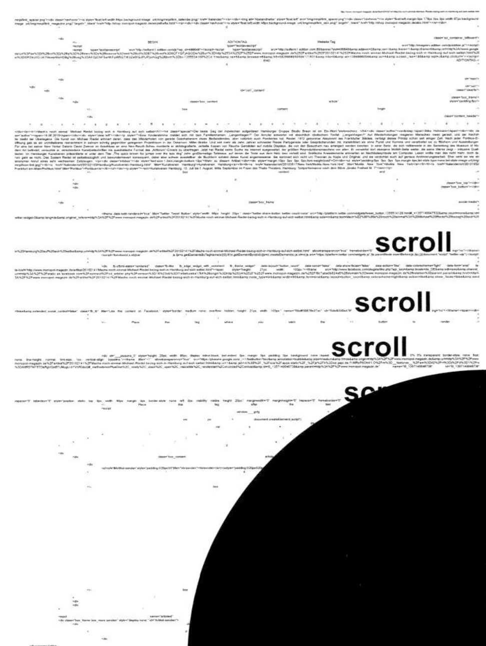

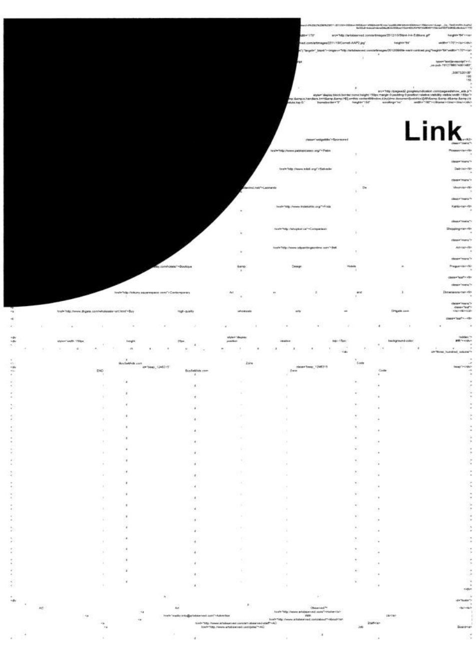

Untitled (method), *Untitled (Slideshow)*, *Untitled (print)*,
Untitled (return), *Untitled (scroll)*, *Untitled (Link)*, 2010–2013
Offset print
Each: 23 x 16 1/2 inches
(58.4 x 41.9 cm)

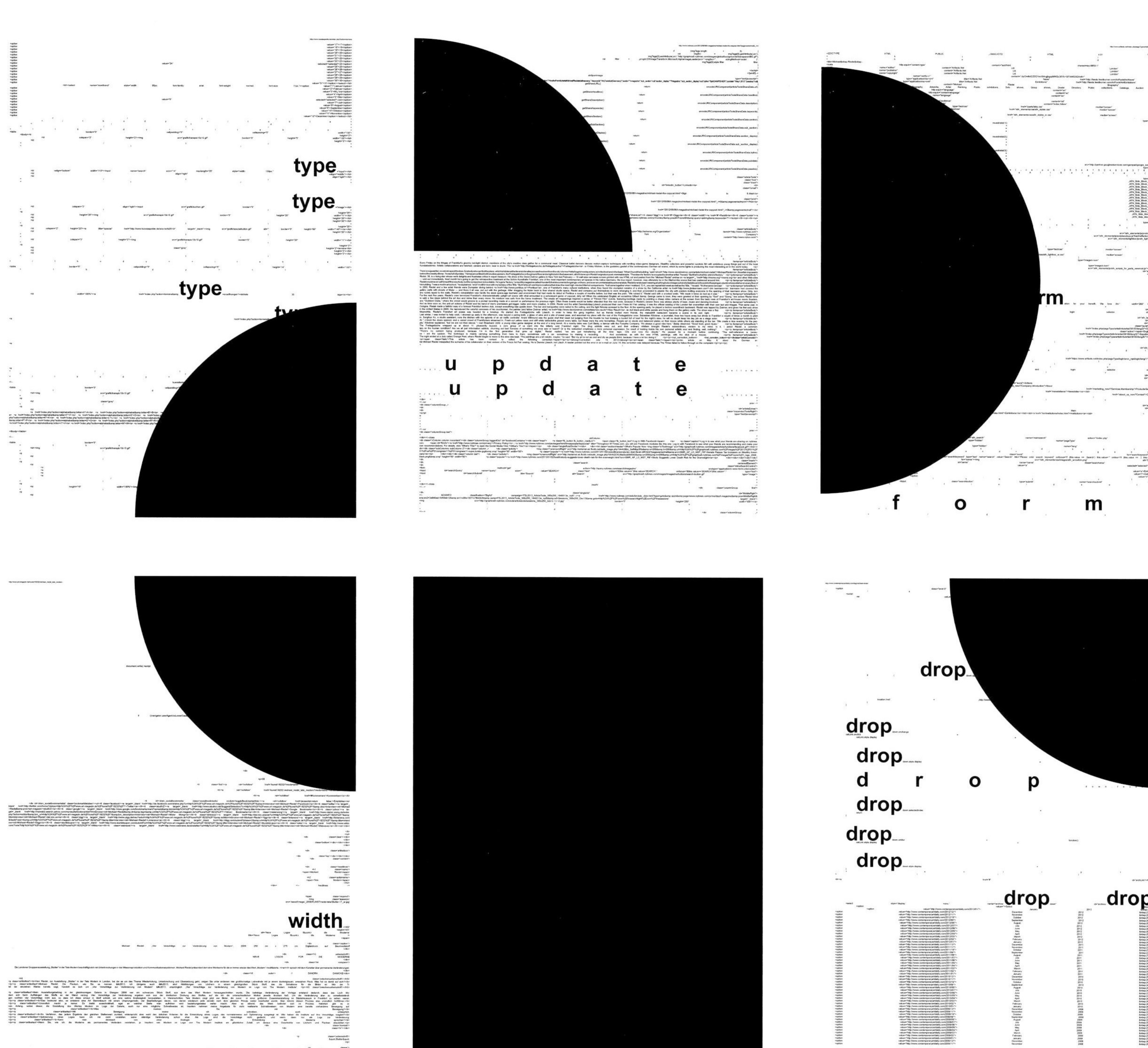

Untitled (type), *Untitled (update)*, *Untitled (form)*,
Untitled (width), *Untitled (solid black)*, *Untitled (drop)*, 2010–2013
Offset print
Each: 23 x 16 1/2 inches
(58.4 x 41.9 cm)

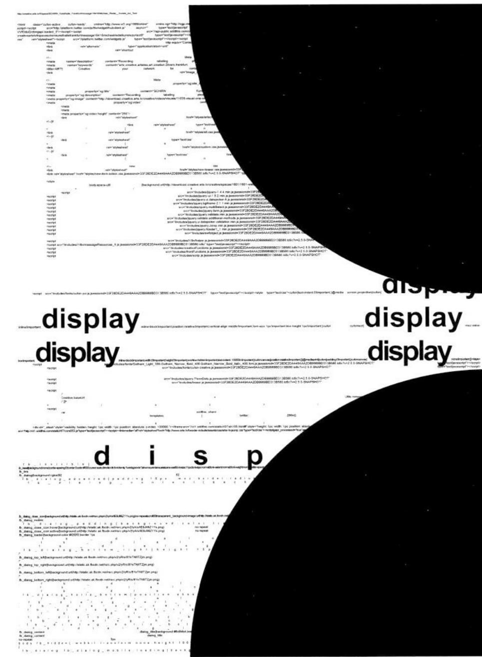
display
display
display
display
display
d i s p
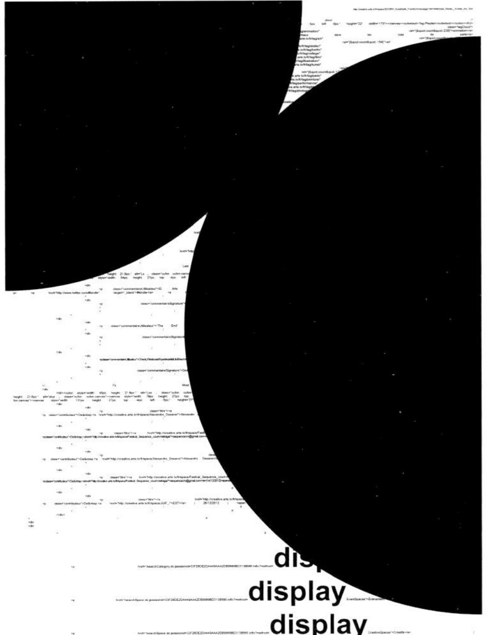
disp
display
display
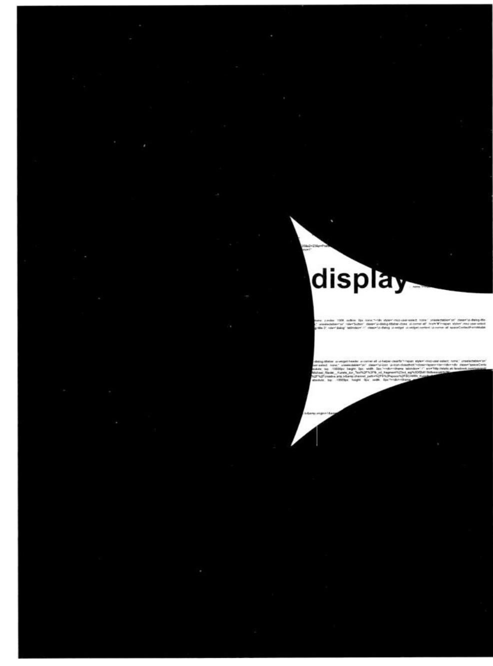
display
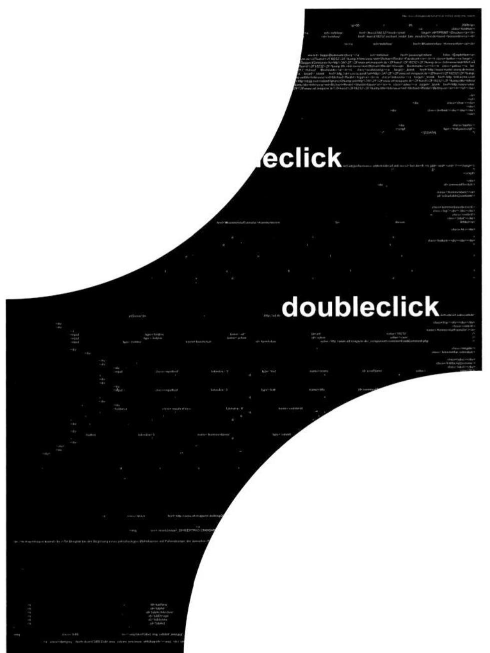
eclick
doubleclick
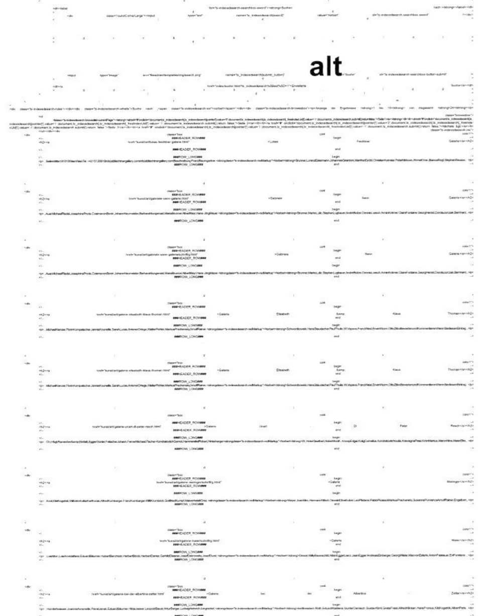
alt
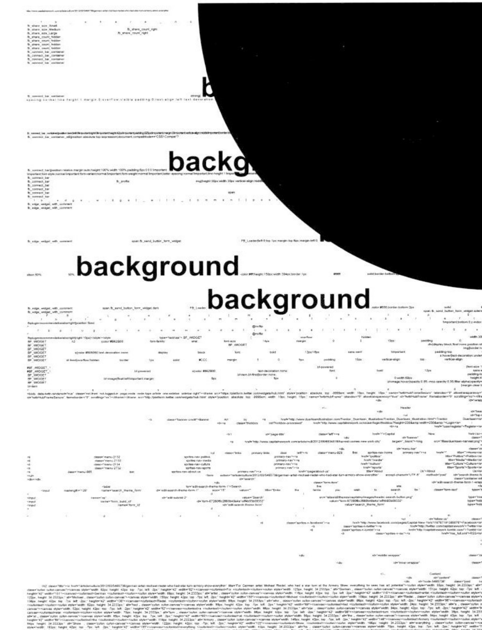
background
background

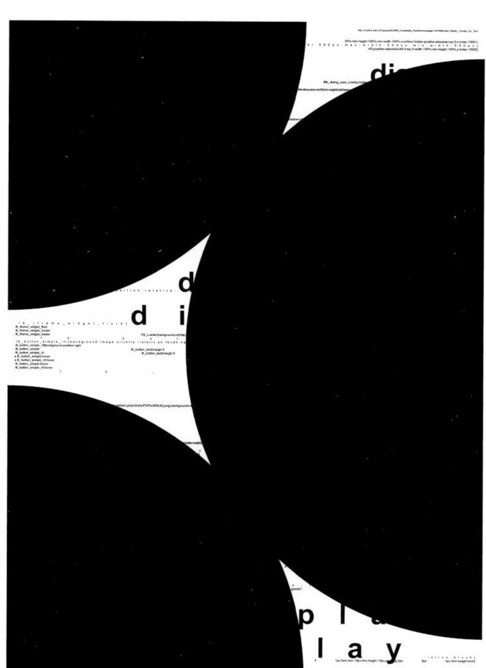

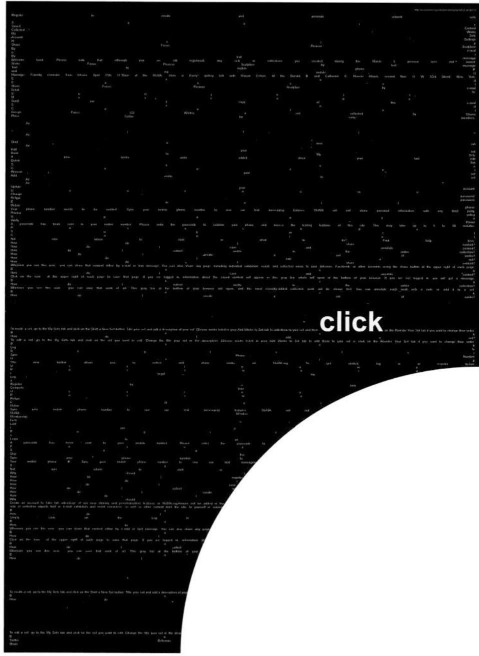

Untitled (display 3), *Untitled (display 4)*, *Untitled (display 1)*, *Untitled (display 2)*,
Untitled (doubleclick), *Untitled (alt)*, *Untitled (background)*, *Untitled (click 1)*, 2010–2013
Offset print
Each: 23 x 16 1/2 inches
(58.4 x 41.9 cm)

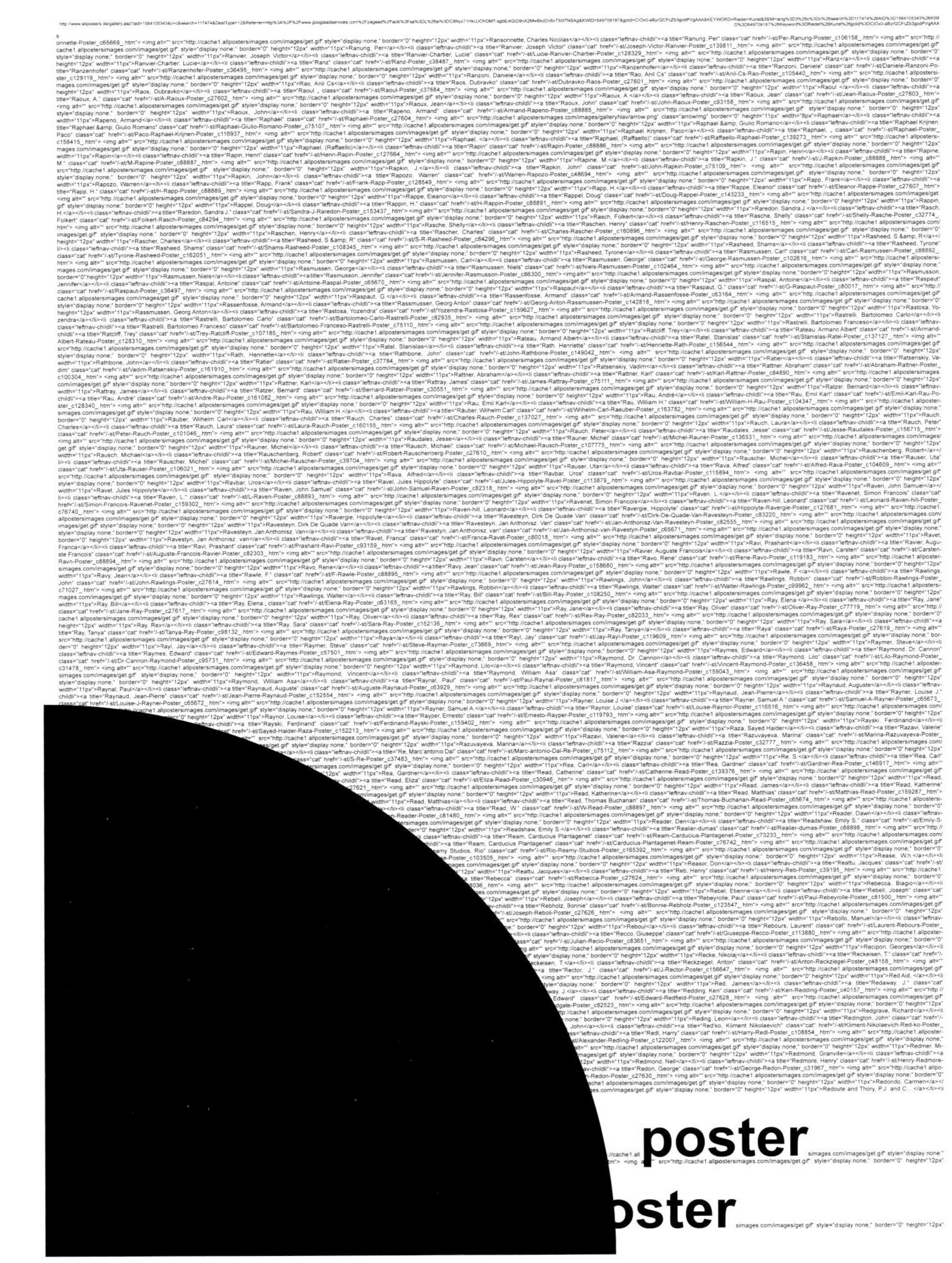

Untitled (poster), 2013
Offset print
23 x 16 1/2 inches
(58.4 x 41.9 cm)

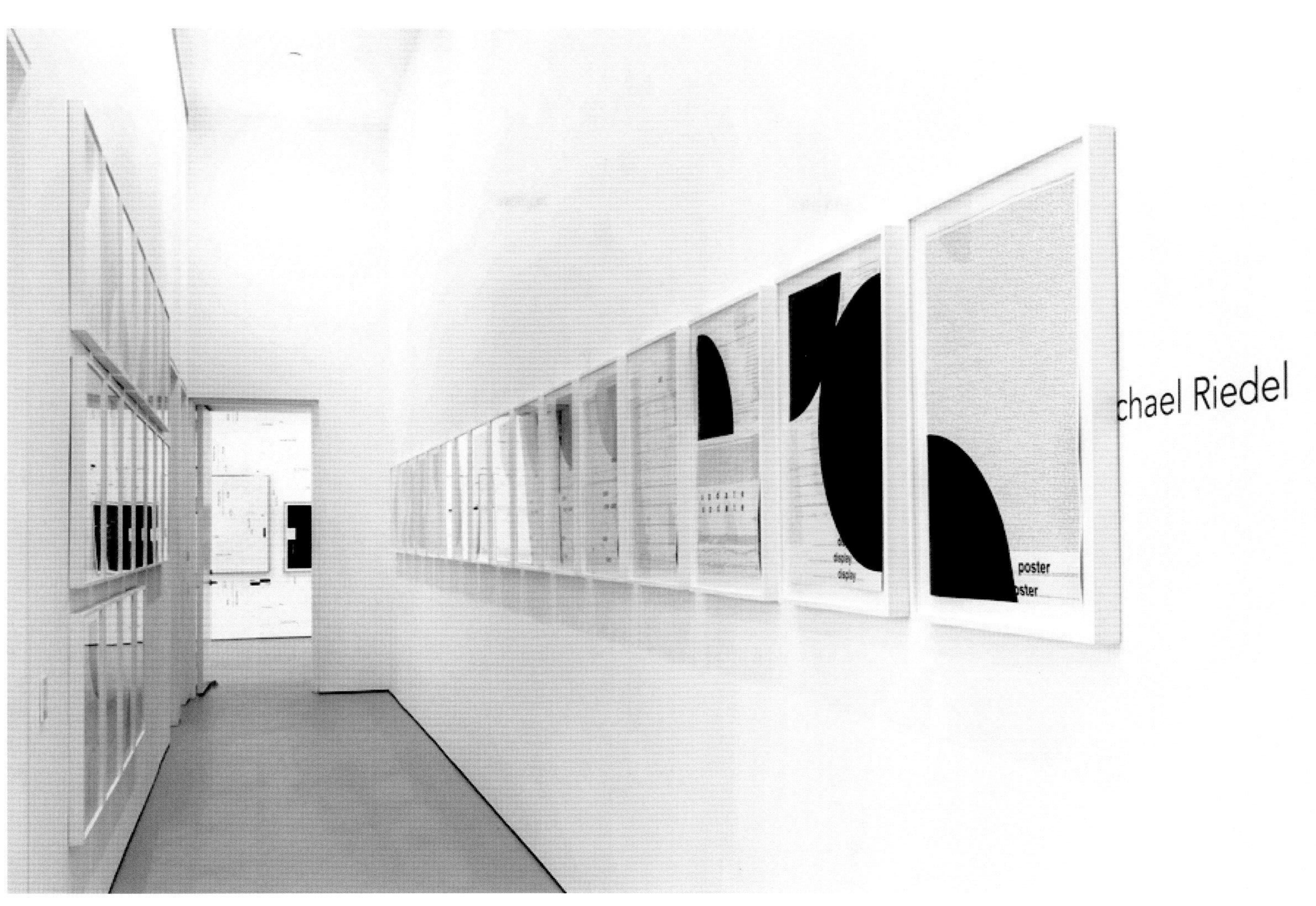

Untitled (34 Posters for Poster Paintings), 2010–2013
Installation view, *Michael Riedel: PowerPoint*
David Zwirner, New York, 2013

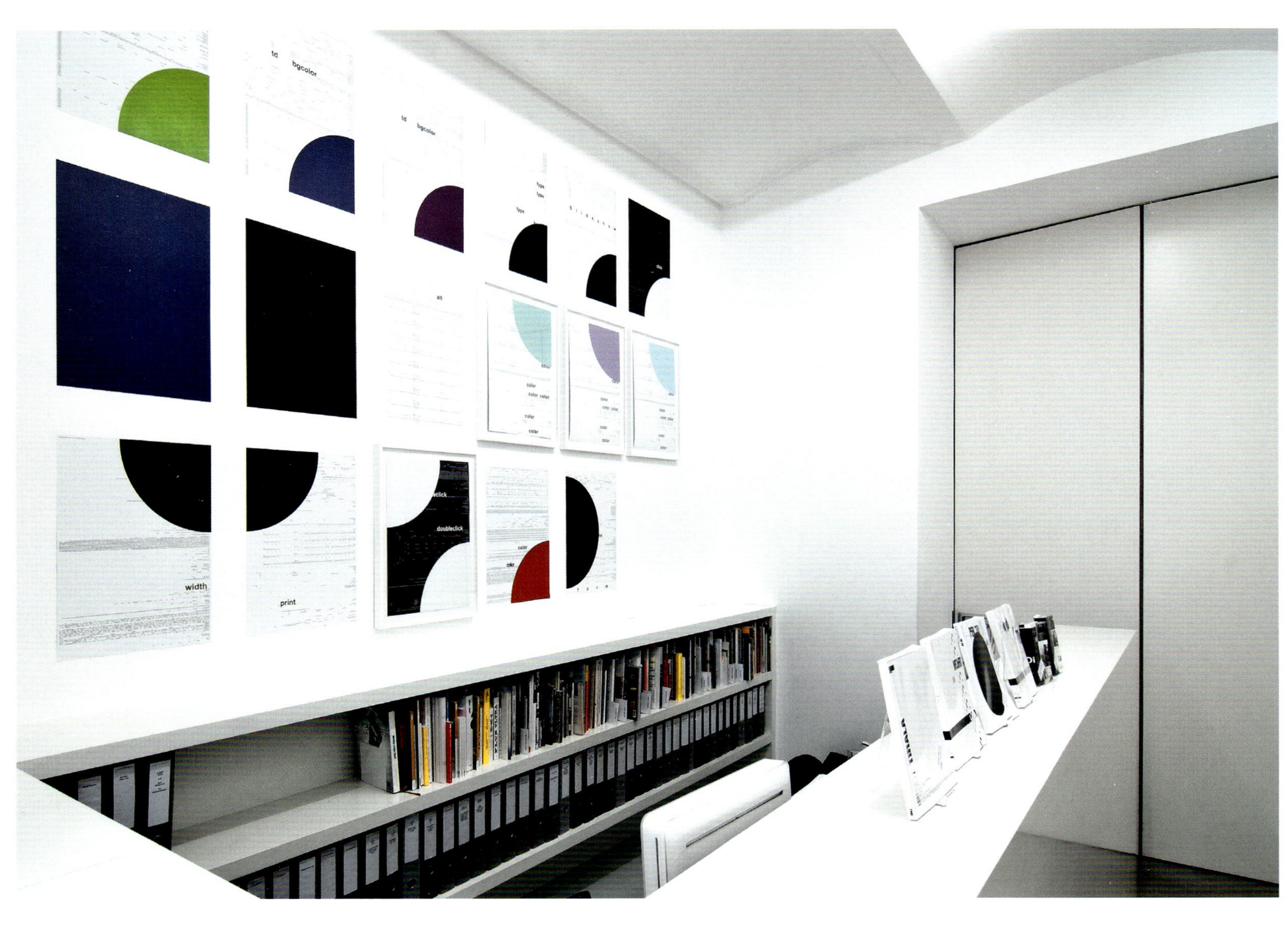

Untitled (Posters for Poster Paintings), 2010–2013
Installation view, *Michael Riedel: The quick brown fox jumps over the lazy dog*
Gabriele Senn Galerie, Vienna, 2011

Untitled (color, light green), *Untitled (color, yellow)*, *Untitled (color, red)*, *Untitled (color, green)*, *Untitled (color, purple)*, *Untitled (color, light purple)*, *Untitled (color, blue)*, *Untitled (clear 1)*, *Untitled (clear 2)*, 2010–2013
Offset print
Each: 23 x 16 1/2 inches
(58.4 x 41.9 cm)

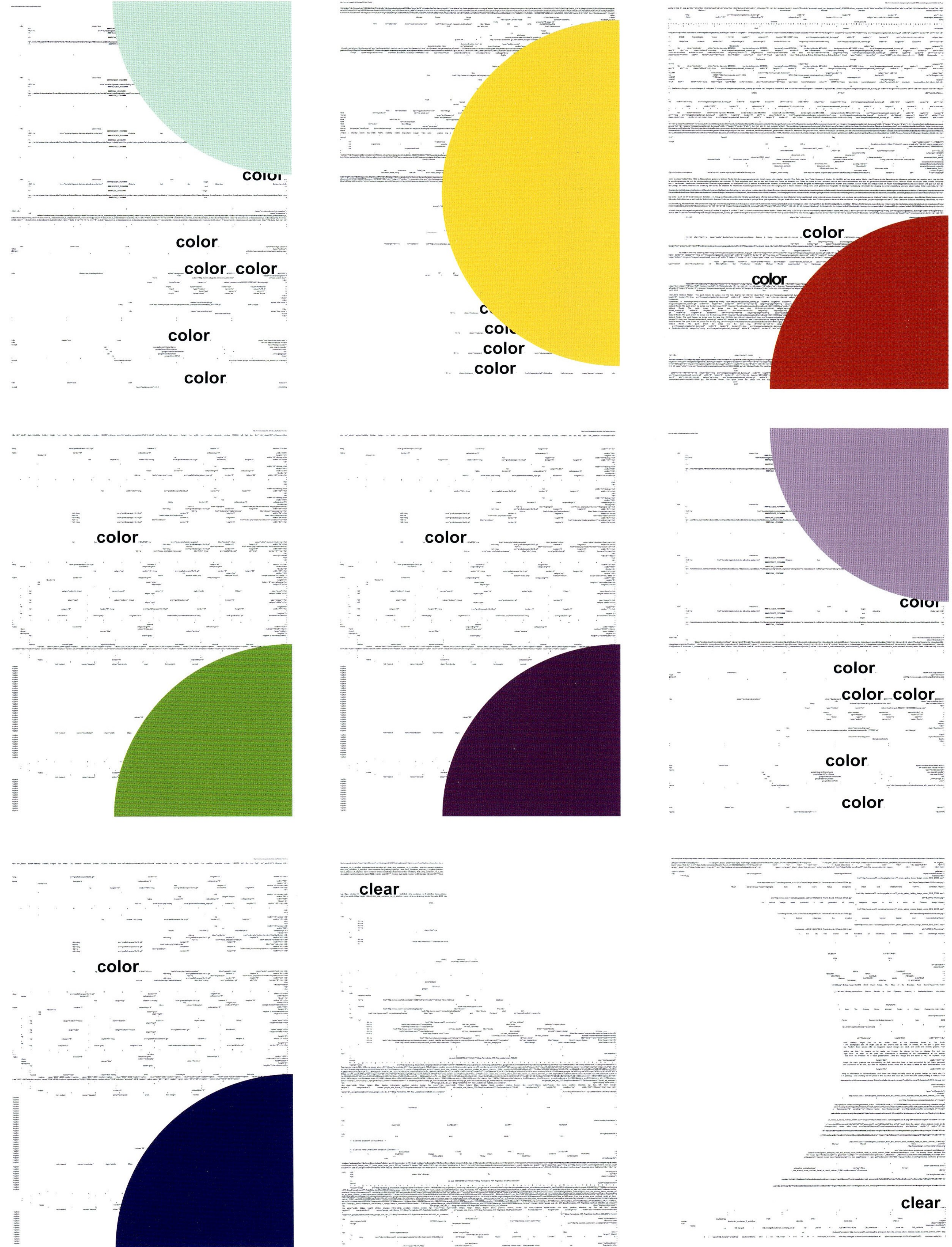
color
color
color color
color
color
color
color
color
color
color
color
color
color
color color
color
color
color
clear
clear

color

http://www.kunstmarkt.com/pagesmag/kunst/_id215769-/ausstellungen_berichtdetail.html
(Accessed June 7, 2010)

```
<!DOCTYPE HTML PUBLIC „-//W3C//DTD HTML 4.01 Transitional//EN“ „http://www.w3.org/TR/html4/loose.dtd“>
<html>
<head>
<!-- <base target=Kunstmarkt> -->
        <title>Ausstellung Michael Riedel. The  Kunst-Messe-Berichte News</title>
<meta http-equiv=“Content-Type“ content=“text/html; charset=iso-8859-1“>
<meta name=“description“ content=“&#9658; Ausstellung Michael Riedel. The:  The quick brown fox jumps over the lazy dog Der flinke braune
Fuchs springt über den faulen Hund so „>

<meta name=“keywords“ content=“Riedel, Michael, Satz, MoMA, Ausstellung, Kunstverein, Internetseiten, Quellcodes, Farbkreisen, Hinsehen,
Material, Postern, Rätsel, Format, Zentimeter, Betrachter, Bildfläche, Buchstabenfolgen, Termine, Picasso, Eröffnungen, Sculpture, Grafik,
Kunstbetrieb, Begriffe, Befehlen, Leinwände, Informatik, Insidern, HTML, Blindtext, Kunstwart, Fuchs, Hund, Titel, de, Art, Hamburg, York,
Museum, Modern, Frankfurter, Künstlers, Testen, Schreibmaschinentastaturen, Willkommen, Reich, Alphabets, Buchstaben, Hamburger,
Bedeutung, Feststellung, Pangramm, Bedeutungslosigkeit“>

<meta name=“author“ content=“Mathias E. Koch - http://www.AdOptimize.de“>
<meta name=“publisher“ content=“Kunstmarkt Media GmbH & Co KG“>
<meta name=“copyright“ content=“Kunstmarkt.com AG“>
<meta name=“robots“ content=“index,follow“>

<link rel=“SHORTCUT ICON“ href=“http://www.kunstmarkt.com/favicon.ico“ type=“image/ico“>

<script language=“JavaScript“ type=“text/javascript“ src=“http://www.kunstmarkt.com/javascript/browser.js“></script>
<script language=“JavaScript“ type=“text/javascript“ src=“http://www.kunstmarkt.com/javascript/div_fly_header.js“></script><script
language=“JavaScript“ type=“text/javascript“>
<!--
var bild=“;
function bild_over(id, obj)        {
bild = document.images[id].src;
document.images[id].src = ‚/images/navigation/all_pfeil.gif‘;
dynmen(id);
}
function bild_out(id) {
document.images[id].src = bild;
}
// -->
</script>

</head>


<body bgcolor=“#fff8ea“ alink=“#000000“ link=“#033365“ vlink=“#777777“ text=“#000000“ leftmargin=“0“ topmargin=“0“ marginwidth=“0“
marginheight=“0“ border=“0“>
<!-- IVW-Zaehlpixel !-->
<a name=“Magazin kunstmarkt“></a>
<!-- Logo-Template -->
<table width=“100%“ border=“0“ cellspacing=“0“ cellpadding=“0“>
<tr>

        <!-- Spanner -->
  <td width=“25%“><img src=“/images/navigation/all_dummy.gif“ width=“1“ height=“1“ border=“0“ alt=““></td>
  <td><img src=“/images/navigation/all_dummy.gif“ width=“1“ height=“1“ border=“0“ alt=““></td>
  <td><img src=“/images/navigation/all_dummy.gif“ width=“1“ height=“1“ border=“0“ alt=““></td>
  <td><img src=“/images/navigation/all_dummy.gif“ width=“1“ height=“1“ border=“0“ alt=““></td></tr>
        <tr>
        <td align=“left“ ><img src=“/images/navigation/all_dummy.gif“ width=“10“ height=“10“ border=“0“ alt=““><br>  <!-- LOGO -->
        <p class=“copyfont“><img src=“/images/navigation/all_dummy.gif“ width=“47“ height=“1“ border=“0“ alt=““>Die Kunst, online zu
lesen.</p><a href=“http://www.kunstmarkt.com“ target=“_self“ title=“Kunstmarkt.com“><img src=“/images/navigation/kunstmarkt.com_logo.
gif“ width=“260“ height=“36“ hspace=“9“ alt=“Home“ border=“0“></a><br /><img src=“/images/navigation/all_dummy.gif“ width=“20“ height=“20“
border=“0“ alt=““>     </td>

        <td colspan=“2“ valign=“top“ align=“center“><img src=“/images/navigation/all_dummy.gif“ width=“1“ height=“1“ border=“0“ alt=““><br>
        <noscript><center><img src=“/images/navigation/enable_javascript.gif“ width=“140“ height=“60“ border=“1“ alt=“Please enable
Javascript“></center></noscript></td>

<td valign=“top“ align=“right“>

<img src=“/images/navigation/all_dummy.gif“ width=“9“ height=“6“ border=“0“ alt=““><br>
```

Untitled (solid blue), 2010
Offset print
23 x 16 1/2 inches
(58.4 x 41.9 cm)

```
<!--/* werbung_header_right  */-->
<!--/* OpenX Javascript Tag v2.8.5-rc7 */-->

<script type=‘text/javascript‘><!--//<![CDATA[
   var m3_u = (location.protocol==‘https:‘?‘https://d1.openx.org/ajs.php‘:‘http://d1.openx.org/ajs.php‘);
   var m3_r = Math.floor(Math.random()*99999999999);
   if (!document.MAX_used) document.MAX_used = ‚,‘;
   document.write („<scr“+“ipt type=‘text/javascript‘ src=‘“+m3_u);
   document.write („?zoneid=139046“);
   document.write (‚&amp;cb=‘ + m3_r);
   if (document.MAX_used != ‚,‘) document.write („&amp;exclude=“ + document.MAX_used);
   document.write (document.charset ? ‚&amp;charset=‘+document.charset : (document.characterSet ? ‚&amp;charset=‘+document.characterSet
: ‚‘));
   document.write („&amp;loc=“ + escape(window.location));
   if (document.referrer) document.write („&amp;referer=“ + escape(document.referrer));
   if (document.context) document.write („&context=“ + escape(document.context));
   if (document.mmm_fo) document.write („&amp;mmm_fo=1“);
   document.write („‘><\/scr“+“ipt>“);
//]]>--></script><noscript><a href=‘http://d1.openx.org/ck.php?n=a4aa196a&amp;cb=5748‘ target=‘_blank‘><img src=‘http://d1.openx.org/avw.ph
p?zoneid=139046&amp;cb=5748&amp;n=a4aa196a‘ border=‘0‘ alt=‘‘ /></a></noscript>

    </div><img src=“/images/navigation/all_dummy.gif“ width=“9“ height=“9“ border=“0“ alt=““></td></tr></table><table border=“0“ width=“100%“

cellspacing=“0“ cellpadding=“0“ bgcolor=“#E7A300“>

<tr><td valign=“top“ colspan=“3“ bgcolor=“#676568“><img src=“/images/navigation/all_dummy.gif“ width=“10“ height=“2“ border=“0“
alt=““></td></tr>
<tr>
    <td><img src=“/images/navigation/all_dummy.gif“ width=“1“ height=“1“ border=“0“ alt=““></td>
    <td valign=“top“ nowrap><ul class=“mainMenu“>
                <li class=“firstItem“><a href=“/pages/mag/magazin_uebersicht.html?word=Magazin“ title=“Magazin“ class=“activeMenu““><b
class=“topfont“>Magazin</b></a></li>
                <li><a href=“/pages/kuk/kunstundkapital_uebersicht.html?word=Kunst+%2B+Kapital“ title=“Kunst + Kapital“ class=“white“><b
class=“topfont“>Kunst + Kapital</b></a></li>
                <li><a href=“/pages/kal/kalender_uebersicht.html?word=Kalender“ title=“Kalender“ class=“white“><b class=“topfont“>Kalender</b></
a></li>

                <li><a href=“/pages/wis/wissen_uebersicht.html?word=Wissen“ title=“Wissen“ class=“white“><b class=“topfont“>Wissen</b></a></li>
                <li><a href=“/pages/kue/kuenstler_uebersicht.html?word=K%26uuml%3Bnstler“ title=“K&uuml;nstler“ class=“white“><b
class=“topfont“>K&uuml;nstler</b></a></li>
                <li><a href=“/pages/job/kunst_kaufen.html?word=Kunst+kaufen“ title=“Kunst kaufen“ class=“white“><b class=“topfont“>Kunst kaufen</
b></a></li>
                <li><a href=“/pages/auk/auktionen_wochenuebersicht.html?word=Auktionen“ title=“Auktionen“ class=“white“><b
class=“topfont“>Auktionen</b></a></li>
                <li><a href=“/pages/prz/adressen_startseite.html?word=Galerien“ title=“Galerien“ class=“white“><b class=“topfont“>Galerien</b></
a></li>
                <li><a href=“/pages/prz/kunsthandel_adressen.html?word=Kunsthandel“ title=“Kunsthandel“ class=“white“><b
class=“topfont“>Kunsthandel</b></a></li>

                <li><a href=“/pages/adr/adressen_startseite.html?word=Adressen“ title=“Adressen“ class=“white“><b class=“topfont“>Adressen</b></
a></li>
                <div class=“clear:both“></div>
                </ul>
    </td>    <td><img src=“/images/navigation/all_dummy.gif“ width=“18“ height=“1“ border=“0“ alt=““></td>
</tr>
<tr><td colspan=“3“><img src=“/images/navigation/all_dummy.gif“ width=“9“ height=“5“ border=“0“ alt=““></td></tr>

<tr><td valign=“top“ colspan=“3“ bgcolor=“#676568“><img src=“/images/navigation/all_dummy.gif“ width=“10“ height=“1“ border=“0“
alt=““></td></tr>
<tr><td valign=“top“ colspan=“3“ bgcolor=“#676767“><img src=“/images/navigation/all_dummy.gif“ width=“10“ height=“1“ border=“0“
alt=““></td></tr>
<tr><td valign=“top“ colspan=“3“ bgcolor=“#8a8a8a“><img src=“/images/navigation/all_dummy.gif“ width=“10“ height=“1“ border=“0“
alt=““></td></tr>
<tr><td valign=“top“ colspan=“3“ bgcolor=“#b3b3b3“><img src=“/images/navigation/all_dummy.gif“ width=“10“ height=“1“ border=“0“
alt=““></td></tr>


</table>
<!--- left empty no Ads serving --><iframe src=“/includes/werbung_headder.php3?k=werbung“ title=“werbung“ class=“iframeBanner“
width=“100%“

border=“0“ style=“background-color:#FFF8EA; border:none; height:110px; padding-top:0; overflow: hidden; border-top:1px solid black;“
scrolling=“no“ marginheight=“0“ marginwidth=“0“ frameborder=“0“></iframe><!-- Content-Bereich (Aufteilung) -->
<table width=“100%“ border=“0“ cellspacing=“0“ cellpadding=“0“>
<tr>
    <!-- Spalte mit Bild unten und Unterrubriken -->

<td width=“50“ align=“left“ valign=“top“ bgcolor=“#fff8ea“><img src=“/images/navigation/all_dummy.gif“ width=“18“ height=“18“ border=“0“
alt=““><!-- Linke Teasespalte - EINE TABELLENZELLE -->
```

```
<!-- LFTOUT HEADER -->
bgcolor=“#E7A300“><img src=“/images/navigation/all_dummy.gif“ width=“1“ height=“1“ border=“0“ alt=““></td></tr><tr><td
colspan=“12“ valign=“top“><img src=“/images/navigation/all_dummy.gif“ width=“9“ height=“9“ border=“0“ alt=““></td></tr><tr><td valign=“top“
colspan=“12“align=“left“><p class=“quelleb“><b>Weitere Inhalte: </b></p></td></tr><tr><td colspan=“12“ valign=“top“><img src=“/images/
navigation/all_dummy.gif“ width=“9“ height=“9“ border=“0“ alt=““></td></tr><tr><td valign=“top“ align=“right“><p class=“quelleb“><b>&#8226;<img
src=“/images/navigation/all_dummy.gif“ width=“2“ height=“2“ border=“0“><img src=“/images/navigation/all_dummy.gif“ width=“4.5“ height=“4.5“
border=“0“ alt=““></b></p></td><td valign=“top“align=“left“><p class=“quelleb“><b>Veranstaltung vom: </b></p><p class=“quelle“><a
href=“http://www.kunstmarkt.de/pageskal/kunst/_id214467-/event_detail.html?_q=%20“ title=“
10.07.2010, Michael Riedel - The quick brown fox jumps over the lazy dog“><br>

10.07.2010, Michael Riedel - The quick brown fox jumps over the lazy dog</a></p></td><td valign=“top“><img src=“/images/navigation/
all_dummy.gif“ width=“9“ height=“9“ border=“0“ alt=““></td><td valign=“top“ align=“right“><p class=“quelleb“><b>&#8226;<img src=“/images/
navigation/all_dummy.gif“ width=“2“ height=“2“ border=“0“><img src=“/images/navigation/all_dummy.gif“ width=“4.5“ height=“4.5“ border=“0“
alt=““></b></p></td><td valign=“top“align=“left“><p class=“quelleb“><b>Bei: </b></p><p class=“quelle“><a href=“http://www.kunstmarkt.de/
pagesall/kunst/_id65525-/notdoneyet.html?_q=%20“ title=“
Kunstverein in Hamburg“><br>
Kunstverein in Hamburg</a></p></td><td valign=“top“><img src=“/images/navigation/all_dummy.gif“ width=“9“ height=“9“ border=“0“
alt=““></td><td valign=“top“ align=“right“><p class=“quelleb“><b>&#8226;<img src=“/images/navigation/all_dummy.gif“ width=“2“ height=“2“
border=“0“><img src=“/images/navigation/all_dummy.gif“ width=“4.5“ height=“4.5“ border=“0“ alt=““></b></p></td><td valign=“top“align=“left“><p
class=“quelleb“><b>Variabilder: </b></p><p class=“quelle“><a href=“http://www.kunstmarkt.de/pagesmag/kunst/_id215773-/marktberichte_
grossbildansicht.html?_q=%20“ title=“
Michael Riedel, The quick brown fox jumps over the lazy dog, 2010“><img src=“/kunstmarkt/cms/upload/news/thumb100/l1160060.jpg“
width=“100“ height=“75“ border=“0“ title=“Michael Riedel, The quick brown fox jumps over the lazy dog, 2010“ alt=“Michael Riedel, The quick
brown fox jumps over the lazy dog, 2010“><br>
Michael Riedel, The quick brown fox jumps over the lazy dog, 2010</a></p></td><td valign=“top“><img src=“/images/navigation/all_dummy.
gif“ width=“9“ height=“9“ border=“0“ alt=““></td></tr><tr><td colspan=“12“ valian=“top“><img src=“/images/navigation/all_dummy.gif“ width=“9“
height=“9“ border=“0“ alt=““></td></tr><tr><td valign=“top“ align=“right“><p class=“quelleb“><b>&#8226;<img src=“/images/navigation/all_
dummy.gif“ width=“2“ height=“2“ border=“0“><img src=“/images/navigation/all_dummy.gif“ width=“4.5“ height=“4.5“ border=“0“ alt=““></b></p></
td><td valign=“top“align=“left“><p class=“quelleb“><b>Variabilder: </b></p><p class=“quelle“><a href=“http://www.kunstmarkt.de/pagesmag/
kunst/_id215774-/marktberichte_grossbildansicht.html?_q=%20“ title=“
Michael Riedel, The quick brown fox jumps over the lazy dog, 2010“><img src=“/kunstmarkt/cms/upload/news/thumb100/l1160061.jpg“
width=“100“ height=“75“ border=“0“ title=“Michael Riedel, The quick brown fox jumps over the lazy dog, 2010“ alt=“Michael Riedel, The quick
brown fox jumps over the lazy dog, 2010“><br>
Michael Riedel, The quick brown fox jumps over the lazy dog, 2010</a></p></td><td valign=“top“><img src=“/images/navigation/all_dummy.
gif“ width=“9“ height=“9“ border=“0“ alt=““></td><td valign=“top“ align=“right“><p class=“quelleb“><b>&#8226;<img src=“/images/navigation/
all_dummy.gif“ width=“2“ height=“2“ border=“0“><img src=“/images/navigation/all_dummy.gif“ width=“4.5“ height=“4.5“ border=“0“ alt=““></b></
p></td><td valign=“top“align=“left“><p class=“quelleb“><b>Variabilder: </b></p><p class=“quelle“><a href=“http://www.kunstmarkt.de/pagesmag/
kunst/_id215775-/marktberichte_grossbildansicht.html?_q=%20“ title=“
Michael Riedel, The quick brown fox jumps over the lazy dog, 2010“><img src=“/kunstmarkt/cms/upload/news/thumb100/l1160073.jpg“
width=“100“ height=“133“ border=“0“ title=“Michael Riedel, The quick brown fox jumps over the lazy dog, 2010“ alt=“Michael Riedel, The quick
brown fox jumps over the lazy dog, 2010“><br>
Michael Riedel, The quick brown fox jumps over the lazy dog, 2010</a></p></td><td valign=“top“><img src=“/images/navigation/all_dummy.
gif“ width=“9“ height=“9“ border=“0“ alt=““></td><td valign=“top“ align=“right“><p class=“quelleb“><b>&#8226;<img src=“/images/navigation/all_
dummy.gif“ width=“2“ height=“2“ border=“0“><img src=“/images/navigation/all_dummy.gif“ width=“4.5“ height=“4.5“ border=“0“ alt=““></b></p></
td><td valign=“top“align=“left“><p class=“quelleb“><b>K&uuml;nstler: </b></p><p class=“quelle“> Michael Riedel</p></td><td valign=“top“><img
src=“/images/navigation/all_dummy.gif“ width=“9“ height=“9“ border=“0“ alt=““></td></tr><tr><td colspan=“12“ valian=“top“><img src=“/images/
navigation/all_dummy.gif“ width=“9“ height=“9“ border=“0“ alt=““></td></tr></table><script type=“text/javascript“><!--
    google_ad_client = „pub-2901863932883369“;
    google_ad_width = 300;
    google_ad_height = 250;
    google_ad_format = „300x250_as“;
    google_color_border = „0C0F85“;
    google_color_bg = „FFF8EA“;
    google_color_link = „0000FF“;
    google_color_url = „0000FF“;
    google_color_text = „000000“;
    //--></script>

<br><div align=“center“><script type=“text/javascript“ src=“http://pagead2.googlesyndication.com/pagead/show_ads.js“>
</script></div><br>

        <!-- table mit Logo und Copyright-Text -->
        <table width=“100%“ border=“0“ cellspacing=“0“ cellpadding=“0“ align=“left“ valign=“top“ bgcolor=“#fff8ea“>

                <tr><td height=“1“ ><img src=“/images/navigation/all_dummy.gif“ width=“9“ height=“1“ border=“0“ alt=““></td>
<td height=“1“ ><img src=“/images/navigation/all_dummy.gif“ width=“132“ height=“1“ border=“0“ alt=““></td>
<td height=“1“ ><img src=“/images/navigation/all_dummy.gif“ width=“9“ height=“1“ border=“0“ alt=““></td></tr>
                <tr>
                <td width=“9“></td><td align=“right“ valign=“bottom“><br><br></td>
                <td width=“9“></td></tr>
        <tr>
                <td></td><td width=“100%“ align=“right“ valign=“middle“ nowrap>
```

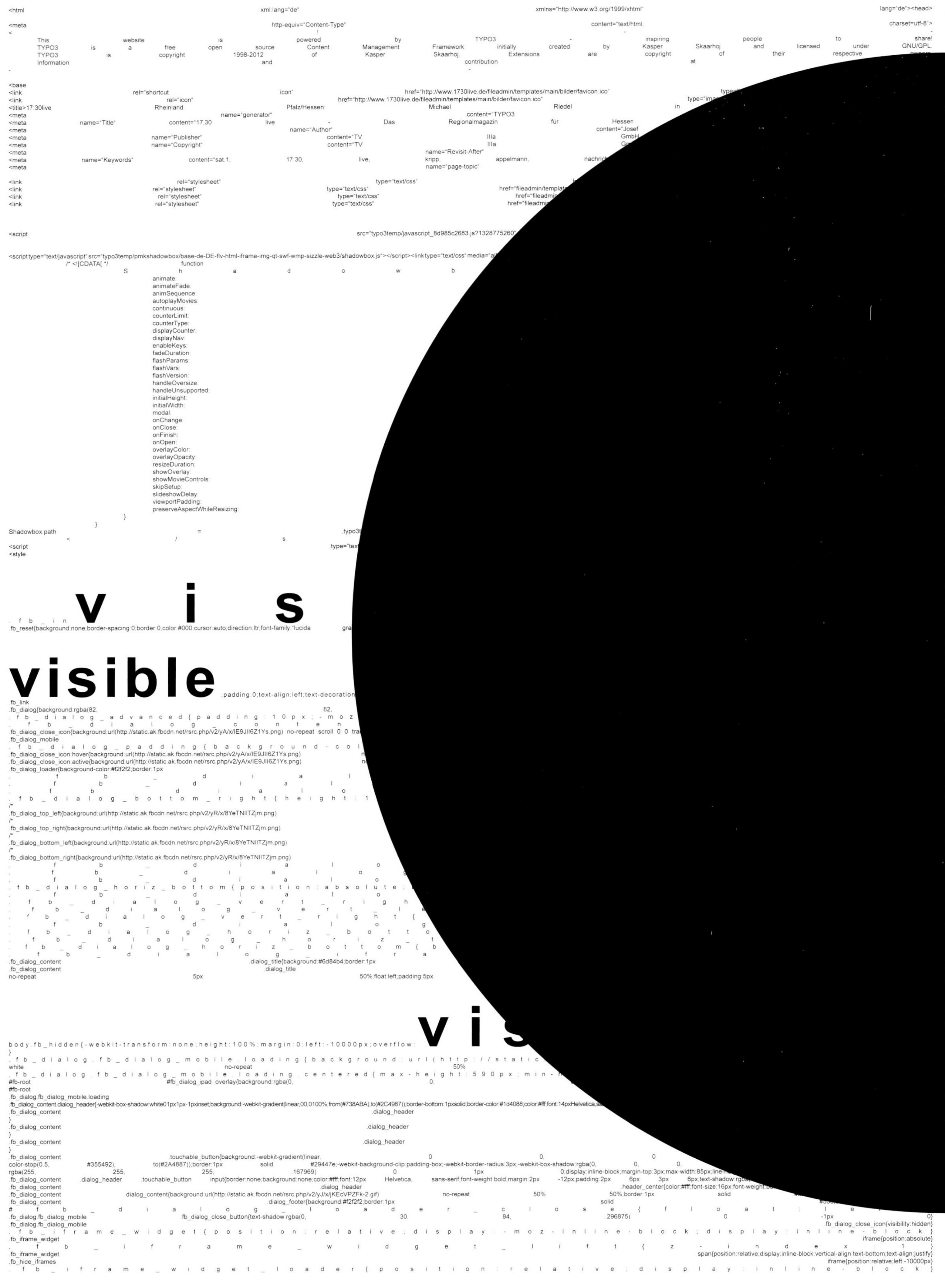
v i s
visible
v i s

visible

http://archive.1730live.de/archiv/news-details/datum/2012/06/18/michael-riedel-in-der-schirn.html
(Accessed June 23, 2012)

```
<html xml:lang=“de“ xmlns=“http://www.w3.org/1999/xhtml“ lang=“de“><head>

<meta http-equiv=“Content-Type“ content=“text/html; charset=utf-8“>
<!--
	This website is powered by TYPO3 - inspiring people to share!
	TYPO3 is a free open source Content Management Framework initially created by Kasper Skaarhoj and licensed under GNU/GPL.
	TYPO3 is copyright 1998-2012 of Kasper Skaarhoj. Extensions are copyright of their respective owners.
	Information and contribution at http://typo3.org/
-->
<script src=“typo3temp/javascript_8d985c2683.js?1328775260“ type=“text/javascript“></script>
<script type=“text/javascript“ src=“typo3temp/pmkshadowbox/base-de-DE-flv-html-iframe-img-qt-swf-wmp-sizzle-web3/shadowbox.js“></
script><link type=“text/css“ media=“all“ rel=“stylesheet“ href=“typo3temp/pmkshadowbox/base-de-DE-flv-html-iframe-img-qt-swf-wmp-sizzle-
web3/shadowbox.css“><script type=“text/javascript“>
		/* <![CDATA[ */			function shadowBoxInit() {
				Shadowbox.init({
					animate: 1,
					animateFade: 1,
					animSequence: ‚sync‘,
					autoplayMovies: 1,
					continuous: 0,
					counterLimit: 10,
					counterType: ‚default‘,
					displayCounter: 1,
					displayNav: 1,
					enableKeys: 1,
					fadeDuration: 0.35,
					flashParams: {bgcolor:“#000000“,allowfullscreen:“true“},
					flashVars: {},
					flashVersion: ‚9.0.0‘,
					handleOversize: ‚resize‘,
					handleUnsupported: ‚link‘,
					initialHeight: 630,
					initialWidth: 820,
					modal: 0,
					onChange: function() {},
					onClose: function() {},
					onFinish: function() {},
					onOpen: function() {},
					overlayColor: ‚#333333‘,
					overlayOpacity: 0.5,
					resizeDuration: 0.35,
					showOverlay: 1,
					showMovieControls: 1,
					skipSetup: 0,
					slideshowDelay: 0,
					viewportPadding: 20,
					preserveAspectWhileResizing: 0
				});
			}
Shadowbox.path = ‚typo3temp/pmkshadowbox/base-de-DE-flv-html-iframe-img-qt-swf-wmp-sizzle-web3/‘;shadowBoxInit();;/* ]]> */
		</script>
<script type=“text/javascript“ src=“http://www.1730live.de/typo3conf/ext/rgmediaimages/res/swfobject.js“></script>
<style type=“text/css“>.fb_hidden{position:absolute;top:-10000px;z-index:10001}

.fb_invisible{display:none}
.fb_reset{background:none;border-spacing:0;border:0;color:#000;cursor:auto;direction:ltr;font-family:“lucida grande“, tahoma, verdana, arial,

sans-serif;font-size:11px;font-style:normal;font-variant:normal;font-weight:normal;letter-spacing:normal;line-height:1;margin:0;overflow:
visible;padding:0;text-align:left;text-decoration:none;text-indent:0;text-shadow:none;text-transform:none;visibility:visible;white-
space:normal;word-spacing:normal}
.fb_link img{border:none}
.fb_dialog{background:rgba(82, 82, 82, .7);position:absolute;top:-10000px;z-index:10001}
.fb_dialog_advanced{padding:10px;-moz-border-radius:8px;-webkit-border-radius:8px;border-radius:8px}
.fb_dialog_content{background:#fff;color:#333}
.fb_dialog_close_icon{background:url(http://static.ak.fbcdn.net/rsrc.php/v2/yA/x/IE9JII6Z1Ys.png) no-repeat scroll 0 0 transparent;_background-
image:url(http://static.ak.fbcdn.net/rsrc.php/v2/y6/x/s816eWC-2sl.gif);cursor:pointer;display:block;height:15px;position:absolute;right:18px;top:17p
x;width:15px;top:8px\9;right:7px\9}
```

Untitled (visible), 2013
Offset print
23 x 16 1/2 inches
(58.4 x 41.9 cm)

click

print

http://slash-paris.com/en/evenements/michael-riedel/
(Accessed June 23, 2012)

```
<!DOCTYPE html>
<html xmlns="http://www.w3.org/1999/xhtml" xml:lang="en" lang="en">

        <head>

                <meta http-equiv="Content-Type" content="text/html; charset=utf-8" />
                <title>Michael Riedel — Michel Rein Gallery — Exhibition —  Slash Paris</title>
                <link rel="shortcut icon" type="image/png" href="/favicon.ico" />


    <meta name="description" content="Whether an artwork be realized or not, is not what matters. What matters is that it exists. And to exist,
the artwork needs to meet an audience. It has to circulate, which happens only thro..." />
                                                        <link rel="alternate" href="/en/lieux/michel-rein/feed" title="Slash — Michel Rein Gallery"
type="application/rss+xml" />

                        <link rel="image_src"                                                                   href="http://
medias.slash.fr/events/images/000/000/699/REIN_RiedelPanopress_grid.jpg?1288801924" />
        <meta name="title"                                                                      content="Michael Riedel" />
        <meta property="og:url"                                                         content="http://www.slash.fr/en/evenements/
michael-riedel" />
        <meta property="og:title"                                               content="Michael Riedel" />
        <meta property="og:type"                                                        content="article"/>
        <meta property="og:url"                                                         content="http://www.slash.fr/en/evenements/
michael-riedel" />
        <meta property="og:image"                                               content="http://medias.slash.fr/events/
images/000/000/699/REIN_RiedelPanopress_grid.jpg?1288801924"/>

        <meta property="og:description"                 content="Whether an artwork be realized or not, is not what matters. What
matters is that it exists. And to exist, the artwork needs to meet an audience. It has to circulate, which happens only thro..."/>

        <meta property="og:latitude"                                    content="48.8578284"/>
<meta property="og:longitude"                   content="2.3644538"/>
<meta property="og:street-address"          content="42, rue de Turenne"/>
<meta property="og:locality"                            content="Paris"/>
<meta property="og:postal-code"                  content="75003"/>
<meta property="og:email"                                       content="galerie@michelrein.com"/>
<meta property="og:phone_number"                content="01 42 72 68 13"/>

                                <meta property="fb:admins" content="643236885" />
                <meta name="zipcode" content="75" />
                <meta name="city" content="Paris" />
                <meta name="country" content="France" />
                <meta name="google-site-verification" content="iY_KcFnOByVCmF0zjTgOwJsjt-4tVsjahMMduE7jiN8" />

         <!-- <meta name="viewport" content="initial-scale=0.47" /> -->
                <meta name="viewport" content="width=661, user-scalable=yes" />
                <meta name="apple-mobile-web-app-capable" content="no" />

                <link href="/stylesheets/application_packaged.css?1289069956" media="all" rel="stylesheet" type="text/css" />

                        <style type="text/css" media="screen">
                #navigator #back, #navigator #previous, #navigator #next {
                        background-color: #265595;
                }
                #event-ticker #kind p {
                        color: #265595;
                }
        </style>
                <script src="/javascripts/base_packaged.js?1289069952" type="text/javascript"></script>

                <div id="wrap">
                        <div id="wrap-inner">                                                   <a class="addthis_
button_email"></a>
                                        </div>
                                        <div                    Screen-printing, son
 id="header">
                                                <ul class='tools'>

                                <li id='search'>
```

Untitled (click 2), 2013
Offset print
23 x 16 1/2 inches
(58.4 x 41.9 cm)

<form action="/en/recherche" id="global-
id='4'><img alt="Rein_riedel_101510_043press_grid" src="http://medias.slash.fr/medias/images/000/002/802/REIN_Riedel_101510_043press_grid.jpg?1288802570" /></a></li>

<li class='last'><a href="#"
id='5'><img alt="Rein_riedel_101510_069press_grid" src="http://medias.slash.fr/medias/images/000/002/801/REIN_Riedel_101510_069press_grid.jpg?1288802496" /></a></li>

</ul>
</div>
<div id="caption">
<small class='dark'>
<strong class='cartel_title'>Vue de l'exposition</strong>
</small>

</div>
</div>

<div id="event-description">
<div class="title">
<h2 class="big_title">
Michael Riedel
<span class='normal'></span>
</h2>
</div>
<div class="paragraph standard_paragraph" lang="en">
<p>
<span class='time_difference'>Ends in 12 days : </span>October 16 → November 20, 2010
</p>

<p>This first solo exhibition of Michael Riedel's work in France announces his entry to the Galerie Michel Rein.</p>

<p>Whether an artwork be realized or not, is not what matters. What matters is that it exists. And to exist, the artwork needs to meet an audience. It has to circulate, which happens only through distribution. In order to exist an artwork must be visible, articles must be written about it, photographs taken and published. It must go through the interpretation of language and be reproduced. The existence of an artwork is therefore dependent on the displacements forced upon it by its distribution. A text always describes it too poorly and offers an interpretation that encloses the questions inherent to the piece. A photograph amputates its volume, its dimensions and a certain number of its aesthetic qualities. Movement only begins when betraying its qualities.</p>
<p>If this movement is central to the existence of an artwork, it seems rather logical to emphasize it, even more so when considering that this circulation will most probably distort the artwork. It is the position that Michael Riedel takes. He feeds the process through which every artwork must go. A circuit made up of exhibitions, media exposures and interpretations. But he feeds it using the modalities belonging to these very displacements. The posters on canvas, Untitled, are in this way made up of information displayed on websites, such as a page from the New York MoMA, describing one of Riedel's pieces from their collection, or a cultural information website, announcing news and events of the art world. In both cases, the information available about Michael Riedel's work is used as material.</p>
<p>This type of information is, furthermore produced on a regular basis by protocols that Riedel himself puts into effect. A poster containing text and images accompanies each of his exhibitions. Photographs are taken on the spot, representing the project as it develops, far from the so-called neutrality of "installation views". The texts are monologues or discussions, sound-recorded through a computer reading device that automatically transcribes text into spoken words. Even though they are produced live and in a mechanical manner, they are, just as any other press release or magazine interview, separate from their subject matter despite their intentions. These posters portray an object from which they are distanced. Their faithfulness is betrayed by their very nature.
The posters have been assembled into a book : Gedruckte und nicht gedruckte Poster 2003-08 (**Print**ed and Un**print**ed Posters, 2003-

2008). The technique used to create the book consisted of assembling the 43 posters onto a unique **print**ing plate that was cut to create a publication much smaller than the posters themselves. Consequently, the book's lay out prevents us from reading its content. Here again we see the adaptation to a format and a means of distribution that distances the object from what it's supposed to represent. These distortions are fundamental to Michael Riedel's work.</p>
<p>The font used by Riedel is Arial, a sort of cheap Helvetica, used by default. His page layouts reveal the same neutrality. They seem to be the result of a copy-paste that is not faithful to its original source. Both are revealing signs of a change of medium producing a change of the content and endangering its ability to be read. The series Four Proposals for the change of modern also displays this type of modification. During an exhibition in 2008 at the Modern Institute in Glasgow, Michael Riedel extracted the word "Modern" from the logo of the institution cutting it into a piece of black

fabric presented as a banner. Using the cut fabric as a stencil the artist creates a series of digital **print**s on white canvas, equal importance being given to the process of production and the final product. Beginning with Four Proposals for the change of Modern in the logo of the Modern Institute, hidden versions of the word Modern have emerged and continue to evolve from each other creating an infinite yet foreseeable number of possibilities. These interpretations do not necessarily give us information about Michael Riedel's work but, as with his posters and postcards, inform us of it's existence and the fact that it is communicated to the world.</p>
</div>

<div class="editor">François Aubart, October 2010 </div>

<div class="facebook_like">

```
<iframe src=“http://www.facebook.com/plugins/like.php?href=http://www.slash.fr/en/evenements/michael-riedel&amp;layout=button_
count&amp;show_faces=false&amp;font=lucida%2Bgrande“ scrolling=“no“ frameborder=“0“ style=“border:none; overflow:hidden; width:450px;
height:23px“ allowTransparency=“true“></iframe>
</div>

        </div>

</div>

<div id=“right-col“>


        <style type=“text/css“ media=“screen“>
                #venue-card {
                        background: url(/images/maps/map_back_3.png) no-repeat 60px 86px;
                }
        </style>

<div id=“venue-card“>

<div id=“top-bar“>

                        <a href=‘/en/lieux/michel-rein‘ id=‘info-bar‘>
                                <span id=“name“ class=‘bold‘>Michel Rein Gallery</span>
                                <span id=“venue-kind“><span class=‘venue_style  k1 full_tag‘>Gallery</span></span>
                                <span id=“button-label“>Details</span>
                </a>
                                <div id=“v-separator“ ><!-- --></div>


   <a href=“javascript:history.back();“ class=“map_button on“>Map</a>
   <a href=“/en/lieux/michel-rein/plan“ class=“map_button off“>Map</a>
        </div>
        <div class=“dotted_line“><!-- --></div>



<div id=“minimap-container“>
                        <span id=“zone-name“>03 Le Marais</span>
                        <a href=‘javascript:history.back();‘ class=‘zoom_button on‘ title=‘Exit the map mode‘>Zoom out</a>

                        <a href=‘/en/lieux/michel-rein/plan‘ class=‘zoom_button off‘ title=‘Zoom on the map‘>Zoom in</a>
                           <a href=“/en/lieux/michel-rein/plan“ class=“flag kind_1“ style=“left:208px; top:90px;“ title=“Michel Rein
Gallery“><!-- --></a>

</div>

                                <div id=“basic-information“>
                                                <p>
                                        42, rue de Turenne<br/>
                                        75003 Paris
                                </p>


                                                                        <p>
                                        T. 01 42 72 68 13
                                        — F. 01 42 72 81 94
                                </p>

<p><a href=“http://www.michelrein.com“ class=“link“ target=“out“>www.michelrein.com</a></p>
                                        </div>

                                        <div id=“subway-lines“>
                                        <div class=“subway_line“>
                                                                <img alt=“Subway_line_10“ class=“subway_
line_number „ src=“/images/subway_line_10.gif?1289069948“ />


        <span>Chemin Vert</span>
</div>
                                </div>


<div id=“opening-information“ class=‘small_paragraph‘>
<h4 class=“bold“>Opening hours</h4>
<p>Tuesday – Saturday, 11am – 7pm<br/></p>


        </div>
```

Painting

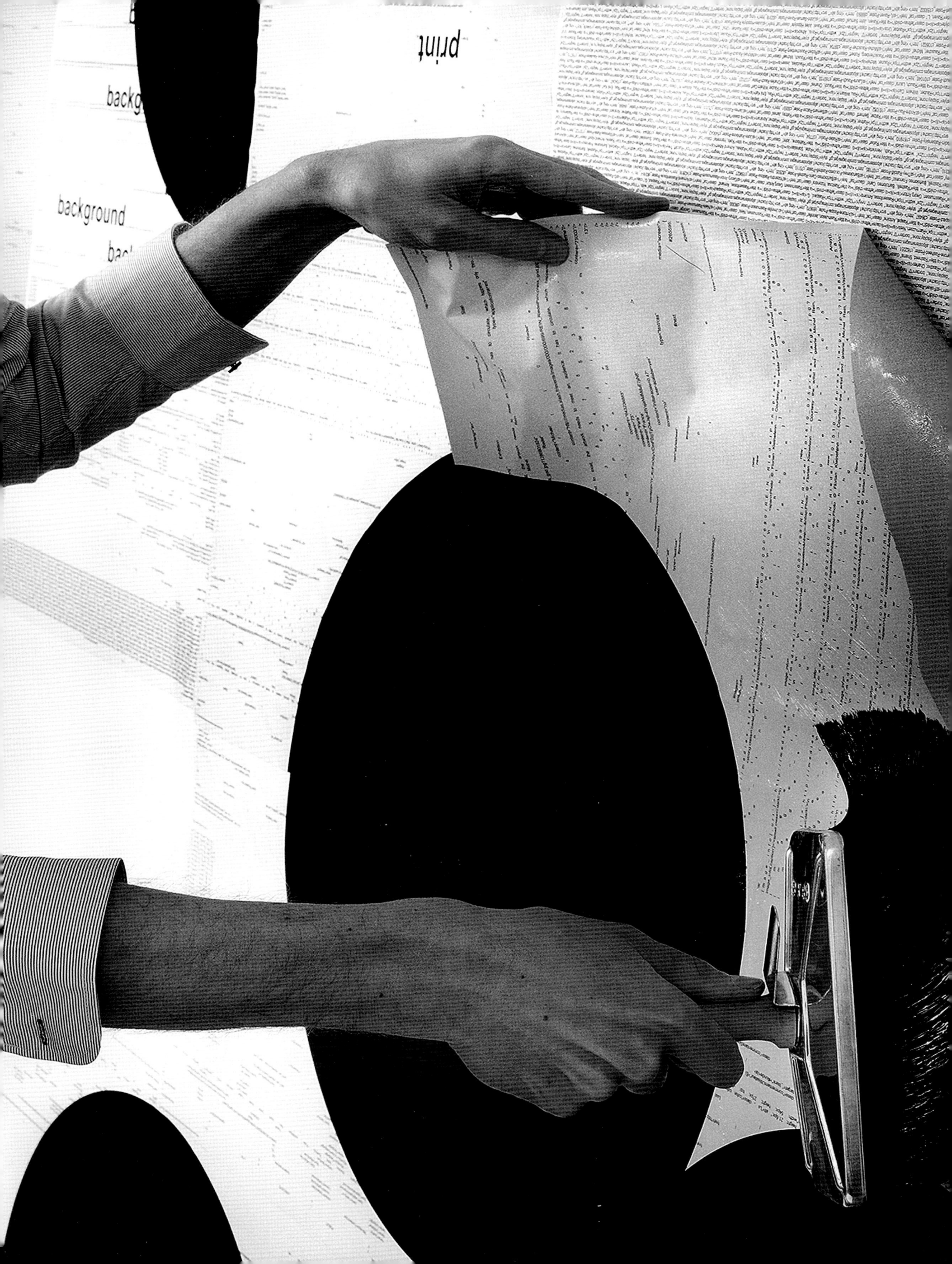
print
background

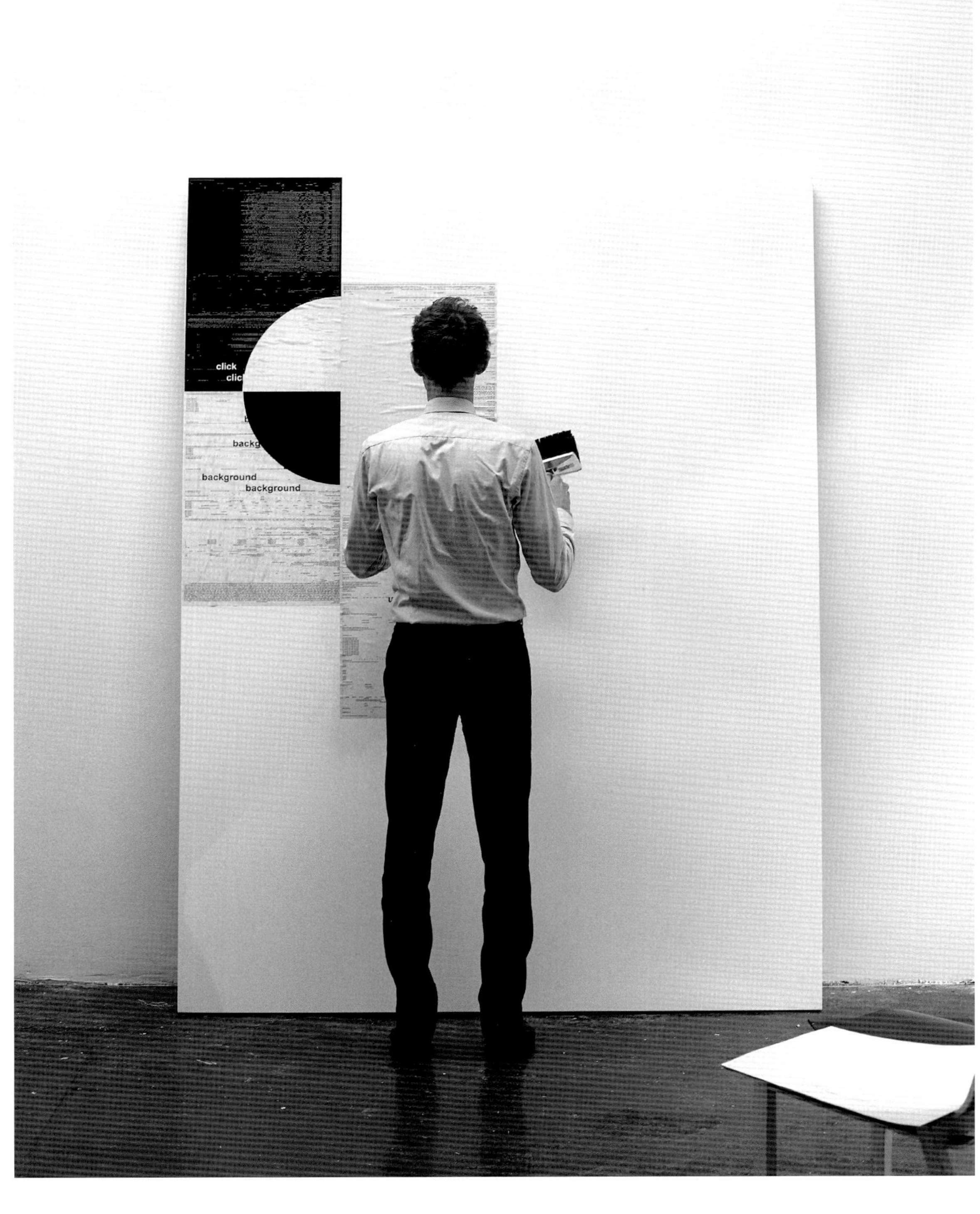

Michael Riedel
London, 2013

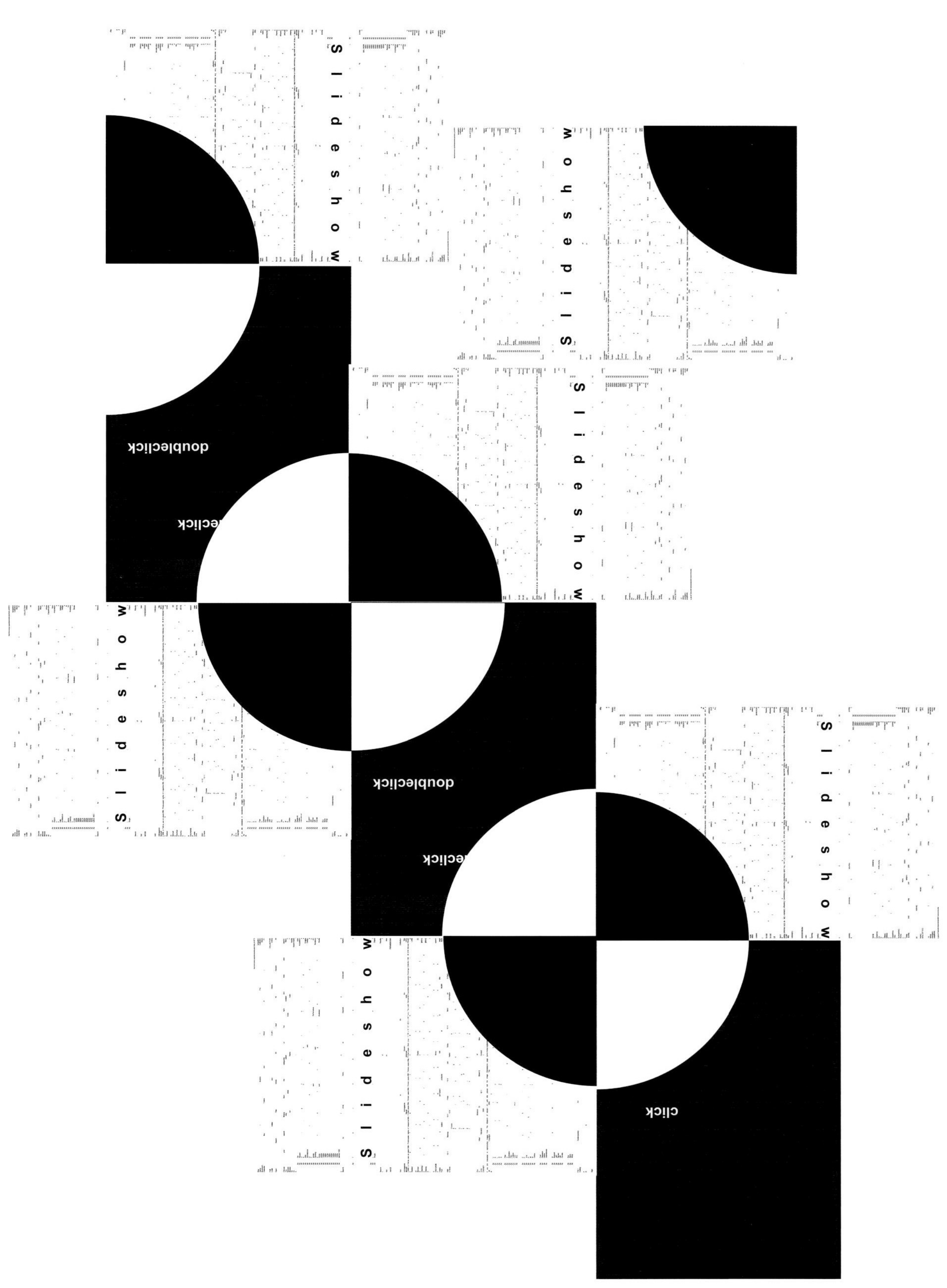

Untitled (Slideshow; doubleclick; click 1), 2011
Silkscreen on linen
90 1/2 x 67 x 2 1/4 inches
(229.9 x 170.2 x 5.7 cm)

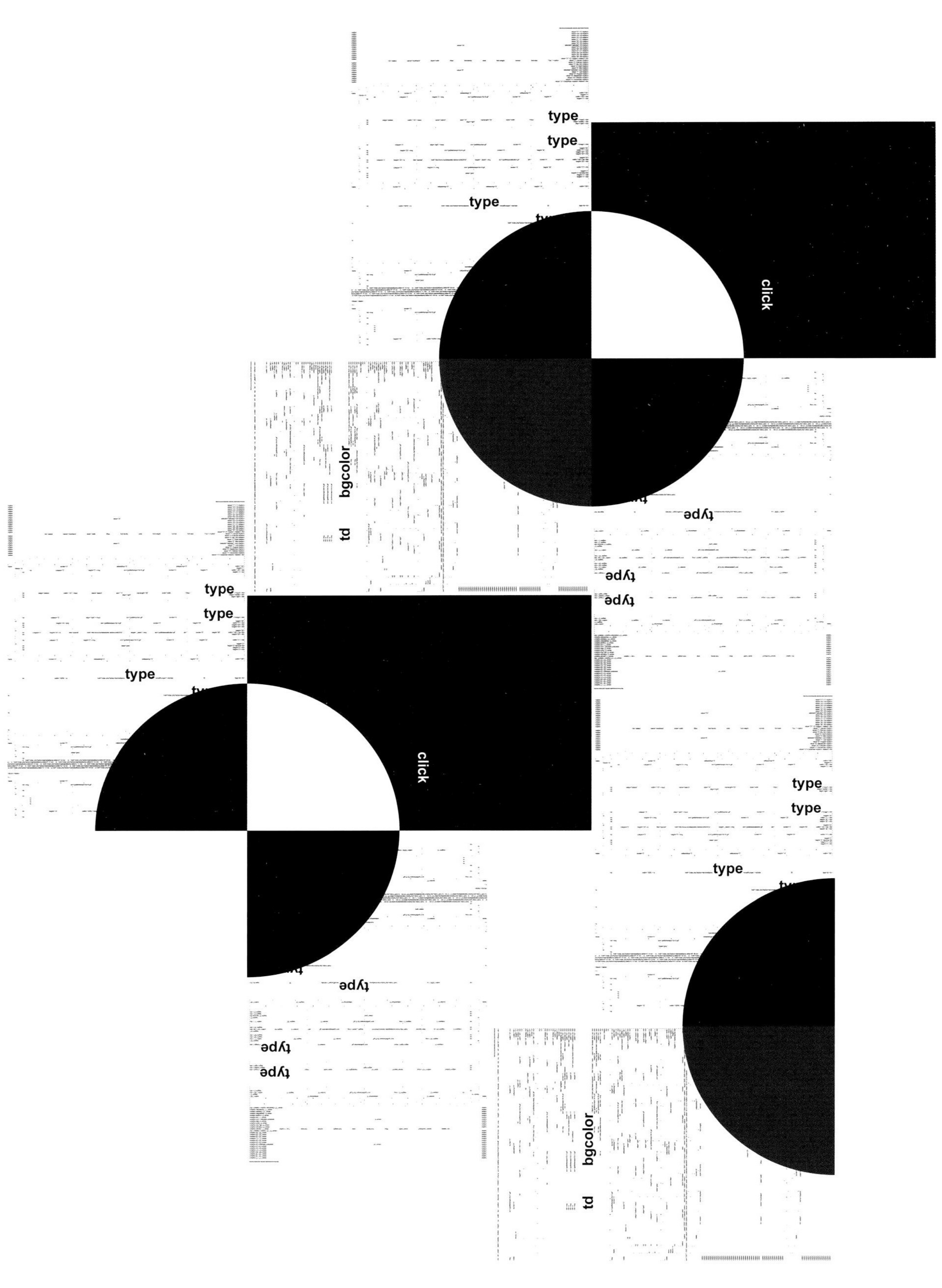

Untitled (type; td bgcolor, purple; click 1), 2010
Posters on linen
90 1/2 x 67 x 2 1/4 inches
(229.9 x 170.2 x 5.7 cm)

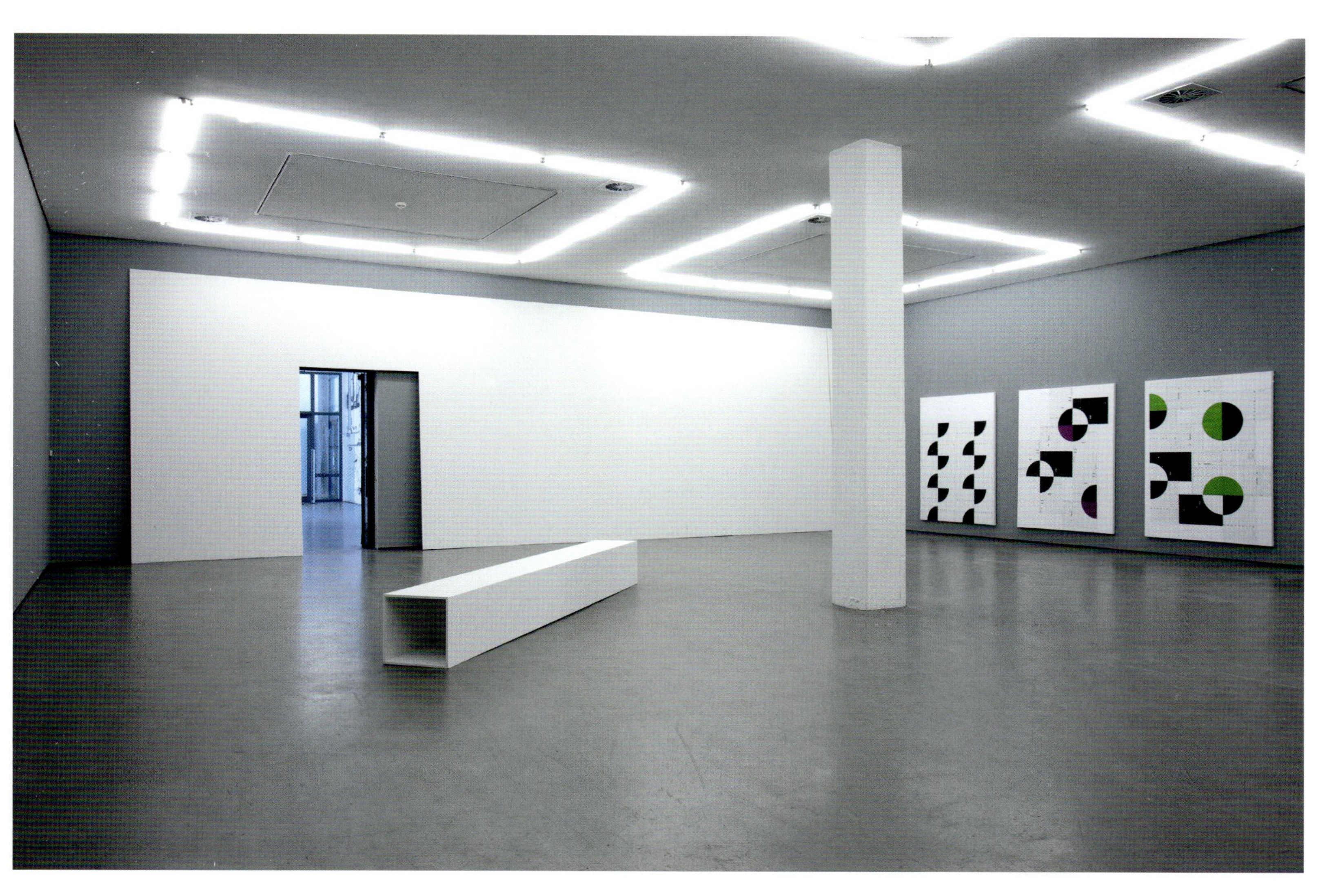

This page & following pages:
Installation views, *Michael Riedel: The quick brown fox jumps over the lazy dog*
Kunstverein Hamburg, 2010

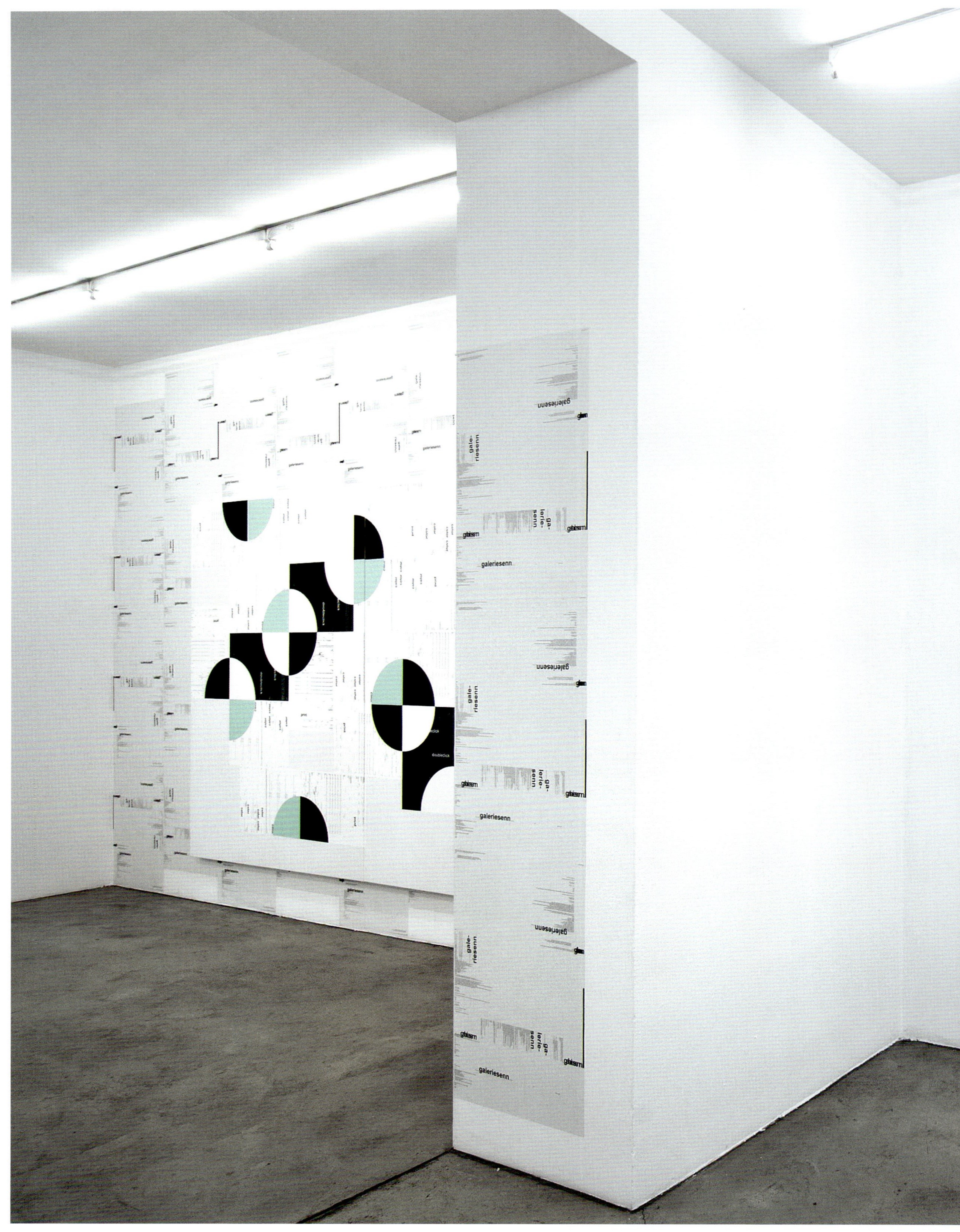
galeriesenn
galeriesenn
galeriesenn

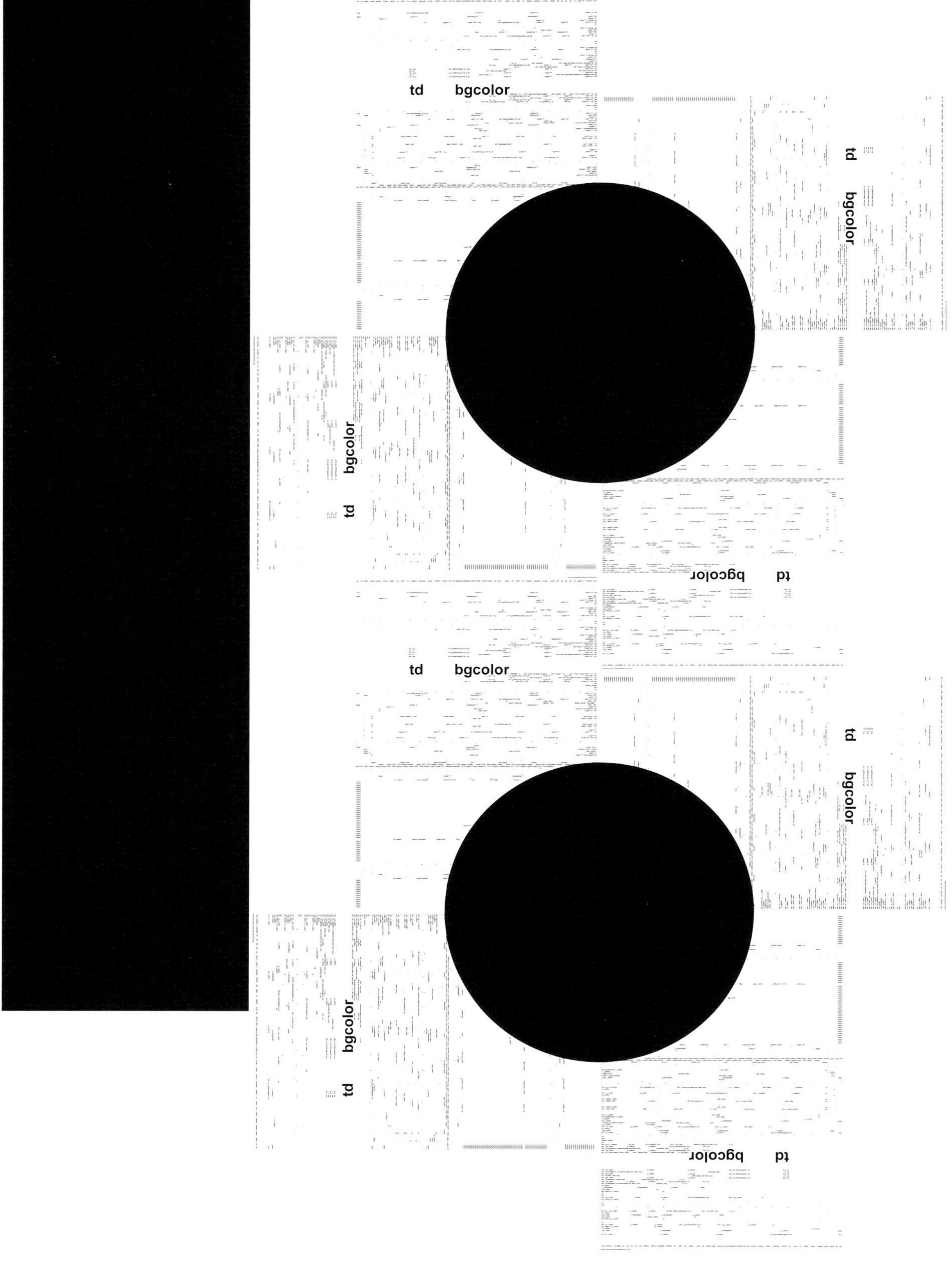
td
bgcolor
td
bgcolor
td
bgcolor
td
bgcolor
td
bgcolor
td
bgcolor
td
bgcolor
td
bgcolor

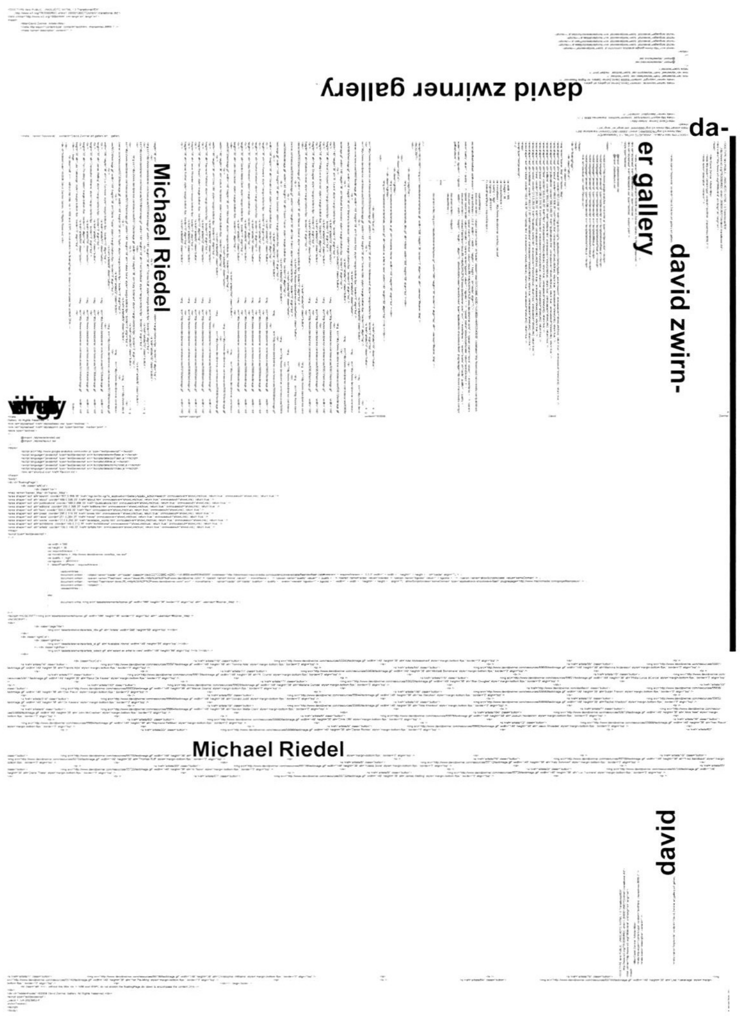

Poster with text from David Zwirner website, http://www.davidzwirner.com/artists/

Untitled (David Zwirner), 2011
Offset print
39 x 27 1/2 inches
(99.1 x 69.9 cm)

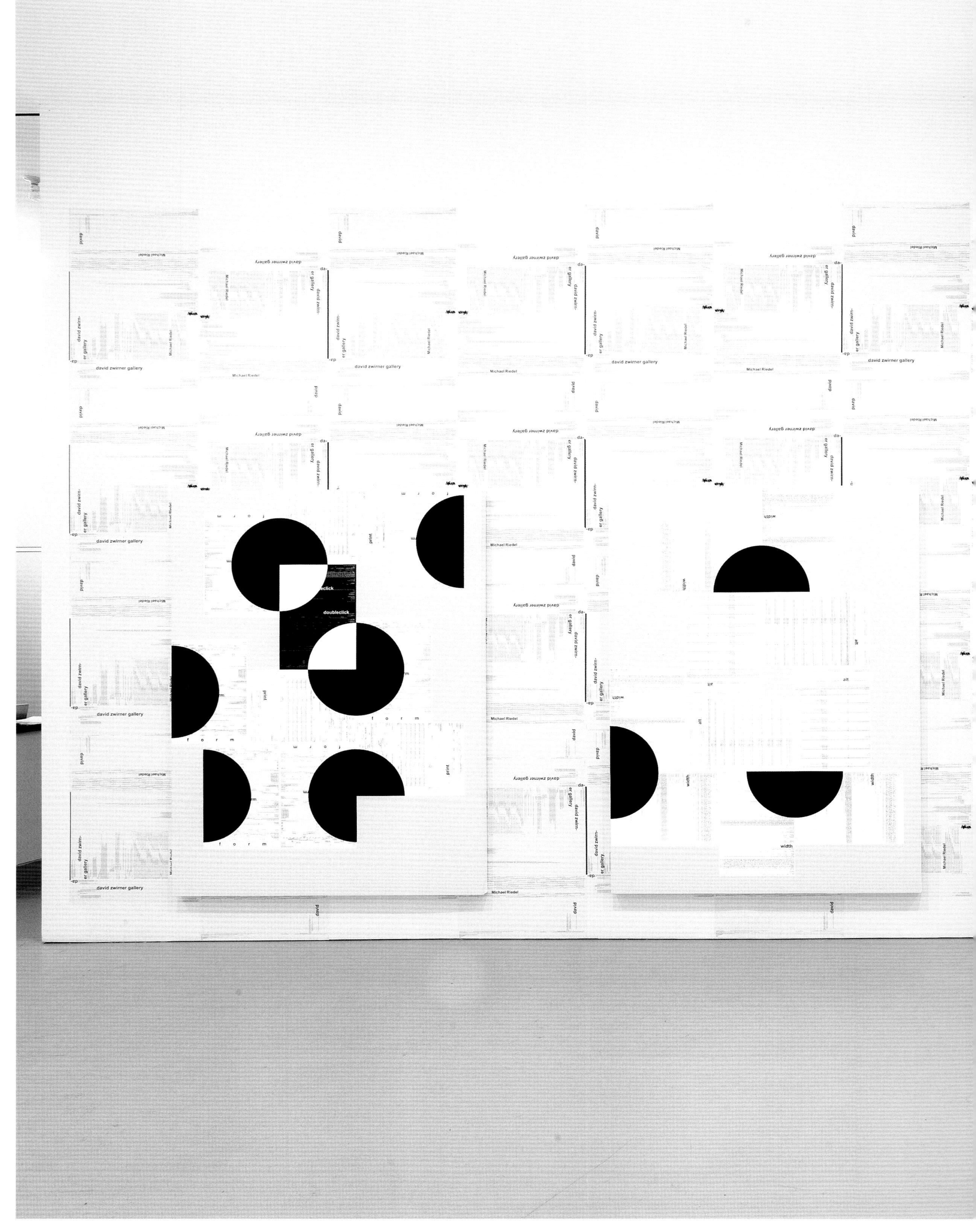
david zwirner gallery
Michael Riedel
doubleclick
form
print
width
alt

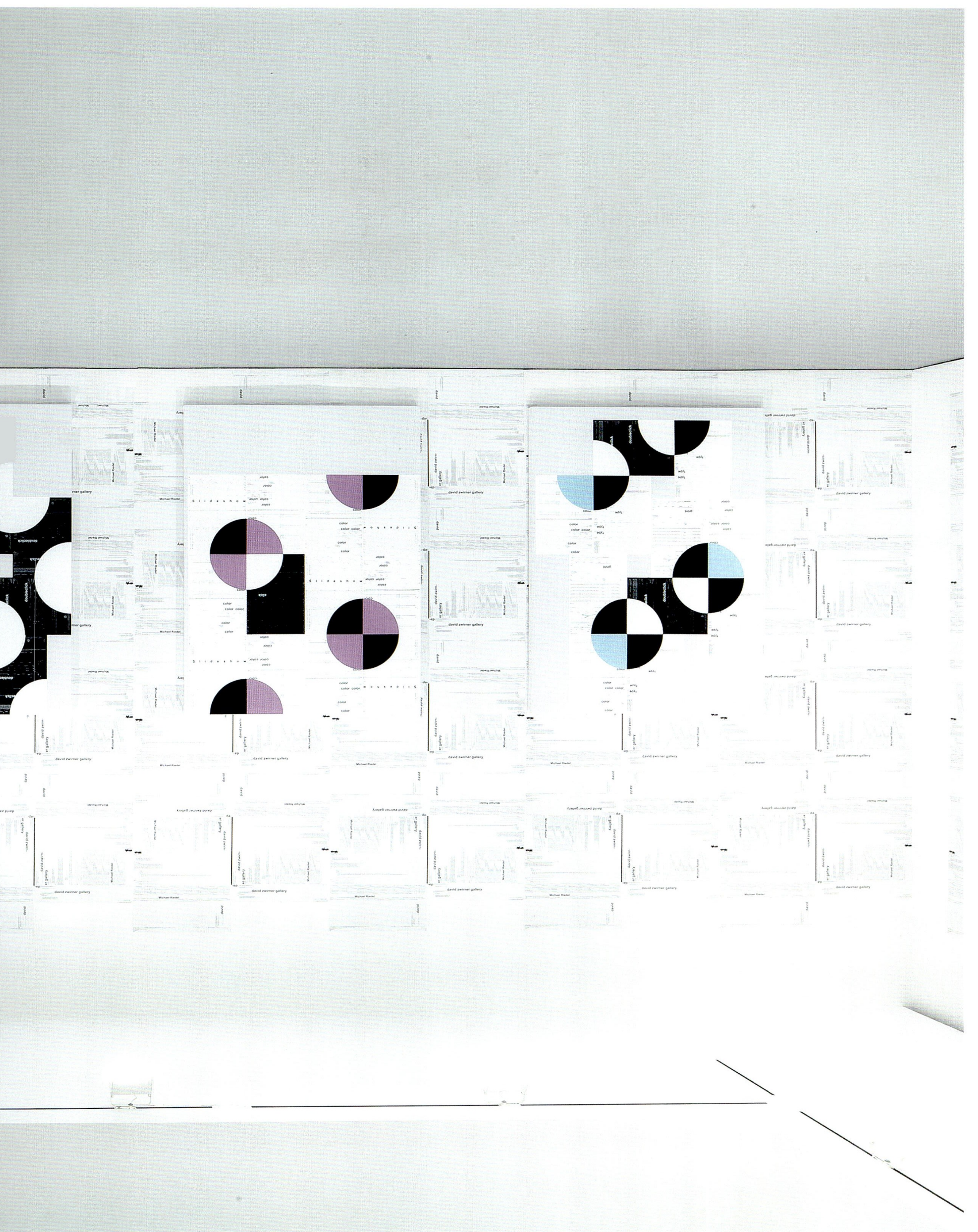
david zwirner gallery
Slideshow
color
doubleclick

Untitled (click 1; form; clear 2; click 2; return; method; poster; display 2; clear 1; print), 2014
Silkscreen on linen
90 1/2 x 67 x 2 1/4 inches
(229.9 x 170.2 x 5.7 cm)

bottom:1px solid;border-color:#1d4088;color:#fff;font:14px Helvetica, sans-serif;font-weight:bold;**text**-overflow:ellipsis;**text**-shadow:rgba(0, 30, 84, .296875) 0 -1px 0;vertical-align:middle;white-space:nowrap}.fb_dialog_content .dialog_header table{-webkit-font-smoothing:subpixel-antialiased;height:43px;width:100%}.fb_dialog_content .dialog_header td.header_left{font-size:12px;padding-left:5px;vertical-align:middle;width:60px}.fb_dialog_content .dialog_header td.header_right{font-size:12px;padding-right:5px;vertical-align:middle;width:60px}.fb_dialog_content .touchable_button{background:-webkit-gradient(linear, 0% 0%, 0% 100%, from(#4966A6), color-stop(.5, #355492), to(#2A4887));border:1px solid #2f477a;-webkit-background-clip:padding-box;-webkit-border-radius:3px;-webkit-box-shadow:rgba(0, 0, 0, .117188) 0 1px 1px inset, rgba(255, 255, 255, .167969) 0 1px 0;display:inline-block;margin-top:3px;max-width:85px;line-height:18px;padding:4px 12px;position:relative}.fb_dialog_content .dialog_header .touchable_button input{border:none;background:none;color:#fff;font:12px Helvetica, sans-serif;font-weight:bold;margin:2px -12px;padding:2px 6px 3px 6px;**text**-shadow:rgba(0, 30, 84, .296875) 0 -1px 0}.fb_dialog_content .dialog_header .header_center{color:#fff;font-size:16px;font-weight:bold;line-height:18px;**text**-align:center;vertical-align:middle}.fb_dialog_content .dialog_content{background:url(http://static.ak.fbcdn.net/rsrc.php/v2/y9/r/jKEcVPZFk-2.gif) no-repeat 50% 50%;border:1px solid #555;border-bottom:0;border-top:0;height:150px}.fb_dialog_content .dialog_footer{background:#f6f7f8;border:1px solid #555;border-top-color:#ccc;height:40px}#fb_dialog_loader_close{float:left}.fb_dialog.fb_dialog_mobile .fb_dialog_close_button{**text**-shadow:rgba(0, 30, 84, .296875) 0 -1px 0}.fb_dialog.fb_dialog_mobile .fb_dialog_close_icon{visibility:hidden}.fb_iframe_widget{display:inline-block;position:relative}.fb_iframe_widget span{display:inline-block;position:relative;**text**align:justify}.fb_iframe_widget iframe{position:absolute}.fb_iframe_widget_fluid_desktop,.fb_iframe_widget_fluid_desktop span,.fb_iframe_widget_fluid_desktop iframe{max-width:100%}.fb_iframe_widget_fluid_desktop iframe{min-width:220px;position:relative}.fb_iframe_widget_lift{z-index:1}.fb_hide_iframes iframe{position:relative;left:-10000px}.fb_iframe_widget_loader{position:relative;display:inline-block}.fb_iframe_widget_fluid{display:inline}.fb_iframe_widget_fluid span{width:100%}.fb_iframe_widget_loader iframe{min-height:32px;z-index:2;zoom:1}.fb_iframe_widget_loader .FB_Loader{background:url(http://static.ak.fbcdn.net/rsrc.php/v2/y9/r/jKEcVPZFk-2.gif) no-repeat;height:32px;width:32px;margin-left:-16px;position:absolute;left:50%;z-index:4}</style></head>

<body class=“blog“>
<!-- this is for fb comments -->
<div class=“ fb_reset“ id=“fb-root“><div style=“position: absolute; top: -10000px; height: 0px; width: 0px;“><div><iframe src=“http://static.ak.facebook.com/connect/xd_arbiter/1ldYU13brY_.js?version=41#channel=f11f24bb7b1f876&origin=http%3A%2F%2Fwww.papermag.com“ style=“border: medium none;“ tabindex=“-1“ title=“Facebook Cross Domain Communication Frame“ aria-hidden=“true“ id=“fb_xdm_frame_http“ scrolling=“no“ allowfullscreen=“true“ allowtransparency=“true“ name=“fb_xdm_frame_http“ frameborder=“0“></iframe><iframe src=“https://s-static.ak.facebook.com/connect/xd_arbiter/1ldYU13brY_.js?version=41#channel=f11f24bb7b1f876&origin=http%3A%2F%2Fwww.papermag.com“ style=“border: medium none;“ tabindex=“-1“ title=“Facebook Cross Domain Communication Frame“ aria-hidden=“true“ id=“fb_xdm_frame_https“ scrolling=“no“ allowfullscreen=“true“ allowtransparency=“true“ name=“fb_xdm_frame_https“ frameborder=“0“></iframe></div></div><div style=“position: absolute; top: -10000px; height: 0px; width: 0px;“><div><iframe src=“https://www.facebook.com/connect/ping?client_id=139143962828899&domain=www.papermag.com&origin=1&redirect_uri=http%3A%2F%2Fstatic.ak.facebook.com%2Fconnect%2Fxd_arbiter%2F1ldYU13brY_.js%3Fversion%3D41%23cb%3Df1c2e0af2e3d462%26domain%3Dwww.papermag.com%26origin%3Dhttp%253A%252F%252Fwww.papermag.com%252Ff11f24bb7b1f876%26relation%3Dparent&response_type=token%2Csigned_request%2Ccode&sdk=joey“ style=“display: none;“ scrolling=“no“ allowfullscreen=“true“ allowtransparency=“true“ name=“f3ca955be59e404“ frameborder=“0“></iframe></div></div></div>
<script>(function(d, s, id) {
var js, fjs = d.getElementsByTagName(s)[0];
if (d.getElementById(id)) return;
js = d.createElement(s); js.id = id;
js.src = „//connect.facebook.net/en_US/all.js#xfbml=1&appId=139143962828899“;
fjs.parentNode.insertBefore(js, fjs);
}(document, ‚script‘, ‚facebook-jssdk‘));</script>
<!-- this was for fb comments -->

<!-- extra_image: -->

<img alt=“michaelriedel1.jpg“ src=“http://cdn.papermag.com/uploaded_images/michaelriedel1.jpg“ class=“mt-image-center“ style=“**text**-align: center; display: block; margin: 0pt auto 20px;“ height=“359“ width=“478“><b>Michael Riedel</b> is a German artist who uses mixed media (Internet pages, in particular) as source material, exploring their various manifestations. That, or he just really likes to Google himself. With his most recent exhibition, <b>“The Quick Brown Fox Jumps Over The Lazy Dog,“</b> showing at <a href=“http://www.davidzwirner.com/“>David Zwirner</a> through March 19th, Riedel uses bits and portions of Internet pages as source material to create abstract collage pieces. A highlight of the exhibit are Riedel‘s silk-screened „poster paintings,“ which are made from cut-and-pasted web **text**s about his art and career, a highlighted word on each canvas („click,“ „type,“ etc.), referring to technological actions as well as the tasks necessary to produce the pieces. We recently chatted with the artist.

<i><b>Tell me about the lecture you gave in 1997 where you wrote your name on a paper bag and put it on your head. Where did that idea stem, and what was the reaction?</b></i>

The paper bag was made for a talk I held at the Städelschule while I was in college. The talk was about possibilities. In 1997, there were many slogans about possibilities like IKEA‘s Entdecke die Möglichkeiten (Discover the possibilities); Audi‘s Das Leben ist voller Möglichkeiten (Life is full of possibilities); and Toyota‘s Nichts ist unmöglich (Nothing is impossible). Increasingly, it was about possibility itself and existence failing because of the possibility to exist -- at least that‘s what it said in the talk.

At the end of the lecture, I pulled the bag with my name on it over my head said, „I‘m Michael Riedel.“ Labeling is usually added on from the outside but in this case, it‘s me labeling myself. I started being the artist watching myself making art. In the talk, I showed a diagram on art history I had found in a book. It listed art movements from 1800 to the present. In this case, the present was 1980 and 1995 and I continued the writing of art history by copying the diagram to A4 and then A5 format and inserted it back into art history. That way, on the one hand, it was a statement about art history repeating itself in 1995 and on the other hand, it was happening at the same time somehow. But as a result, 1995 is also being repeated within this repetition and so forth, which sets off a perpetual motion.

<b>Of this current exhibit, you have said, „I‘m not just the artist making art but also the artist watching himself making art and perceiving this process as art.“ Can you elaborate on this? </b>

I did a lot of works by labeling existing works. After these overwritings were made and exhibited, they appeared on the Internet in online reviews or interviews -- like the one we‘re doing now. Overwritten again -- descriptions, addresses, comments -- I took whole web pages that were mentioning works of mine to use them as backgrounds in my paintings.

<i><b> Your new work is ultimately based around material from the Internet. Have you always been fascinated with

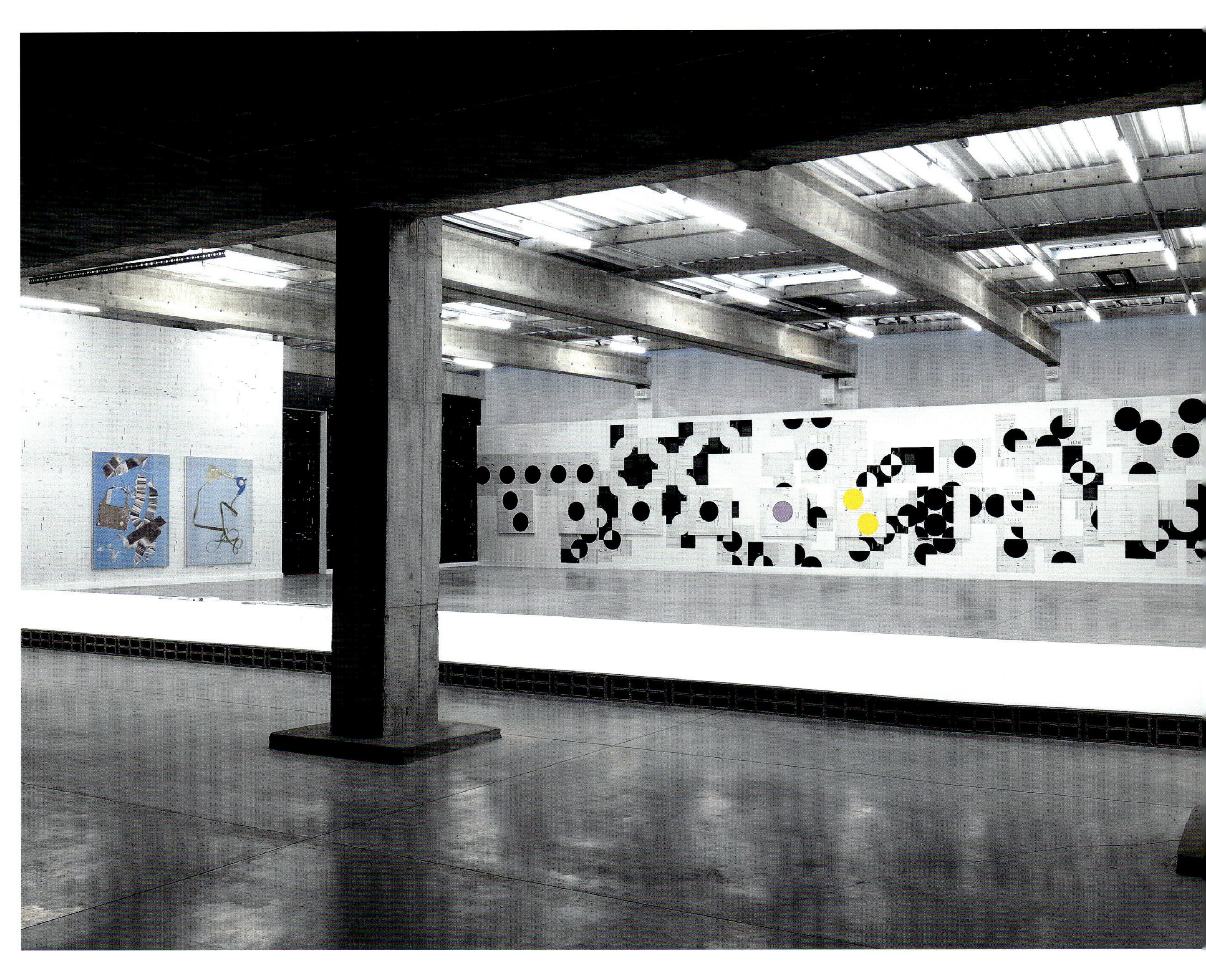

Installation view, *Michael Riedel*
Le Box – Fonds M-ARCO, Marseille, France, 2015

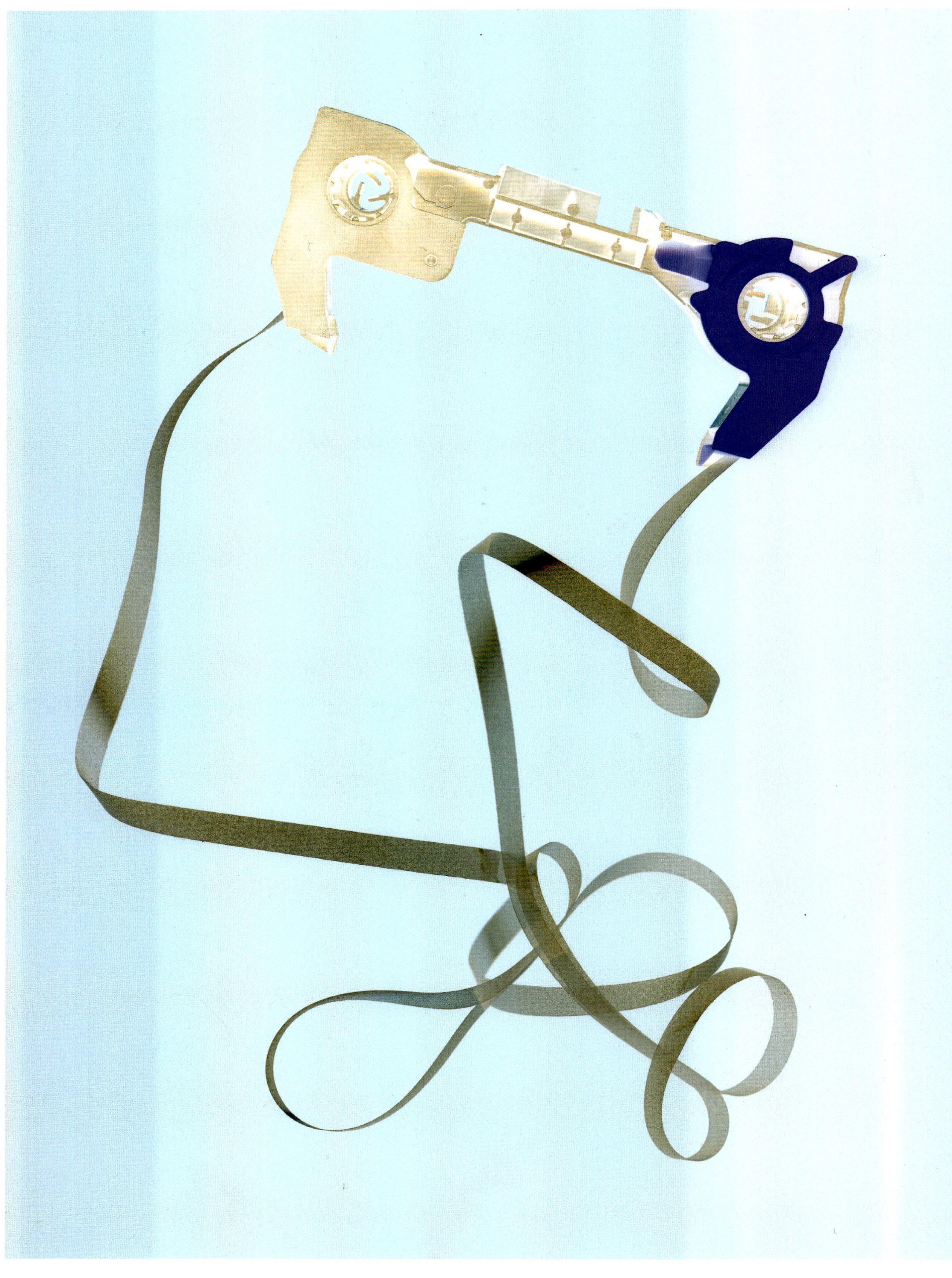

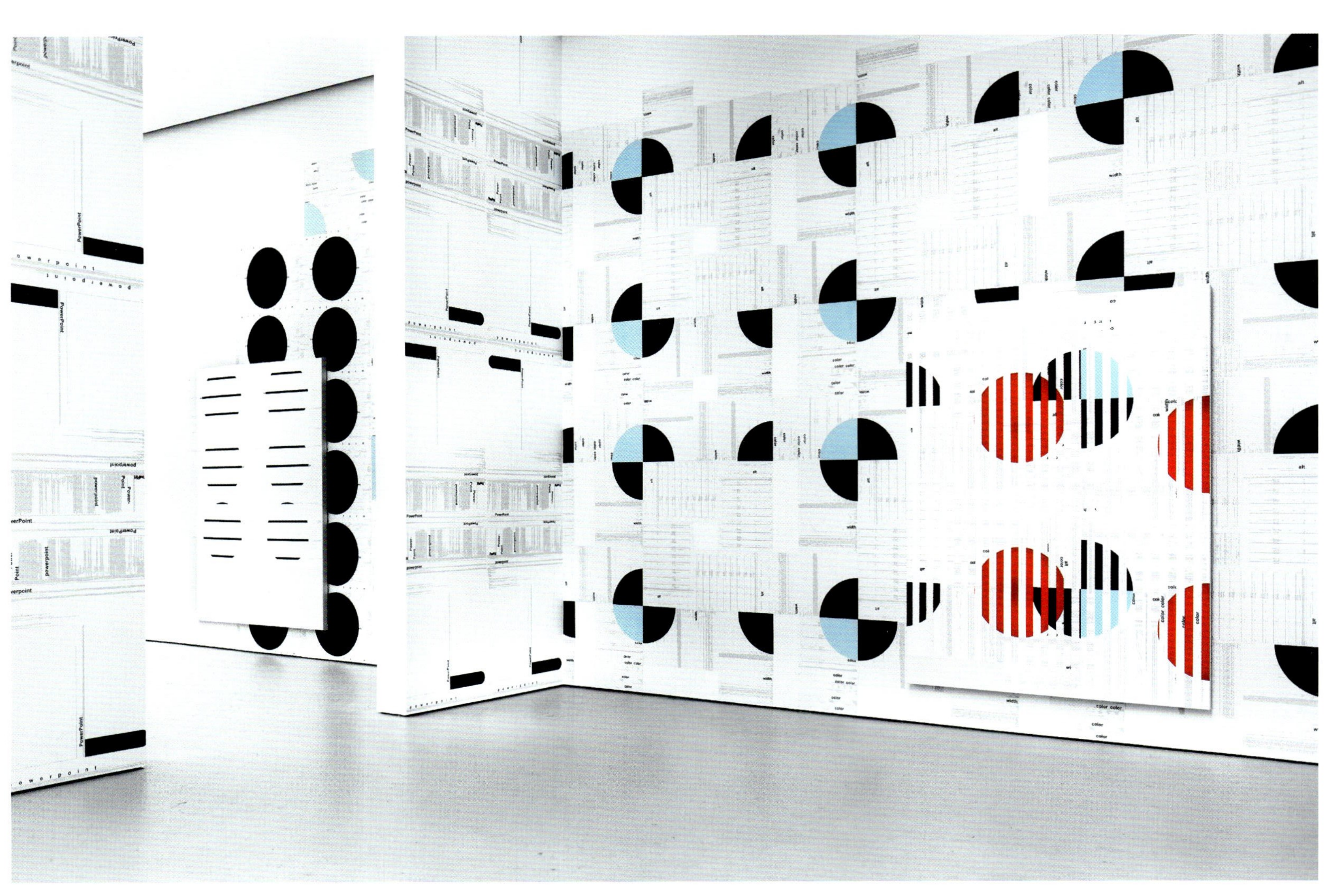

Installation view, *Michael Riedel: PowerPoint*
David Zwirner, New York, 2013

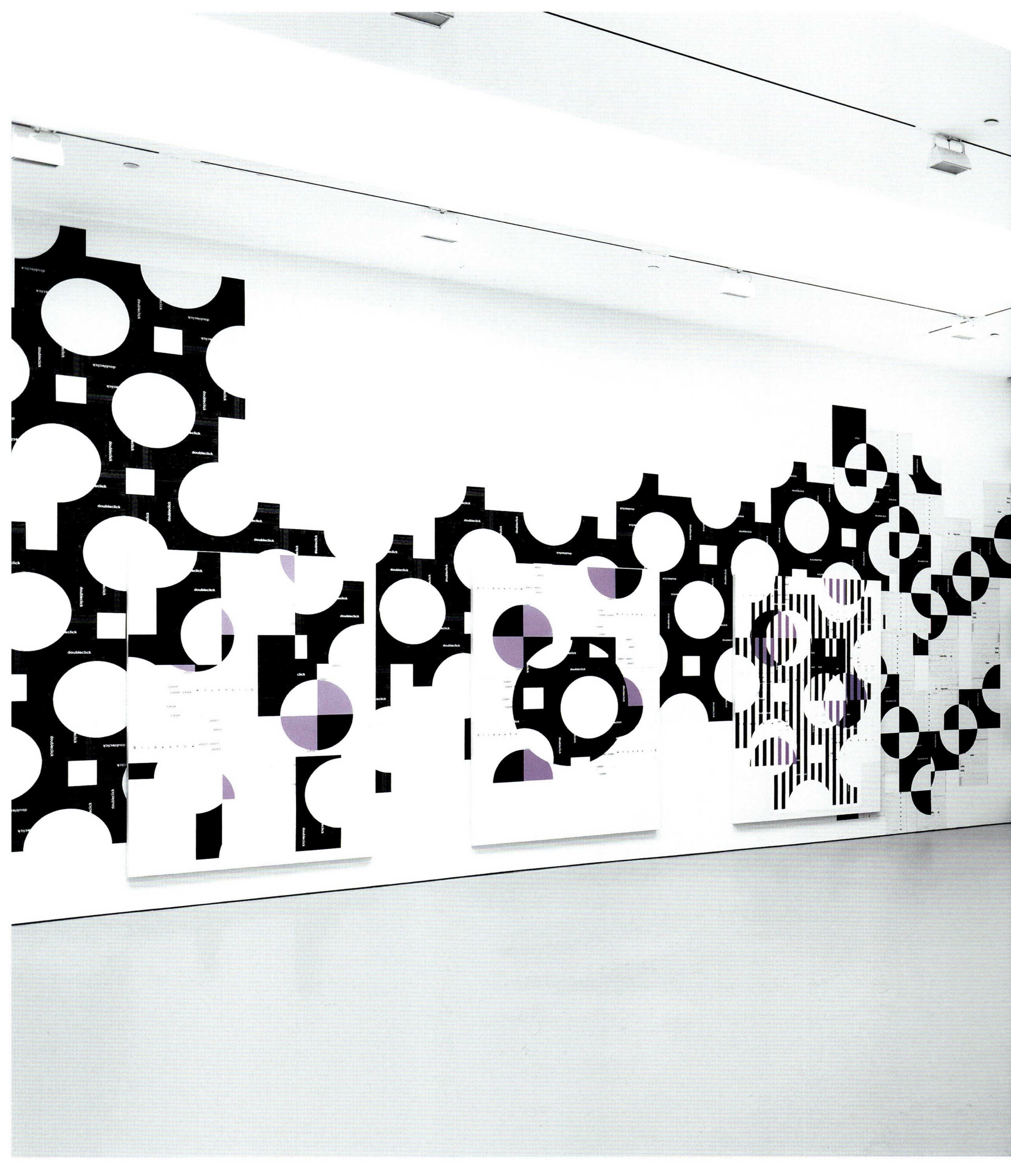

Installation view, *Michael Riedel: PowerPoint*
David Zwirner, New York, 2013

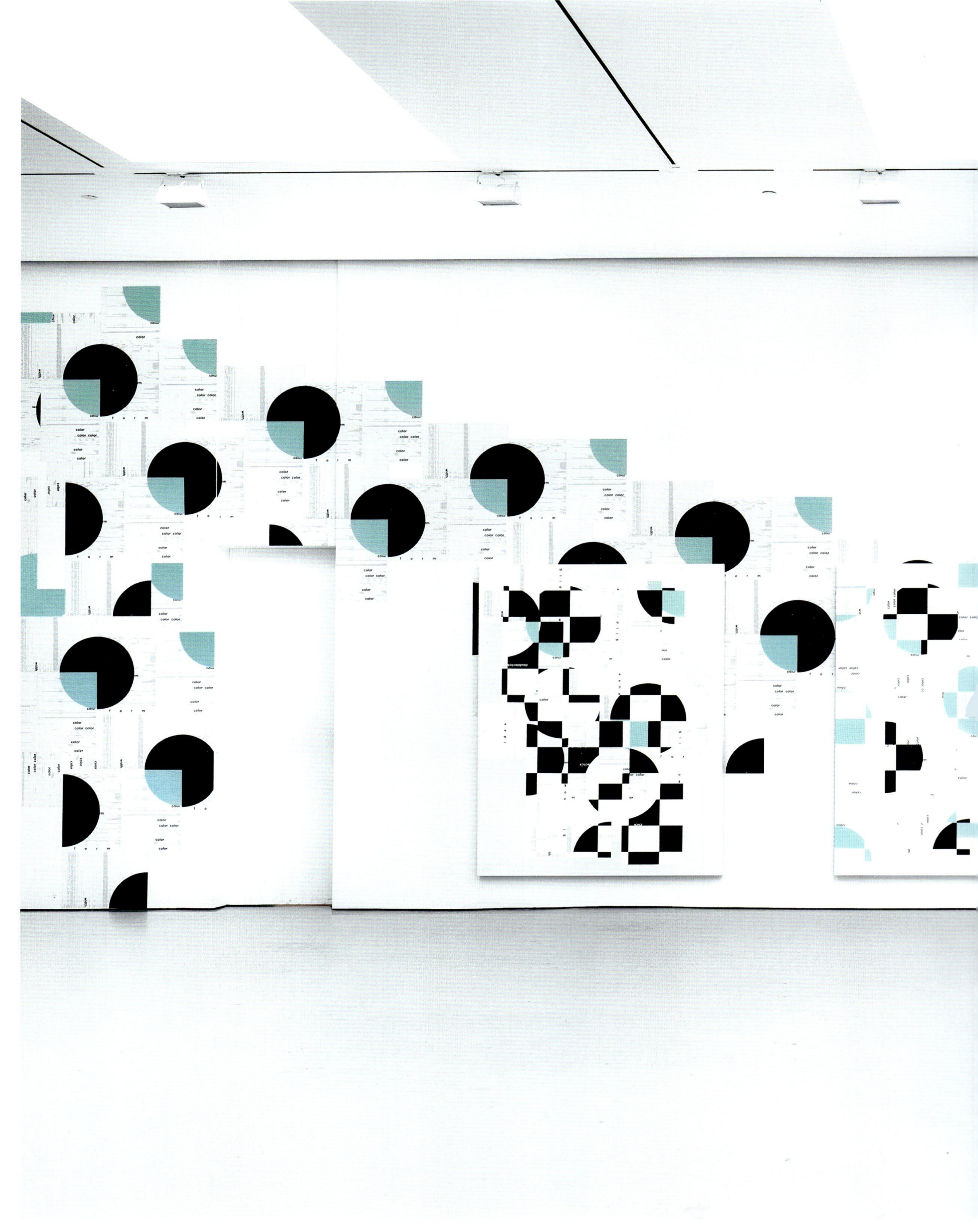

On A Clear Day I Can See Forever, Whatspace, Tilburg, The Netherlands
Stutter, Tate Modern, London

2008
Das Piraterie-Problem, Brandenburgischer Kunstverein, Potsdam, Germany
Depositions, Galerie Francesca Pia, Zürich
The Gallery, David Zwirner, New York
Hotel Marienbad 002: Sammlung Rausch, Kunst-Werke Berlin
Karotten und Schweinehals – Deutsche Kunst seit 1995, Oldenburger Kunstverein, Oldenburg, Germany
No Leftovers, Kunsthalle Bern
P2P, Casino Luxembourg
Records Played Backwards, The Modern Institute, Glasgow

2007
9th Lyon Biennale: The History of a Decade that has not yet been named, La Sucriére, Villeurbanne Institute of Contemporary Art, Bullukian Foundation, and Musée d'art contemporain de Lyon, Lyon, France [catalogue]
Dependance, Galerie Neu, Berlin
The importance of not being seen, Galerie Isabella Bortolozzi/Café Moskau, Berlin
Kiosk, Artists Space, New York
Outside-In I: there have to be many…, Kunstverein Braunschweig, Germany
Not Right But Wrong, Jet, Berlin

2006
Riss, Lücke, Scharnier A/Rift, Gap, Hinge A, Galerie nächst St. Stephan Rosemarie Schwarzwälder, Vienna [catalogue published in 2010]
Villa Jelmini: The Complex of Respect, Kunsthalle Bern

2005
Early Work, David Zwirner, New York
Été Urbain, Gabriele Senn Galerie, Vienna
Les Grands Spectacles, Museum der Moderne, Salzburg, Austria
Moscow Biennale of Contemporary Art, Lenin Museum, Moscow [catalogue]

2004
Black Friday: Exercises in Hermetics, Galerie Kamm, Berlin
Wiener Linien: Kunst und Stadtbeobachtung seit 1960, Wien Museum, Vienna [catalogue]

2003
Kontext, Form, Troja, Secession, Vienna [catalogue]
zeichnen sprechen schreiben, Galerie Krobath Wimmer, Vienna

SOLO EXHIBITION CATALOGUES, ARTIST BOOKS & TEXTS

2015
Michael Riedel: Untitled. Le Box – Fonds M-ARCO, Marseille, France (exh. cat.)

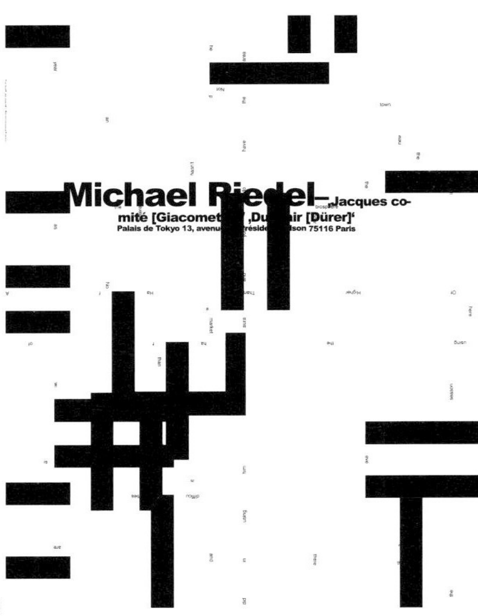

Michael Riedel: Jacques comité [Giacometti] / Dual air [Dürer]. Text by Michael Riedel. Koenig Books, London (exh. cat.)

2005
Momentane Monumente, Aedes West and Berlinische Galerie, Berlin [itinerary: Gió Marconi, Milan] [catalogue *Kühn Malvezzi*]
London Report, Gabriele Senn Galerie, Vienna
Neo, David Zwirner, New York [catalogue]
Frieze Art Fair, London [site-specific project for Gabriele Senn Galerie booth]

2004
Nichael Z. Riebel, Galerie Dépendance, Brussels
NOSNHO.-...... (ROBERT-JOHNSON), Galerie Michael Neff, Frankfurt [catalogue *Johnson-Robert*]
Quasi Portikus, Frieze Art Fair, London [site-specific installation at Portikus booth] [catalogue]

2003
'Au fur et à mesure que la saison s'avança, changea le tableau que je trouvais à la fenêtre.[24] Natürlich wäre hier auch möglich gewesen: Au fur et à mesure que la saison s'avança, le tableau que je trouvais à la fenêtre, changea.' 24 Marcel Proust, Gabriele Senn Galerie, Vienna
Schleifmühlgasse 1A, The Armory Show, New York [site-specific project for Gabriele Senn Galerie booth]
Art Frankfurt 2003 [site-specific installation at Arbeitsgemeinschaft Deutscher Kunstvereine (ADKV) booth]

2002
Opel, Ausstellungshalle A1 Adam Opel AG, Rüsselsheim, Germany

2001
Christopher Wool, Gabriele Senn Galerie, Vienna [two-person exhibition with Achim Lengerer]
Moving Walls, Galerie Michael Neff, Frankfurt [artist's intervention with Achim Lengerer in *Jeppe Hein: Sving*]

SELECTED EXHIBITIONS & EVENTS AT OSKAR-VON-MILLER STRASSE 16

The following is a selection of exhibitions and events held at Oskar-von-Miller Strasse 16, an experimental art space launched by Michael Riedel and Dennis Loesch in 2000 where he restaged cultural events. There have been three iterations of the space to date: Frankfurt, Oskar-von-Miller Strasse 16, 2000–2005; Berlin, Weydinger Strasse 20, 2007–2009; and Frankfurt, Mainzer Landstrasse 105, 2010–2011.

2013
Zweite Anekdotenkonferenz / Second Conference of Anecdotes [catalogue *Oskar*, 2014]

2011
Die Situationistischen Internationalen [together with Daniel Birnbaum, Roberto Ohrt, Kim West]

2007
Riow (part of ongoing event *Club[b]ed Clubs*); *SK N E ST SSE* [catalogue]

2005
Demolition of Oskar-von-Miller Strasse 16

2004
Freitagsküche (ongoing event)
Filmed Film, Deutsches Filmmuseum, Frankfurt

2003
Erste Anekdotenkonferenz/ First Conference of Anecdotes [catalogue *Oskar*]
30.02.2003 [fake event]

2002
Doubled Wall; *Gert & Georg* [artist's intervention in *Gilbert & George: Nine Dark Pictures*]; *Max Goldt & Robert Gernhardt*; *Oskar-von-Miller Strasse 16*; *Remake of New Year's Eve Weekender*; *Simon Starling*

2001
Warhol Shooting; *Jason Rhoades – Wassertest*; *Lola Montez*; *Marco Lulic – Disco Wilhelm Reich Version FFM*; *Remake Atomic Cafe München* (part of ongoing event *Club[b]ed Clubs*); *Remake Club Eleven Köln* (part of ongoing event *Club[b]ed Clubs*); *Rirkrit Tiravanija*

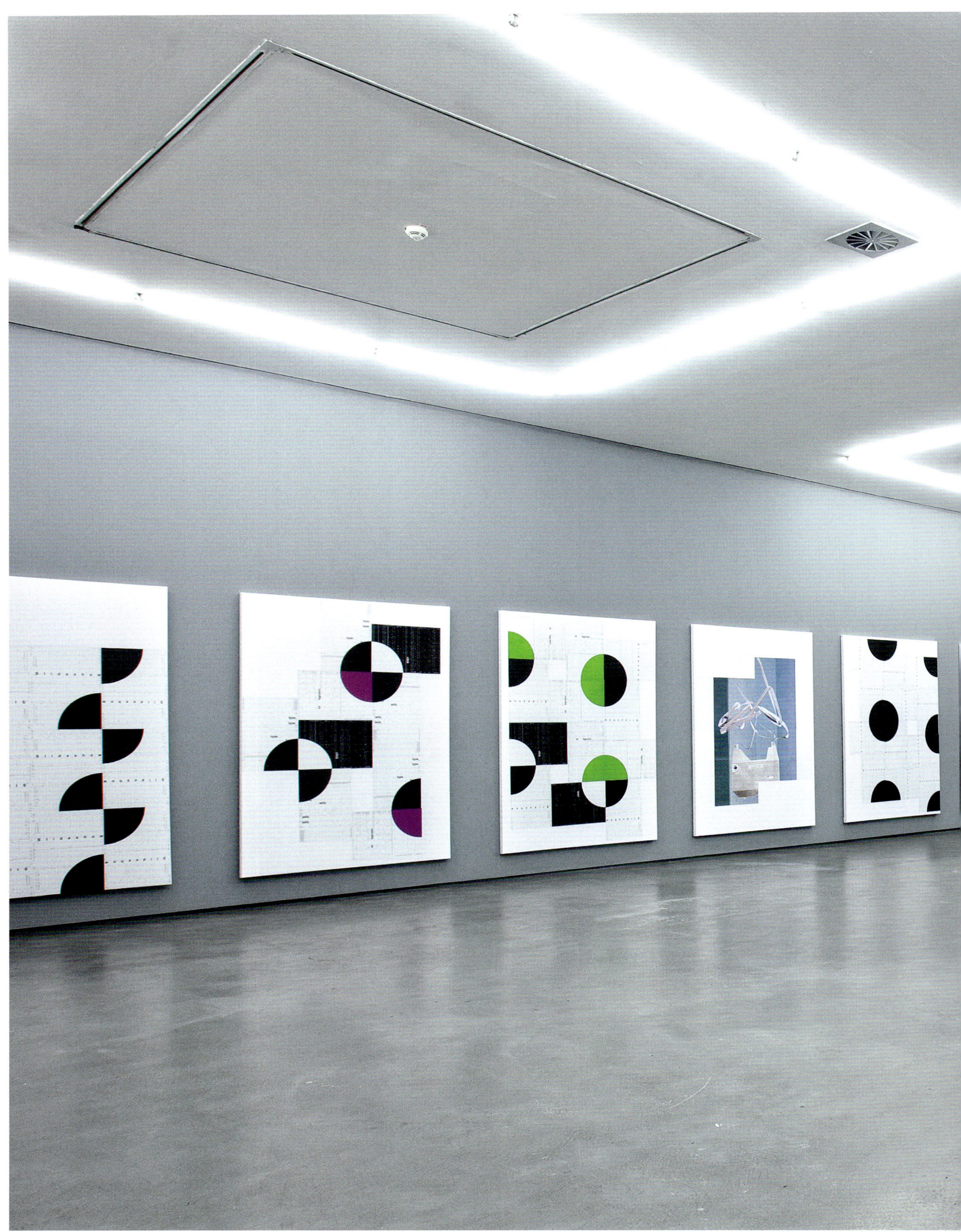

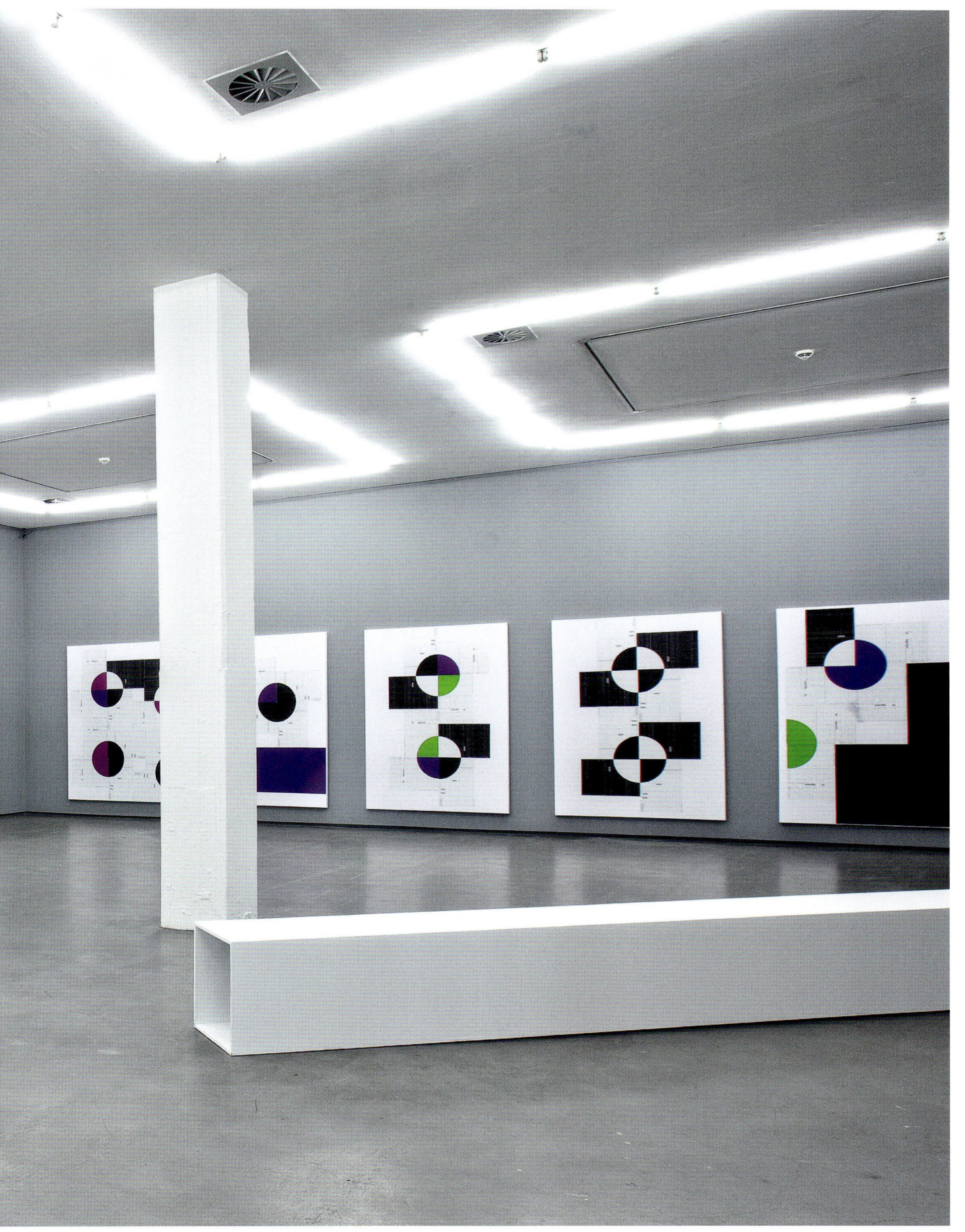

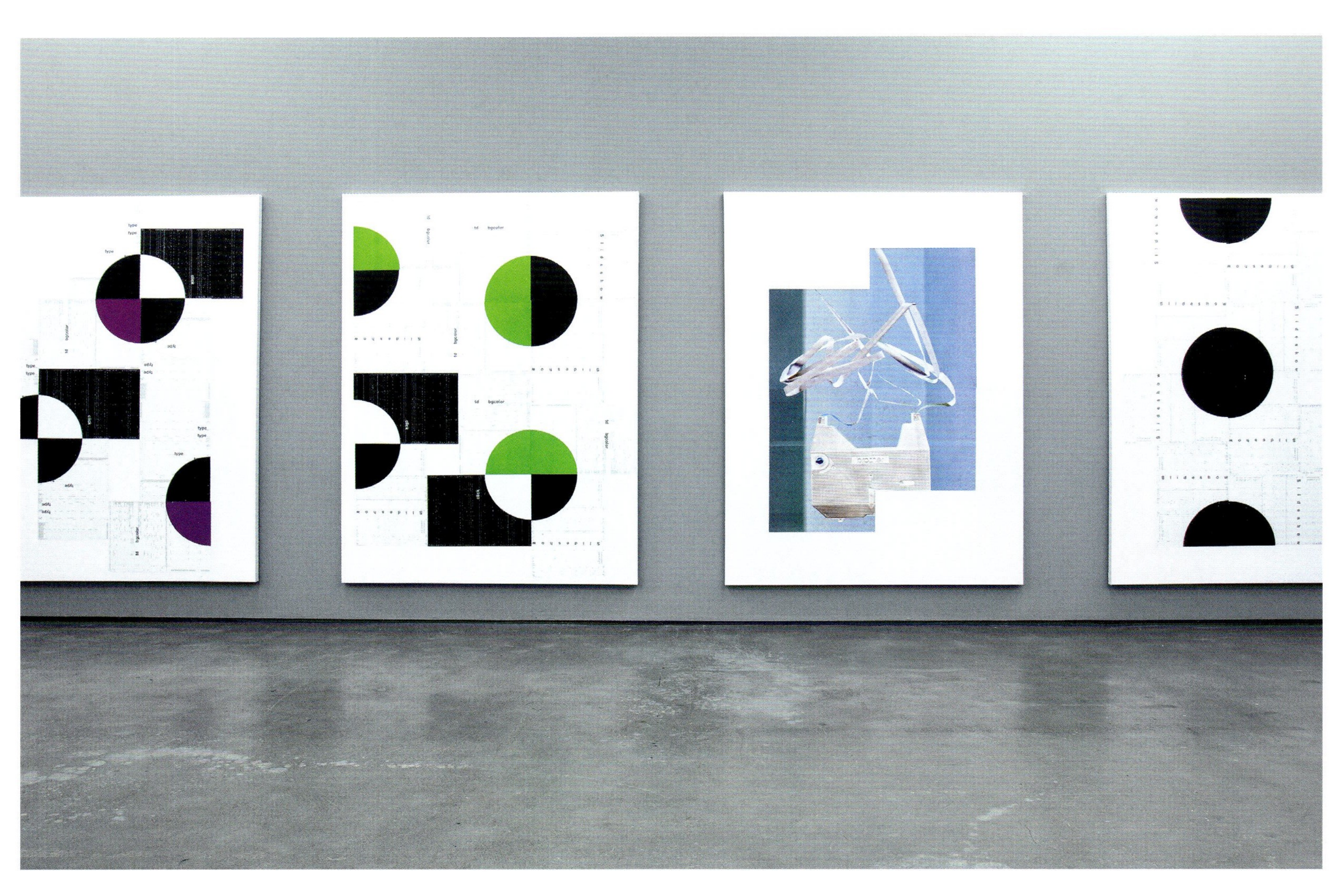

Installation view, *Michael Riedel: The quick brown fox jumps over the lazy dog*
Kunstverein Hamburg, 2010

Untitled (Correctable film ribbon for AX10/20/30), 2010
Paper on linen
90 1/2 x 67 x 2 1/4 inches
(229.9 x 170.2 x 5.7 cm)

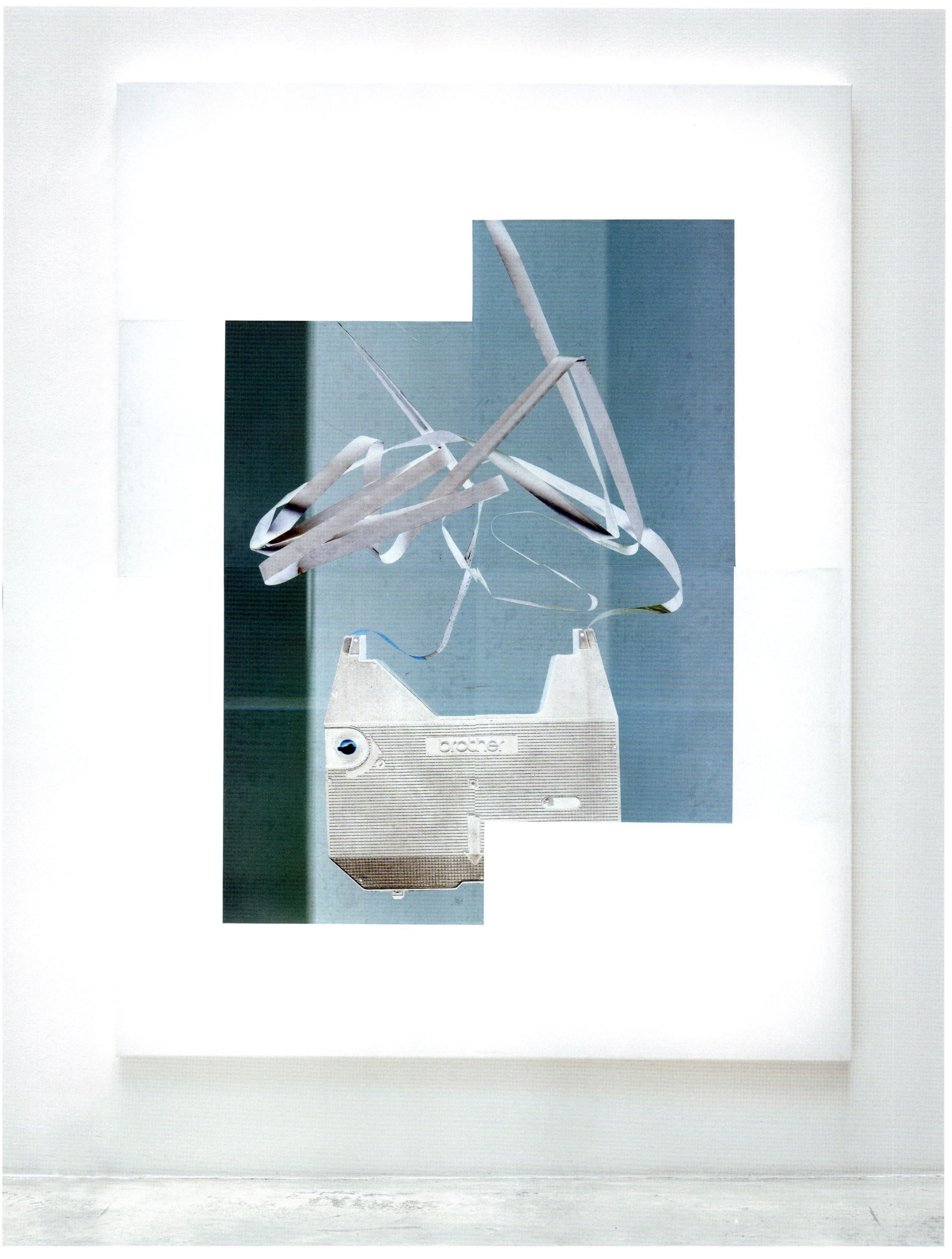
brother

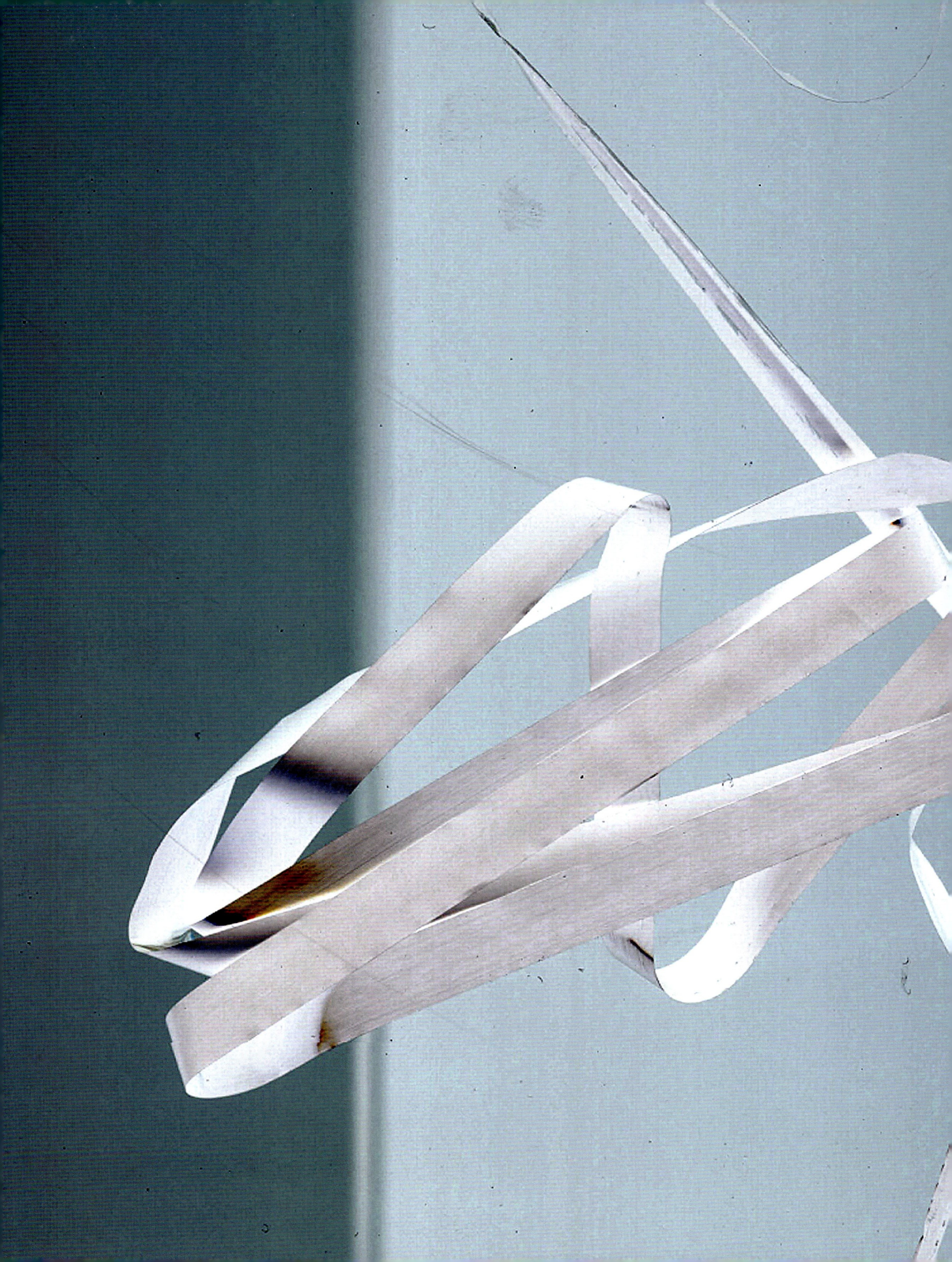

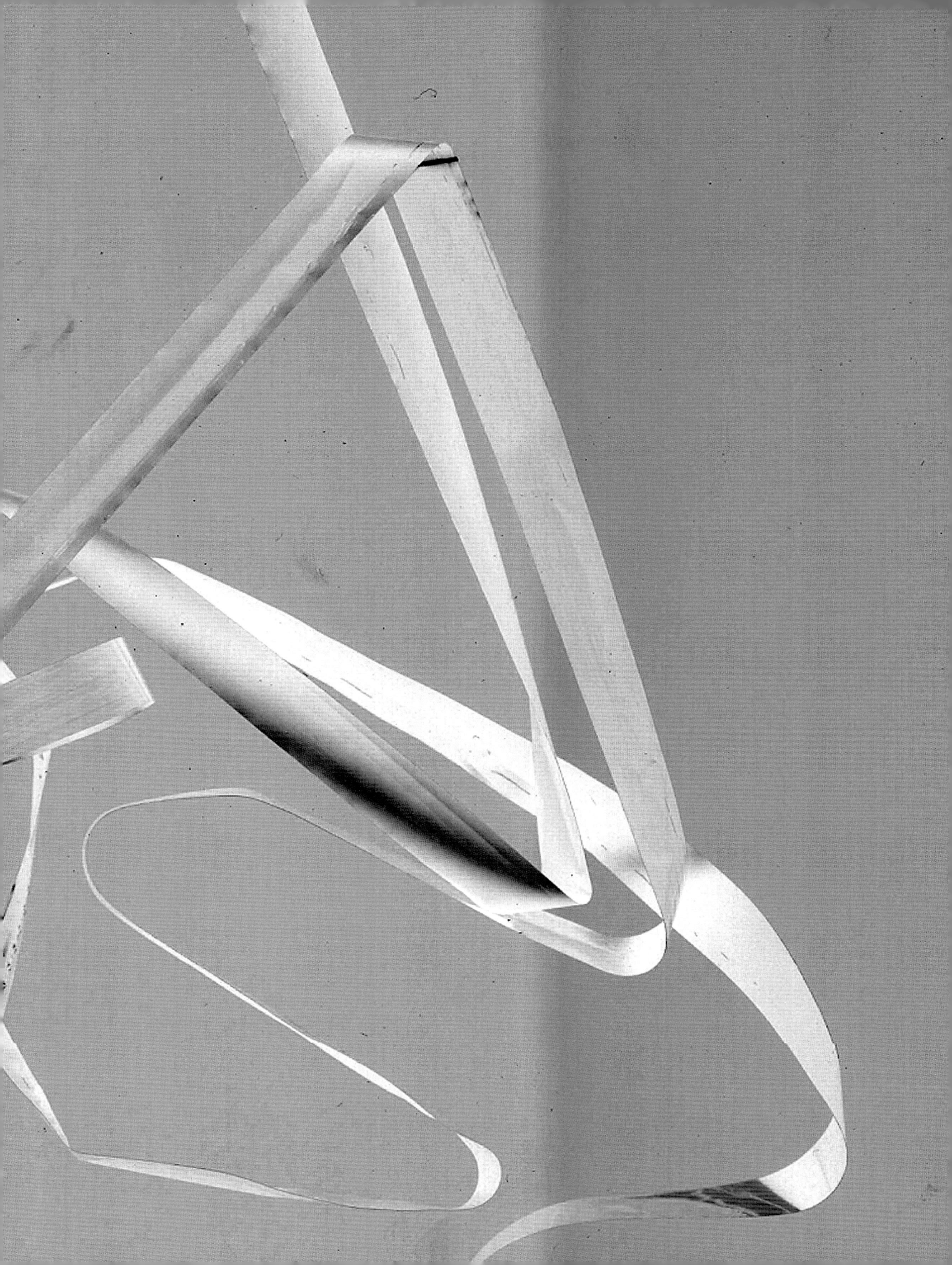

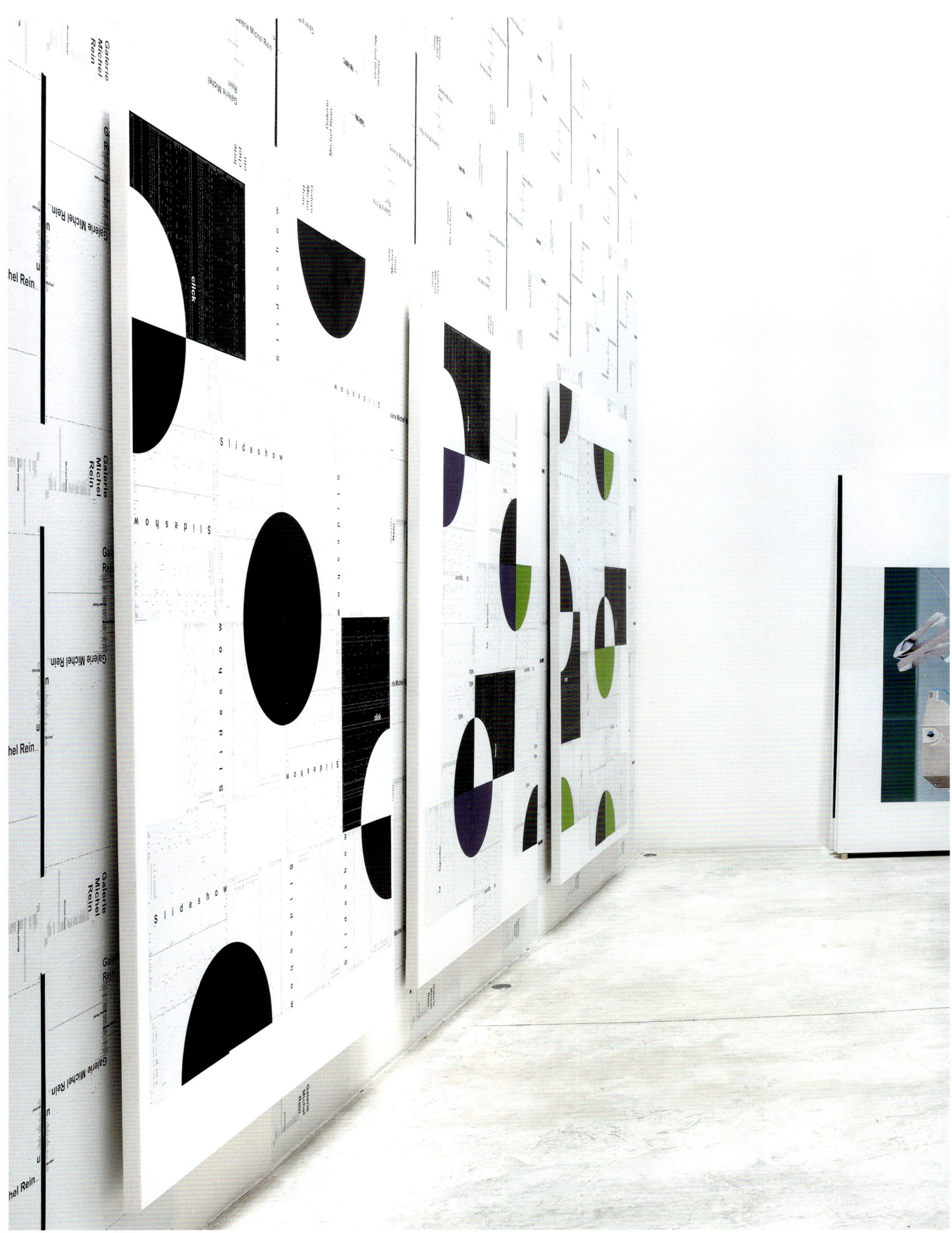
Galerie Michel Rein
Slideshow
click

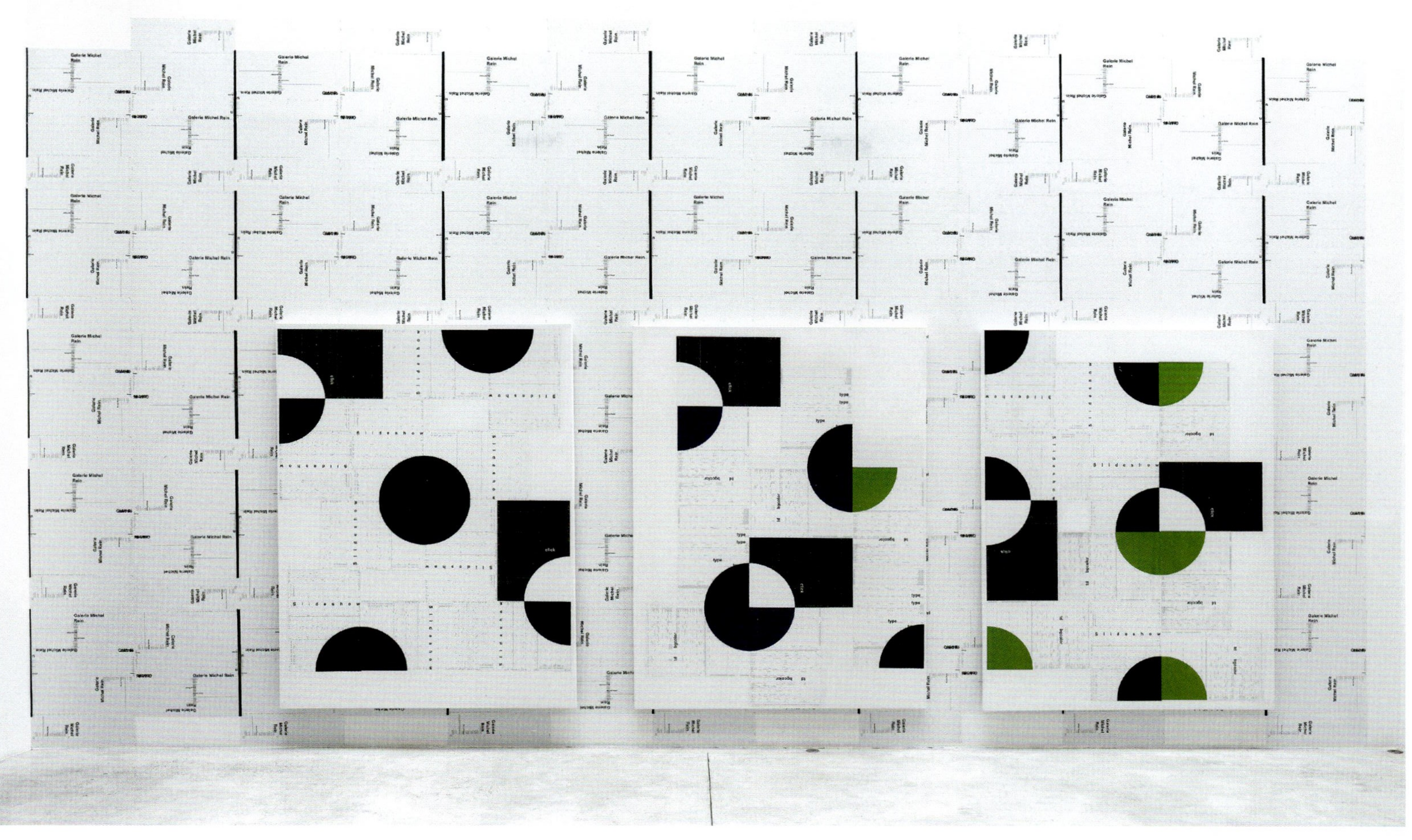

Installation views, *Michael Riedel*
Galerie Michel Rein, Paris, 2010

Following pages:
Installation view, *Michael Riedel: The quick brown fox jumps over the lazy dog*
Gabriele Senn Galerie, Vienna, 2011

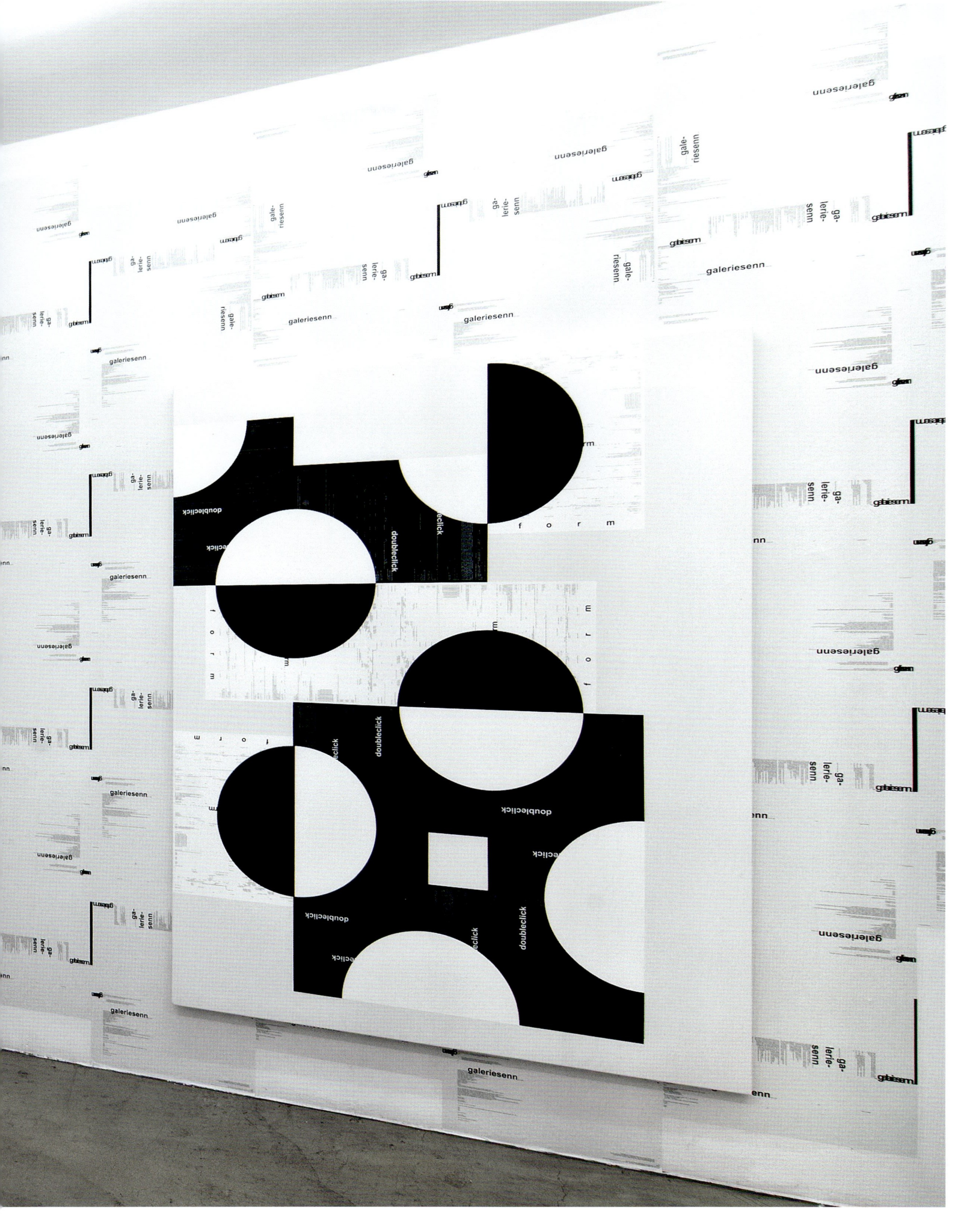
galeriesenn
ga-
lerie-
senn
gale-
riesenn
doubleclick
form

Untitled (form; doubleclick), 2011
Silkscreen on linen
90 1/2 x 67 x 2 1/4 inches
(229.9 x 170.2 x 5.7 cm)

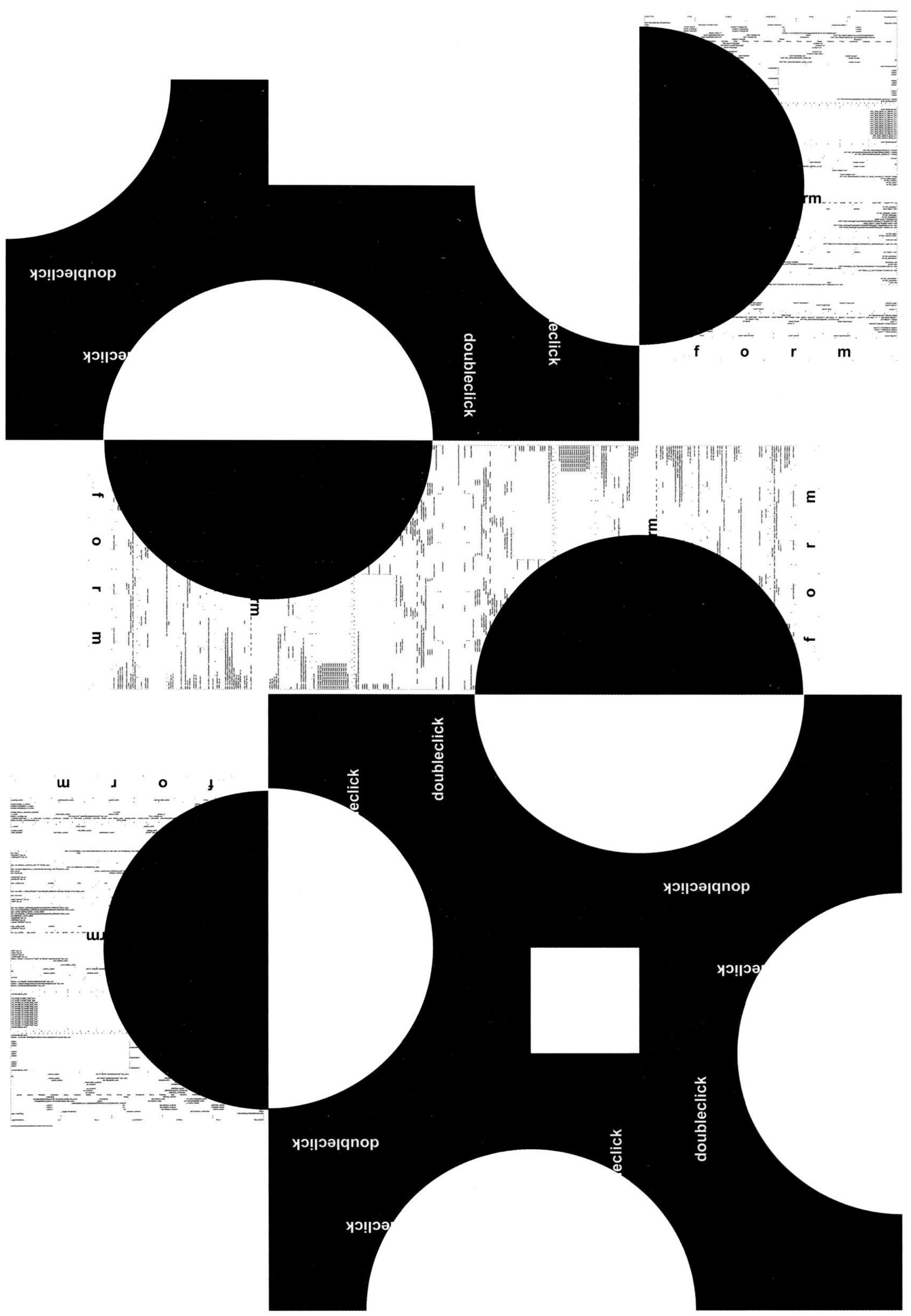
doubleclick
doubleclick
f o r m
f o r m
doubleclick
doubleclick
f o r m
doubleclick
doubleclick
doubleclick

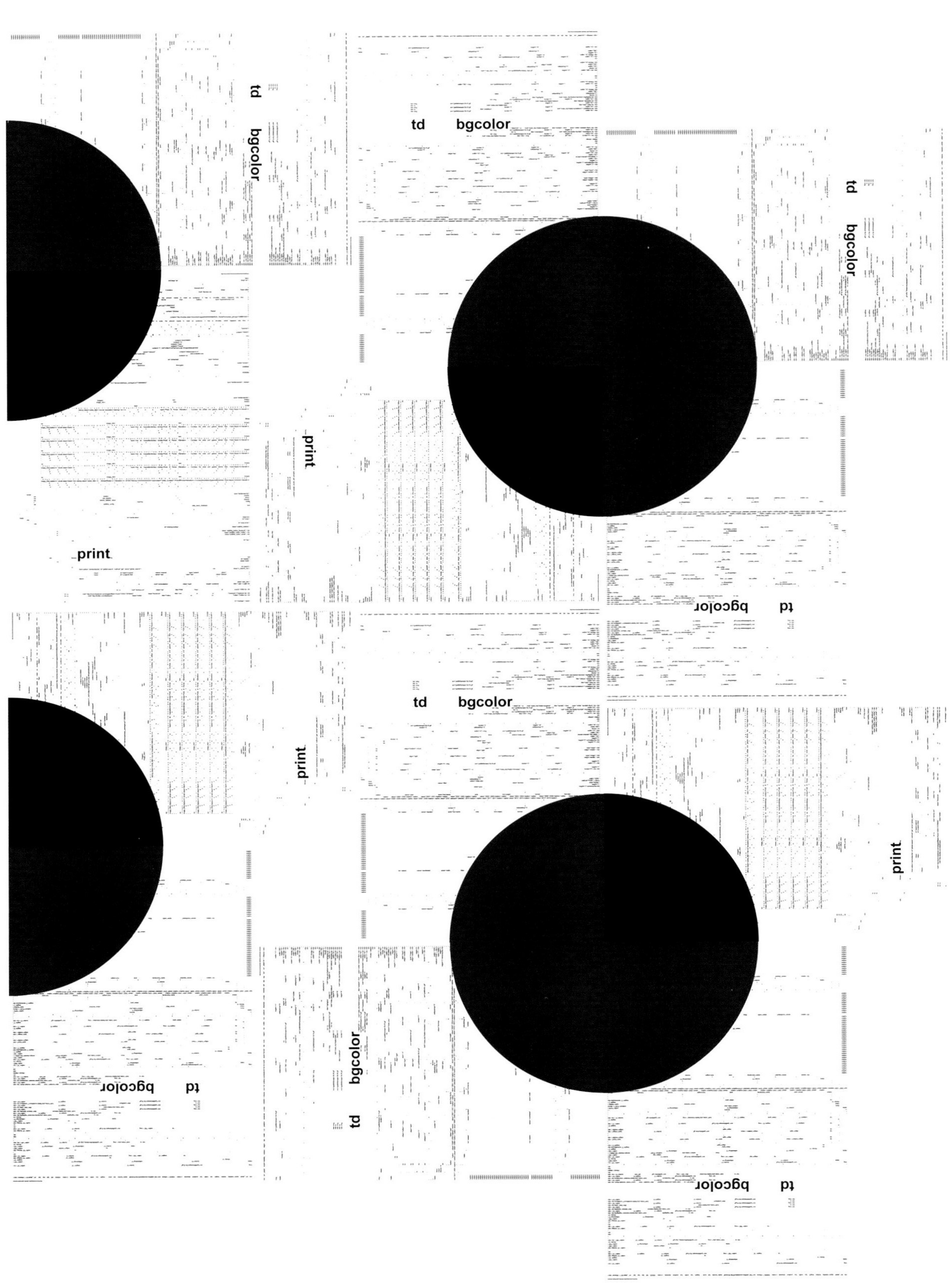

Untitled (td bgcolor, purple; print), 2011
Silkscreen on linen
90 1/2 x 67 x 2 1/4 inches
(229.9 x 170.2 x 5.7 cm)

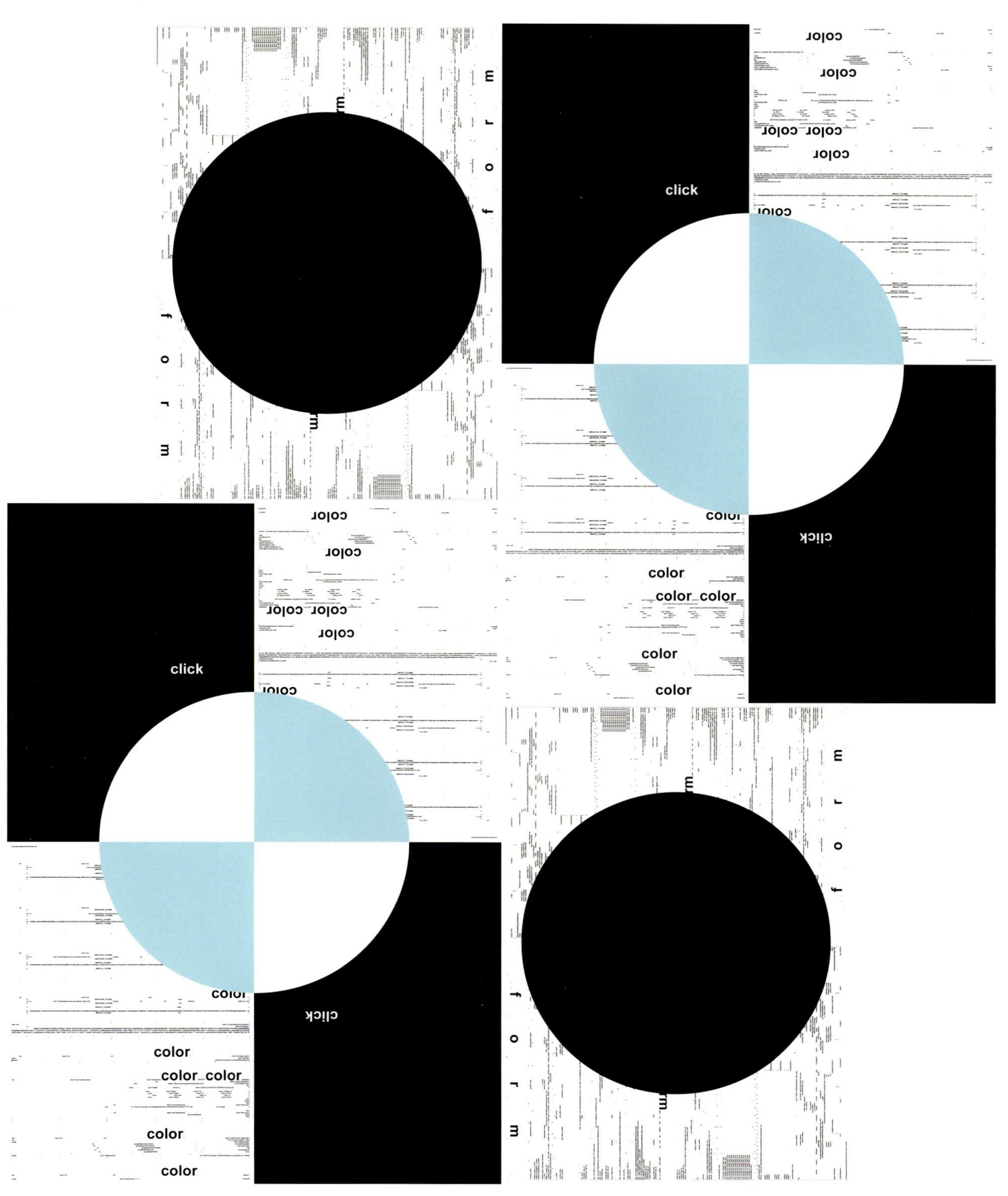

Untitled (form; color, light blue; click 1), 2011
Silkscreen on linen
90 1/2 x 67 x 2 1/4 inches
(229.9 x 170.2 x 5.7 cm)

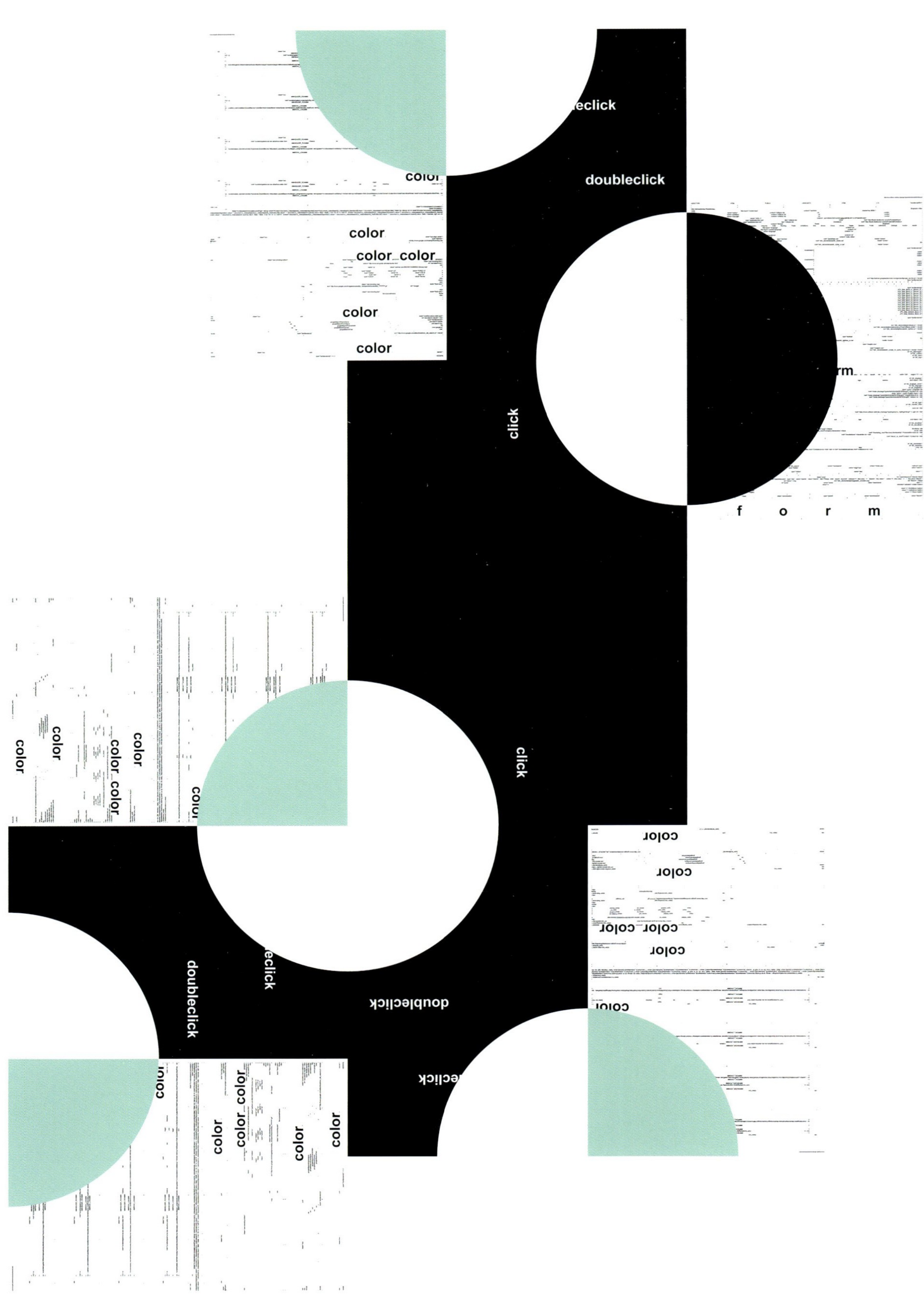

Untitled (color, light green; click 1; doubleclick; form), 2012
Silkscreen on linen
90 1/2 x 67 x 2 1/4 inches
(229.9 x 170.2 x 5.7 cm)

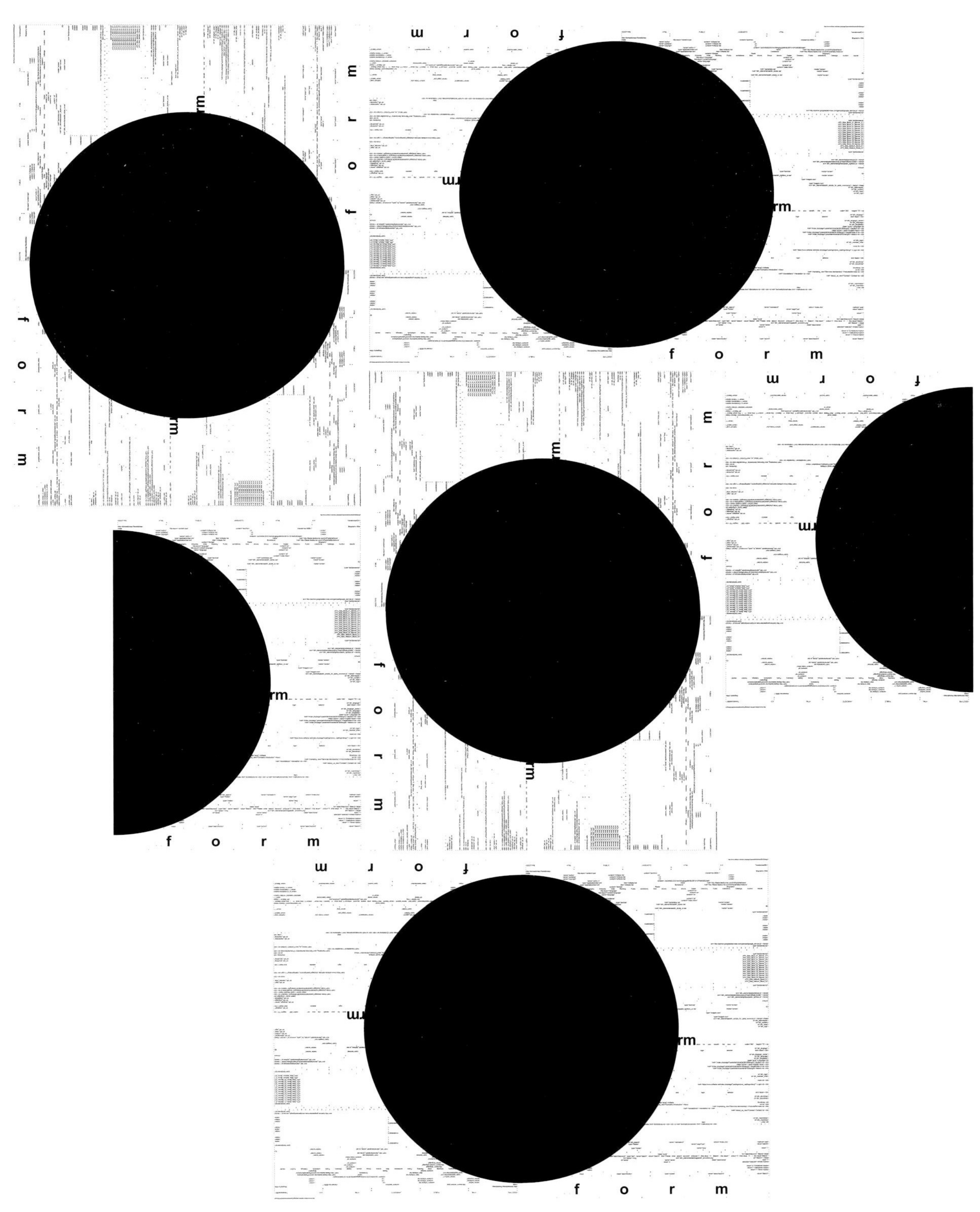

Untitled (form), 2011
Silkscreen on linen
90 1/2 x 67 x 2 1/4 inches
(229.9 x 170.2 x 5.7 cm)

display

http://dailyserving.com/2014/05/michael-riedel-laws-of-form-at-david-zwirner-london/
(Accessed December 3, 2015)

```
        <li class="toplast"><a href="http://dailyserving.com/tag/elsewhere/" style="height:14px;line-height:16px;"><span>ELSEWHERE</
span></a>

        <ul>

                <li><a href="http://dailyserving.com/tag/paris/">Paris</a></li>

                <li><a href="http://dailyserving.com/tag/boston/">Boston</a></li>

                <li><a href="http://dailyserving.com/tag/portland/">Portland</a></li>

                <li><a href="http://dailyserving.com/tag/sao-paulo/">São Paulo</a></li>

                <li><a href="http://dailyserving.com/tag/toronto/">Toronto</a></li>

                <li><a href="http://dailyserving.com/tag/beijing/">Beijing</a></li>

                <li><a href="http://dailyserving.com/tag/shanghai/">Shanghai</a></li>

                <li><a href="http://dailyserving.com/tag/sydney/">Sydney</a></li>

        </ul></li>

</ul>


        </div>



<!-- End Header sub menu -->

        <div class="hr1" style="margin-top:25px;"><!-- <hr /> --> </div>


        </div>

        </div>




  <div id="topnavcontainer">


  <div id="navcontainer">

    <ul id="navlist">

      <li><a href="http://dailyserving.com/">Home</a></li>

      <li class="page_item page-item-1056"><a href="http://dailyserving.com/about/">About Us</a></li>
<li class="page_item page-item-1058"><a href="http://dailyserving.com/contributors/">Contributors</a></li>
<li class="page_item page-item-23299"><a href="http://dailyserving.com/contributors-test/">Contributors test</a></li>
<li class="page_item page-item-23029"><a href="http://dailyserving.com/partners/">Partners</a></li>
<li class="page_item page-item-1073"><a href="http://dailyserving.com/sponsor-us/">Sponsor Us</a></li>
<li class="page_item page-item-1070"><a href="http://dailyserving.com/store/">Store</a></li>
<li class="page_item page-item-1057"><a href="http://dailyserving.com/submit/">Submit</a></li>

    </ul>

        </div>
```

Untitled (solid blue; td bgcolor, blue), 2012
Silkscreen on linen
90 1/2 x 67 x 2 1/4 inches
(229.9 x 170.2 x 5.7 cm)

```
<div id=”divSearchForm”>

  <form method=”get” id=”searchform” action=”http://dailyserving.com/”>

    <div>

      <input value=”1” id=”IncludeBlogs” name=”IncludeBlogs” type=”hidden”>

      <input name=”s” class=”txt” value=”Search Keywords” onfocus=”document.forms[‘searchform’].s.value=‘’;” onblur=”if (document.
forms[‘searchform’].s.value == ‘’) document.forms[‘searchform’].s.value=’Search Keywords’;” type=”text”>

      <input src=”http://dailyserving.com/wp-content/themes/cameron/images/search.gif” alt=”Submit” value=”Search” id=”searchsubmit”
type=”image”>

    </div>

  </form>

</div>


</div>









</div>

<!-- end #header -->

<div id=”container”>

<div id=”content”>




                <div class=”post”>




                        <h4 class=”pagetitle” style=”padding-right:10px;”>London
                        </h4>






                <div class=”postmetadata” style=”padding-top:10px;”>

                                <li>May 14, 2014 Written by <a href=”http://dailyserving.com/author/adam-rompel/” title=”Posts by
Adam Rompel” rel=”author”>Adam Rompel</a></li>



                        </div>

      <h2><a href=”http://dailyserving.com/2014/05/michael-riedel-laws-of-form-at-david-zwirner-london/” rel=”bookmark”>Michael Riedel:
Laws of Form at David Zwirner, London</a></h2>



<!--       <div class=”hr2”></div>                  -->
```

<div class="entry">

<p>"There's no content being produced, because I'm in the first generation that grew up digital.... We are just transferring all the time: tape, CDs, and now the clouds."[1]</p>
<p>Something radical has been happening for a while in art that has been evading easy classification. The digital <a href="http://www.simonosullivan.net/articles/deleuze-dictionary.pdf">fold</a> has facilitated a giant mash-up of layers upon layers of information composed from fragments of fragments. Sound bites, video clips, 140-character quips, and filtered snapshots are curated extracts, continuously looping in a recopied and redistributed cycle. Yet in an age of digital re-pointing, the language used to consider art is still rooted in a Modernist dialogue of movements and styles, and it's inevitable that there would be a notional presupposition about much of the work made today. It would be easy to misclassify an artist's use of <em>digital-processing</em> as part of a conceptual practice, but putting aside dated art-historical constructs, let's incorporate the twenty-year-old foundation of <a href="http://www.kim-cohen.com/seth_texts/artmusictheorytexts/Bourriaud%20Relational%20Aesthetics.pdf">Relational Aesthetics</a> as a jumping-off point instead. Artists now process information rather than material or even constructed experiences; viewed through this theoretic lens, even if an artist paints color-field paintings in 2014, the resulting paint strokes are the consequence of reprocessed information. It's a seemingly subtle shift, but one that accounts for process as the medium for our digital age. This is the access point for <a href="http://www.davidzwirner.com/reader/michael-riedel-reader/">Michael Riedel</a>'s current solo show at <a href="http://www.davidzwirner.com/exhibition/michael-riedel-3/">David Zwirner</a>'s London gallery. Riedel has been making art—collaboratively and individually—for the last 14 years, and one won't get a more succinct example of his mantra of "Record–Label–Playback" than in this exhibition.</p>
<div id="attachment_43926" style="width: 610px" class="wp-caption aligncenter"><img class="size-full wp-image-43926" src="http://dailyserving.com/wp-content/uploads/2014/05/oskar_install.jpg" alt="Michael Riedel. Laws of Form, 2014; installation view, David Zwirner, London. Courtesy the Artists and David Zwirner, New York/London." height="450" width="600"><p class="wp-caption-text">Michael Riedel. <em>Laws of Form</em>, 2014; installation view, David Zwirner, London. Courtesy of the Artists and David Zwirner, New York/London.</p></div>
<p>On the ground floor, the installation <em>Oskar-von-Miller Strasse 16</em> (2000–2011) offers ephemera and documentation of the collaborative activities of the Frankfurt art space that Riedel started with Dennis Loesch. The space is described as a "recording device that would merely replay the cultural offering it had recorded and then marvel at the pops, hisses, crackles, and skips that such playback caused." Oskar-von-Miller Strasse 16 (OMS) opened its doors in 2000 by restaging a deinstalled Jim Isermann show taken from the garbage bins of a nearby museum. Other offerings included film nights that screened handycam-captured films from art theaters, reenactments of talks and readings of cultural importance, club nights that reconstituted other club nights by replacing the recorded sounds from those clubs, numerous copied publications and posters (often produced by printing over the source material), and on one occasion, hired actors to mime Gilbert and George at their own reception; all of which was obsessively documented. This continual outward critique would intermittently point back and copy itself by re-creating exhibitions from documentation of past shows. Each copy, with its flaws and interpretations, creates a new document. This strategy unfailingly extends to the Zwirner show where exhibition fragments, video documentation, and publication byproduct fill the space. One technique that OMS unwaveringly used was that the reproducible images were always done in black-and-white. This furthers the distortion, pushing the work away from its source and toward ambiguity. Framed and orderly, the ground floor has the tangential raw energy of a zine made gigantic, but the fun-spirited energy and prankster aura of the original space is still very much present in this re-presentation. Riedel offers another fold in the ground floor's rear gallery by precisely re-creating the visual elements from <em>Warhol Shooting </em>(2001)—a reenactment of Cecil Beaton's photo <a href="http://www.americanphotomag.com/files/imagecache/ajax_galleries_image_default/gallery-images/Factory2.jpg"><em>Andy Warhol and Members of the Factory</em></a>—complete with a mirrored table, built-out corner with accompanying electrical wire, cheap wood-constructed window facsimile, stripy shirt, and tripod. To complete the install, stacks of the newly published <em>Oskar</em> (2014), the artist book that tallies up ten years of OMS activities, adorn the table as mass-produced props. A contained system of process in itself, the 490 pages of content are a reedited and expanded version of the earlier German version from 2003.</p>
<p><span id="more-43924"></span></p>
<div id="attachment_43929" style="width: 610px" class="wp-caption aligncenter"><img class="size-full wp-image-43929" src="http://dailyserving.com/wp-content/uploads/2014/05/warhol_shooting.jpg" alt="Michael Riedel. Warhol Shooting, 2001
; MDF and silver foil table, camera, tripod, sweater, cable, wood;
Dimensions variable. Courtesy the Artist and David Zwirner, New York/London." height="711" width="600"><p class="wp-caption-text">Michael Riedel. <em>Warhol Shooting</em>, 2001
; MDF and silver foil table, camera, tripod, sweater, cable, wood;
dimensions variable. Courtesy of the Artist and David Zwirner, New York/London.</p></div>
<p>If the activities at Oskar-von-Miller Strasse 16 were a continual transmission of processing copy after copy, then Riedel's post-OMS work is the continual practice of copying process after process, and reveling in the resulting distorted byproduct. The gallery's first floor feels much more grown-up and somber, with the polished<em> PowerPoint Paintings</em> series being the central axis of the show. This series is constructed from PowerPoint images that are interrupted at the moment of transition between one slide and the next; the content of those two separate images is fractured and merged to create a new aesthetic offering. This new image is captured and silkscreened onto a honeycomb panel and framed. The source material for these paintings is from Riedel's previous projects, which themselves are the byproduct of a process that references older work.</p>
<div id="attachment_43930" style="width: 610px" class="wp-caption aligncenter"><img class="wp-image-43930 size-full" src="http://dailyserving.com/wp-content/uploads/2014/05/powerpoint3wide.jpg" alt="(from left to right) Michael Riedel. Untitled (Circle), 2014; Untitled (Wheel 4 spoke), 2014; Untitled (Dissolve), 2014; each work, silkscreen on honeycomb panel; 100 3/8 x 56 3/4 inches (255 x 144 cm). Courtesy the Artist and David Zwirner, New York/London." height="317" width="600"><p class="wp-caption-text">(from left to right) Michael Riedel. Untitled (<em>Circle</em>), 2014; Untitled (<em>Wheel 4 Spoke</em>), 2014; Untitled (<em>Dissolve</em>), 2014; each work, silkscreen on honeycomb panel; 100 3/8 x 56 3/4 in. (255 x 144 cm). Courtesy of the Artist and David Zwirner, New York/London.</p></div>
<p>This system of production is tangible, made visible by the resulting composition of layered panels of reworked and combined fragments. Those individual fragments still reveal their origin but have been subsumed into the larger construct. Riedel has now come to a place in his practice where the source material's original content is still traceable but is so distorted that it renders any original meaning purposeless. What is left is a chain of defused content that can be understood only visually. Adjacent to the paintings are windowed walls that have been papered with passages of repeated and scaled text. The content is taken from a snippet of HTML code on nature.com's <a href="http://www.nature.com/nature/journal/v410/

n6827/full/410417a0.html">"Laws of Form Revisited" webpage</a>. By **display**ing the raw metadata, content, and style, the site's own system of formatting information is revealed. Riedel reorganizes the literal content as a repeated random pattern of perpendicular text segments and highlights the recurring phrase "Laws of Form" by more than quadrupling its size. This simple act of copy–pasting renders the code dysfunctional for its original purpose while leaving its reference points to generate an aesthetic experience.</p>

<div id="attachment_43931" style="width: 610px" class="wp-caption aligncenter"><img class="size-full wp-image-43931" src="http://dailyserving.com/wp-content/uploads/2014/05/lawsofform.jpg" alt="Michael Riedel. Laws of Form, 2014; installation view, David Zwirner, London. Courtesy the Artists and David Zwirner, New York/London." height="437" width="600"><p class="wp-caption-text">Michael Riedel. <em>Laws of Form</em>, 2014; installation view, David Zwirner, London. Courtesy of the Artists and David Zwirner, New York/London.</p></div>

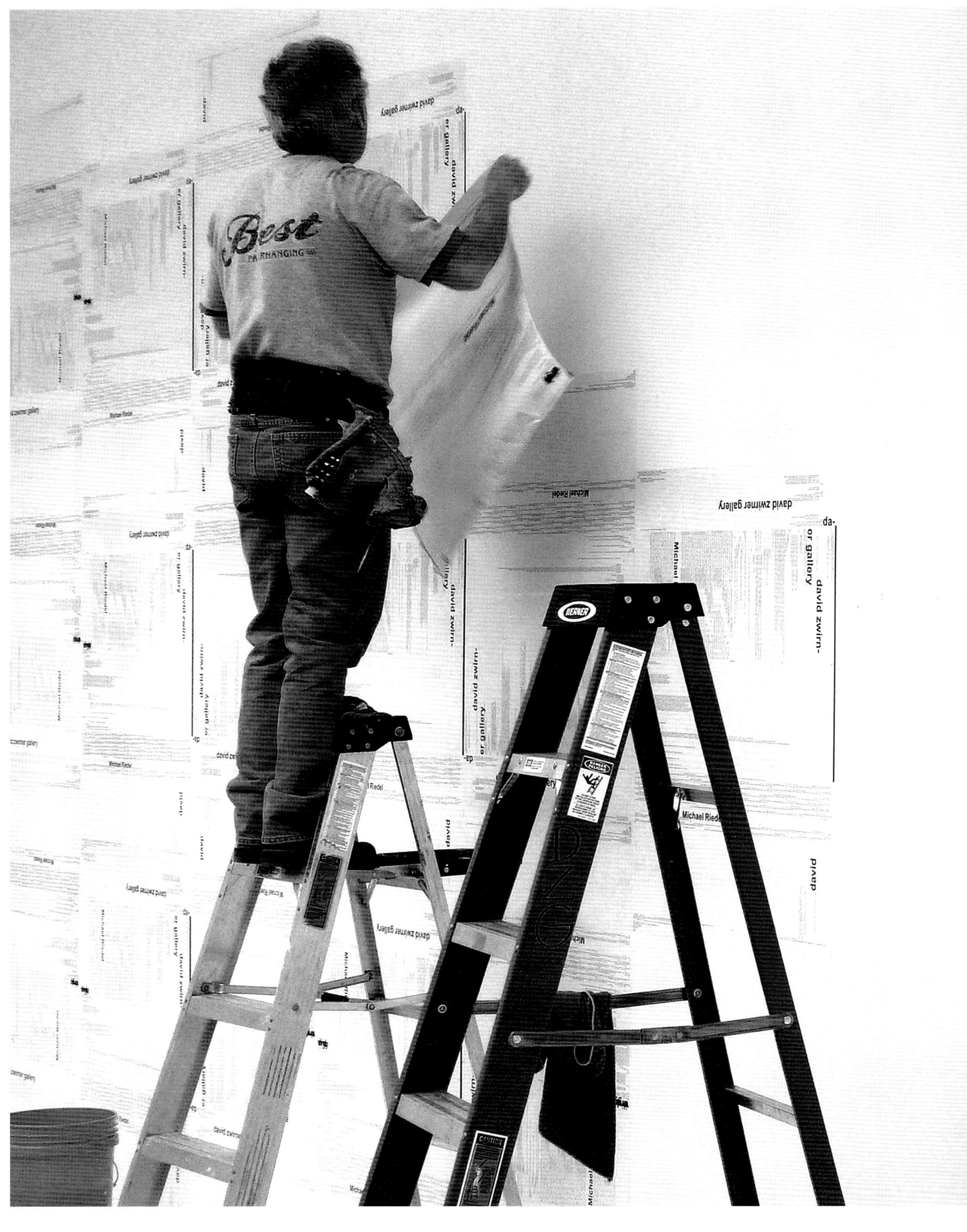
Best
david zwirner gallery
da-
or gallery
david zwirn-
Michael Riedel
david
WERNER

Installation in progress, *Michael Riedel: The quick brown fox jumps over the lazy dog*
David Zwirner, New York, 2011

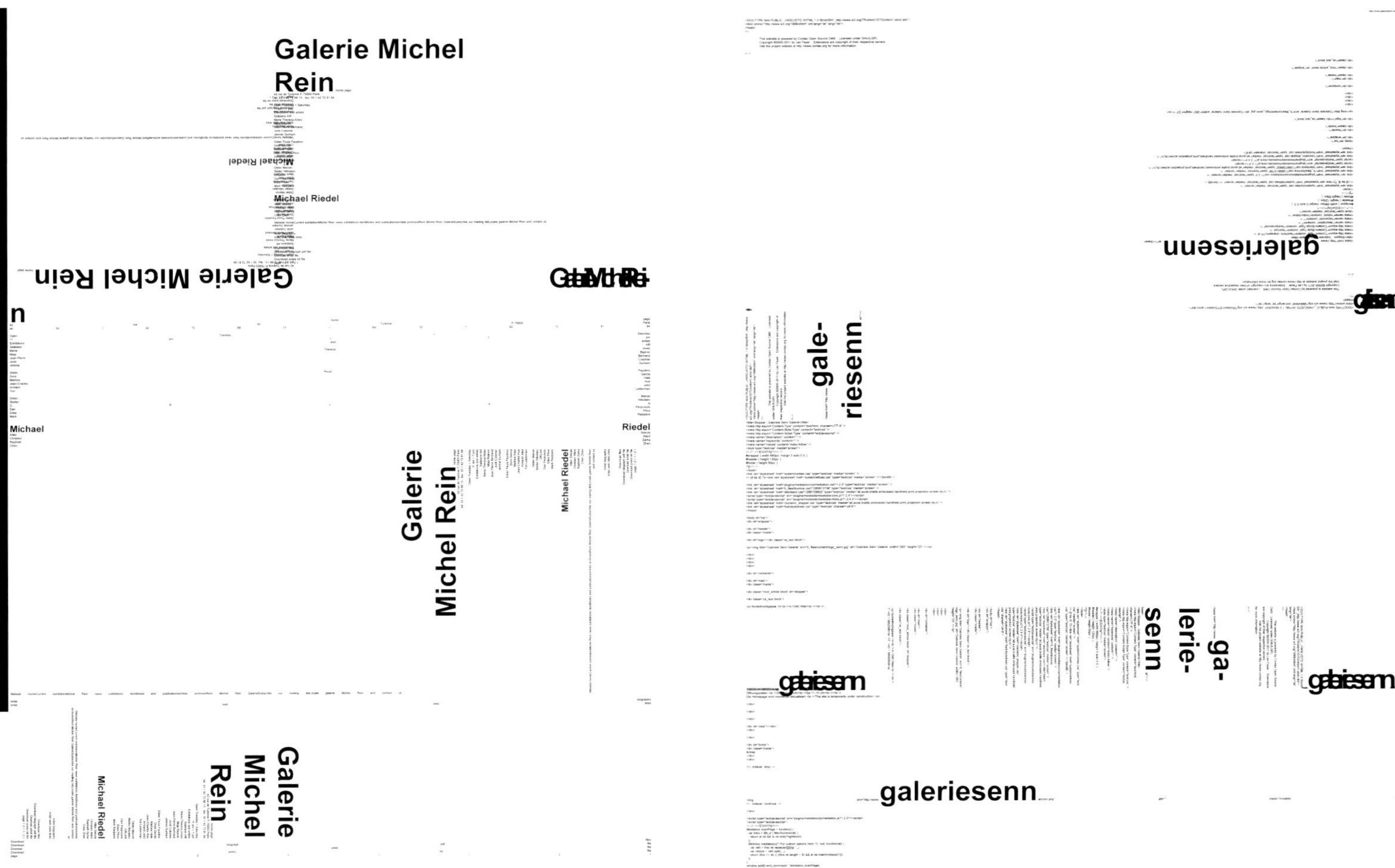

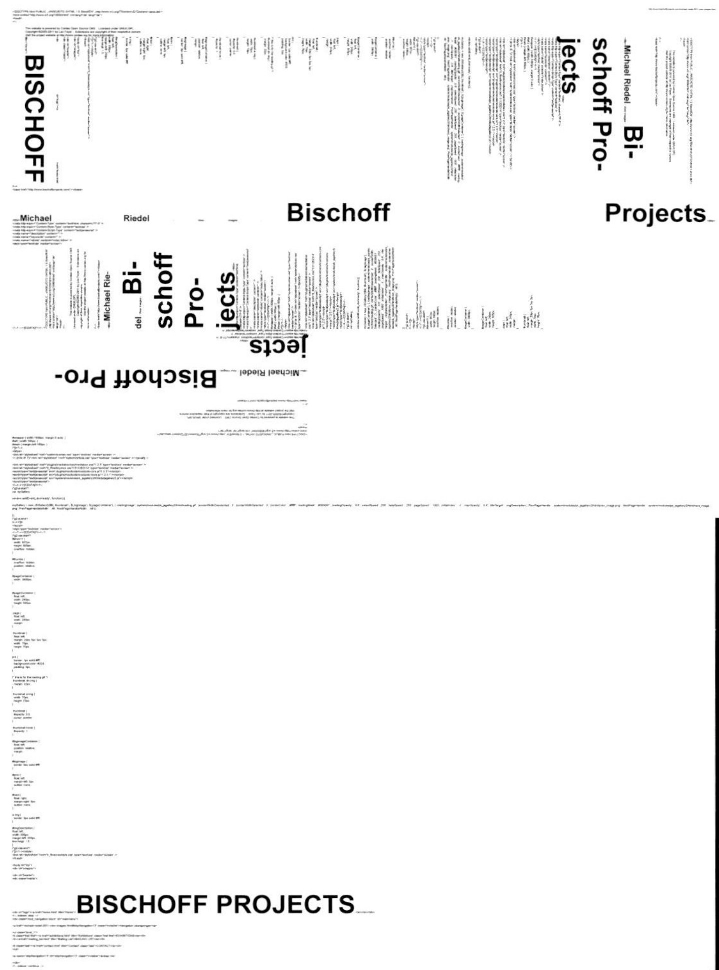

Posters with text from gallery websites

Untitled (Galerie Michel Rein), *Untitled (Galerie Senn)*, *Untitled (Bischoff Projects)*, 2010–2013
Offset print
Each: 33 1/8 x 23 3/8 inches
(84.1 x 59.4 cm)

Additional replicated gallery walls

Installation view, *Michael Riedel: The quick brown fox jumps over the lazy dog*
David Zwirner, New York, 2011

Replicated gallery wall

Installation view, *Michael Riedel: The quick brown fox jumps over the lazy dog*
David Zwirner, New York, 2011

Pattern based on the Poster *Untitled (David Zwirner)*, 2011

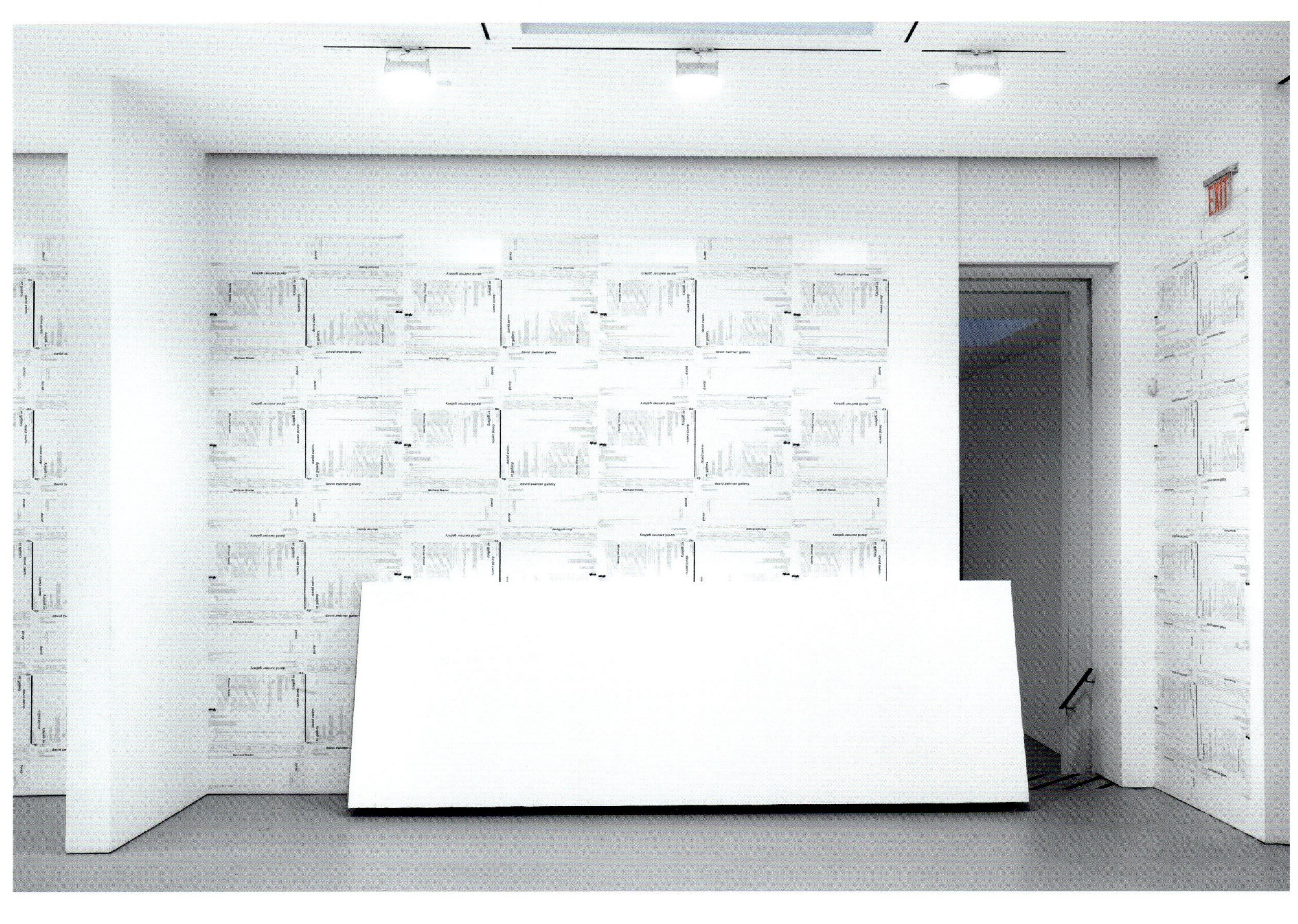

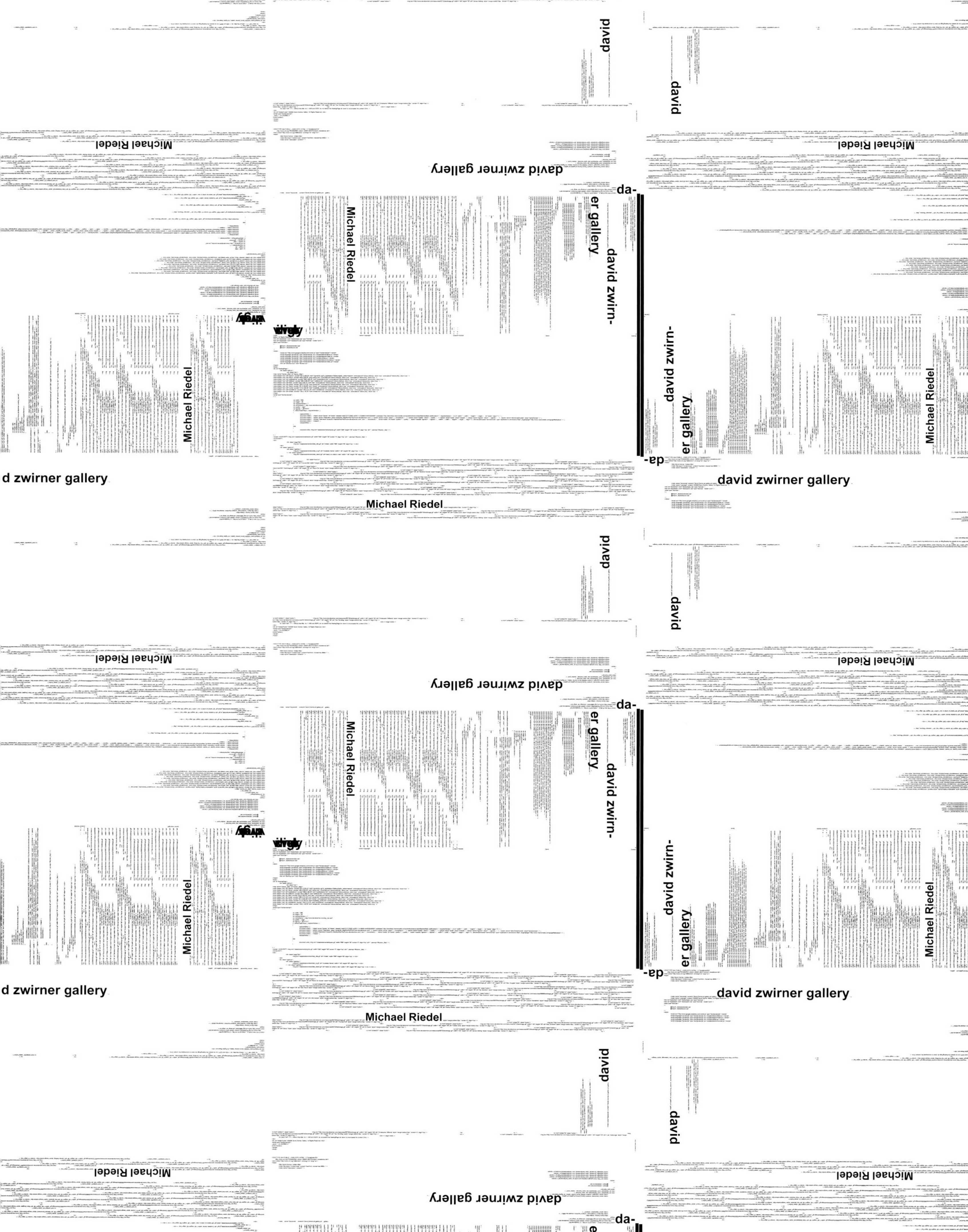

Michael Riedel
david
david zwirner gallery
da-
david zwirn-
er gallery
Michael Riedel
Michael Riedel
d zwirner gallery
david zwirner gallery

```
</div><div id="tw-content-5-1" class="tw-content tw-widget-last"><span style="display:none;">Archives</span><h4 tabindex="-1"
aria-expanded="false" aria-selected="false" aria-controls="ui-accordion-1-panel-1" role="tab" id="tw-title-5-1" class="tw-title ui-accordion-header
ui-helper-reset ui-state-default ui-corner-all ui-accordion-icons"><span class="ui-accordion-header-icon ui-icon ui-icon-triangle-1-e"></span><a
href="#">Archives</a></h4>                    <ul aria-hidden="true" role="tabpanel" aria-labelledby="tw-title-5-1" id="ui-accordion-1-panel-1"

style="display: none; height: 1785px;" class="ui-accordion-content ui-helper-reset ui-widget-content ui-corner-bottom">
        <li><a href="http://dailyserving.com/2015/06/">June 2015</a></li>
        <li><a href="http://dailyserving.com/2015/05/">May 2015</a></li>
        <li><a href="http://dailyserving.com/2015/04/">April 2015</a></li>
        <li><a href="http://dailyserving.com/2015/03/">March 2015</a></li>
        <li><a href="http://dailyserving.com/2015/02/">February 2015</a></li>
        <li><a href="http://dailyserving.com/2015/01/">January 2015</a></li>
        <li><a href="http://dailyserving.com/2014/12/">December 2014</a></li>
        <li><a href="http://dailyserving.com/2014/11/">November 2014</a></li>
        <li><a href="http://dailyserving.com/2014/10/">October 2014</a></li>
        <li><a href="http://dailyserving.com/2014/09/">September 2014</a></li>
        <li><a href="http://dailyserving.com/2014/08/">August 2014</a></li>
        <li><a href="http://dailyserving.com/2014/07/">July 2014</a></li>
        <li><a href="http://dailyserving.com/2014/06/">June 2014</a></li>
        <li><a href="http://dailyserving.com/2014/05/">May 2014</a></li>
        <li><a href="http://dailyserving.com/2014/04/">April 2014</a></li>
        <li><a href="http://dailyserving.com/2014/03/">March 2014</a></li>
        <li><a href="http://dailyserving.com/2014/02/">February 2014</a></li>
        <li><a href="http://dailyserving.com/2014/01/">January 2014</a></li>
        <li><a href="http://dailyserving.com/2013/12/">December 2013</a></li>
        <li><a href="http://dailyserving.com/2013/11/">November 2013</a></li>
        <li><a href="http://dailyserving.com/2013/10/">October 2013</a></li>
        <li><a href="http://dailyserving.com/2013/09/">September 2013</a></li>
        <li><a href="http://dailyserving.com/2013/08/">August 2013</a></li>
        <li><a href="http://dailyserving.com/2013/07/">July 2013</a></li>
        <li><a href="http://dailyserving.com/2013/06/">June 2013</a></li>
        <li><a href="http://dailyserving.com/2013/05/">May 2013</a></li>
        <li><a href="http://dailyserving.com/2013/04/">April 2013</a></li>
        <li><a href="http://dailyserving.com/2013/03/">March 2013</a></li>
        <li><a href="http://dailyserving.com/2013/02/">February 2013</a></li>
        <li><a href="http://dailyserving.com/2013/01/">January 2013</a></li>
        <li><a href="http://dailyserving.com/2012/12/">December 2012</a></li>
        <li><a href="http://dailyserving.com/2012/11/">November 2012</a></li>
        <li><a href="http://dailyserving.com/2012/10/">October 2012</a></li>
        <li><a href="http://dailyserving.com/2012/09/">September 2012</a></li>
        <li><a href="http://dailyserving.com/2012/08/">August 2012</a></li>
        <li><a href="http://dailyserving.com/2012/07/">July 2012</a></li>
        <li><a href="http://dailyserving.com/2012/06/">June 2012</a></li>
        <li><a href="http://dailyserving.com/2012/05/">May 2012</a></li>
        <li><a href="http://dailyserving.com/2012/04/">April 2012</a></li>
        <li><a href="http://dailyserving.com/2012/03/">March 2012</a></li>
        <li><a href="http://dailyserving.com/2012/02/">February 2012</a></li>
        <li><a href="http://dailyserving.com/2012/01/">January 2012</a></li>
        <li><a href="http://dailyserving.com/2011/12/">December 2011</a></li>
        <li><a href="http://dailyserving.com/2011/11/">November 2011</a></li>
        <li><a href="http://dailyserving.com/2011/10/">October 2011</a></li>
        <li><a href="http://dailyserving.com/2011/09/">September 2011</a></li>
        <li><a href="http://dailyserving.com/2011/08/">August 2011</a></li>
        <li><a href="http://dailyserving.com/2011/07/">July 2011</a></li>
        <li><a href="http://dailyserving.com/2011/06/">June 2011</a></li>
        <li><a href="http://dailyserving.com/2011/05/">May 2011</a></li>
        <li><a href="http://dailyserving.com/2011/04/">April 2011</a></li>
        <li><a href="http://dailyserving.com/2011/03/">March 2011</a></li>
        <li><a href="http://dailyserving.com/2011/02/">February 2011</a></li>
        <li><a href="http://dailyserving.com/2011/01/">January 2011</a></li>
        <li><a href="http://dailyserving.com/2010/12/">December 2010</a></li>
        <li><a href="http://dailyserving.com/2010/11/">November 2010</a></li>
        <li><a href="http://dailyserving.com/2010/10/">October 2010</a></li>
        <li><a href="http://dailyserving.com/2010/09/">September 2010</a></li>
        <li><a href="http://dailyserving.com/2010/08/">August 2010</a></li>
        <li><a href="http://dailyserving.com/2010/07/">July 2010</a></li>
        <li><a href="http://dailyserving.com/2010/06/">June 2010</a></li>
        <li><a href="http://dailyserving.com/2010/05/">May 2010</a></li>
        <li><a href="http://dailyserving.com/2010/04/">April 2010</a></li>
        <li><a href="http://dailyserving.com/2010/03/">March 2010</a></li>
        <li><a href="http://dailyserving.com/2010/02/">February 2010</a></li>
        <li><a href="http://dailyserving.com/2010/01/">January 2010</a></li>
        <li><a href="http://dailyserving.com/2009/12/">December 2009</a></li>
        <li><a href="http://dailyserving.com/2009/11/">November 2009</a></li>
        <li><a href="http://dailyserving.com/2009/10/">October 2009</a></li>
        <li><a href="http://dailyserving.com/2009/09/">September 2009</a></li>
        <li><a href="http://dailyserving.com/2009/08/">August 2009</a></li>
        <li><a href="http://dailyserving.com/2009/07/">July 2009</a></li>
```

Installation view, *Michael Riedel: The quick brown fox jumps over the lazy dog*
David Zwirner, New York, 2011

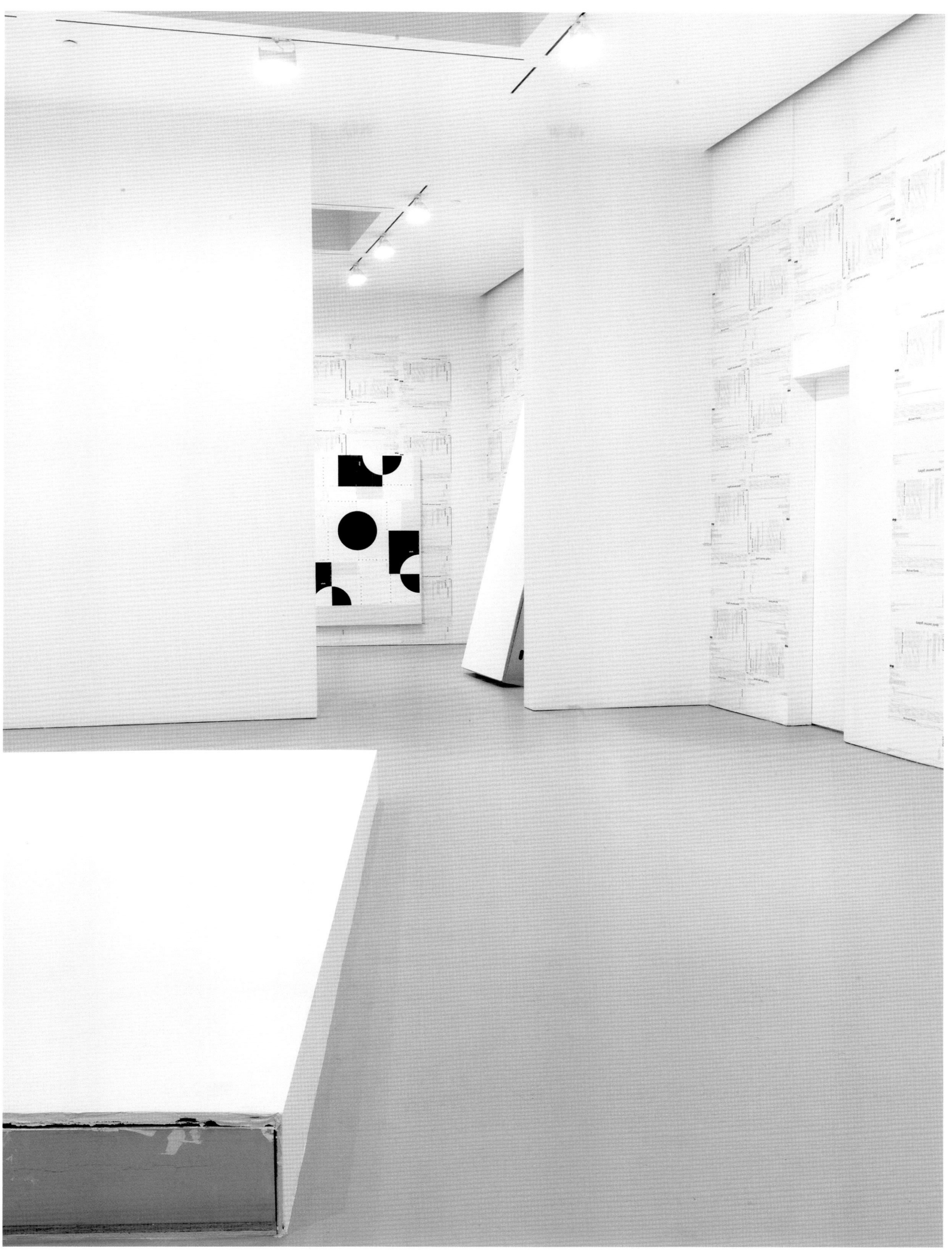

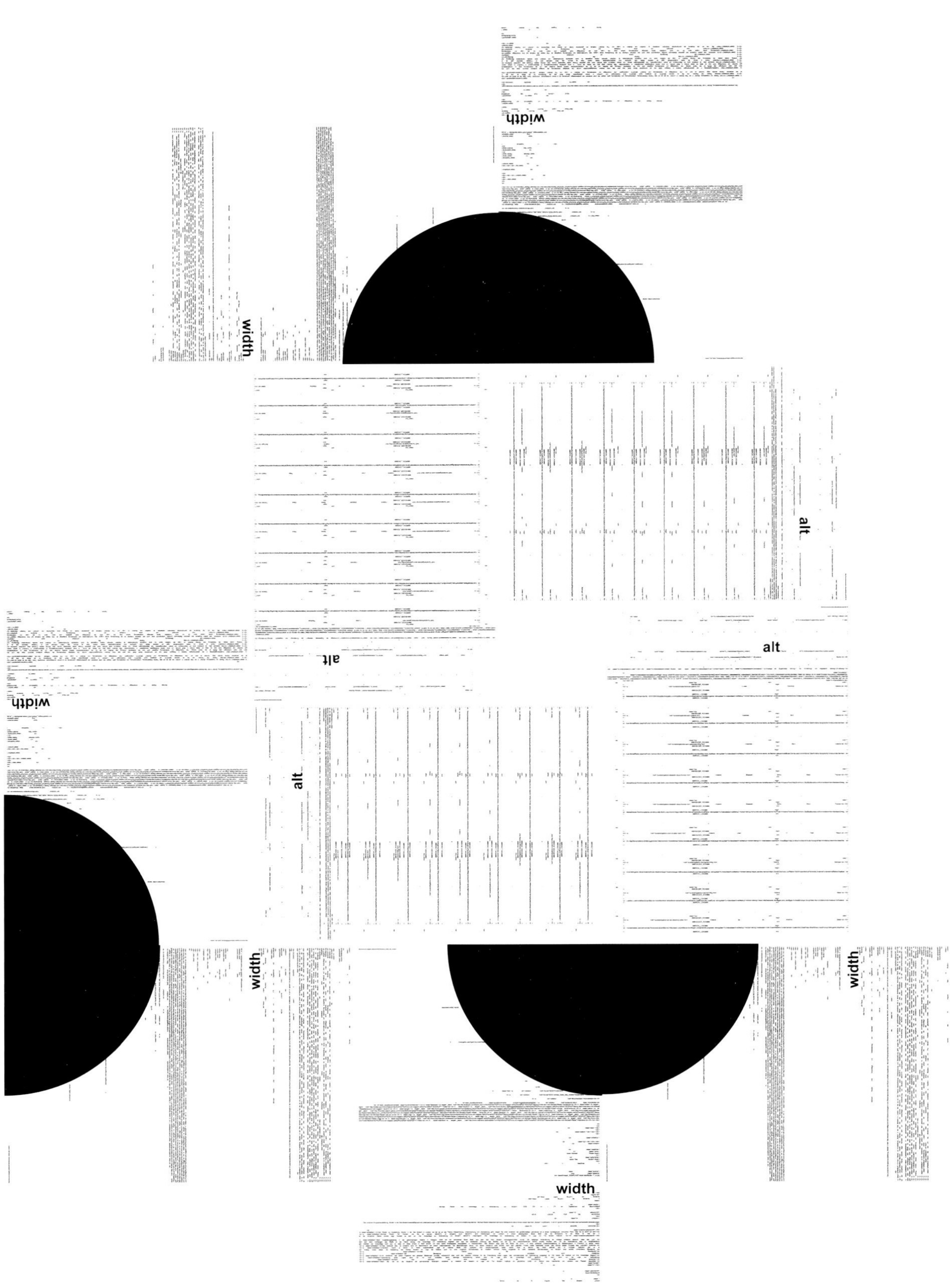

Untitled (width; alt), 2011
Silkscreen on linen
90 1/2 x 67 x 2 1/4 inches
(229.9 x 170.2 x 5.7 cm)

Opposite page & following pages:
Installation views, *Michael Riedel: The quick brown fox jumps over the lazy dog*
David Zwirner, New York, 2011

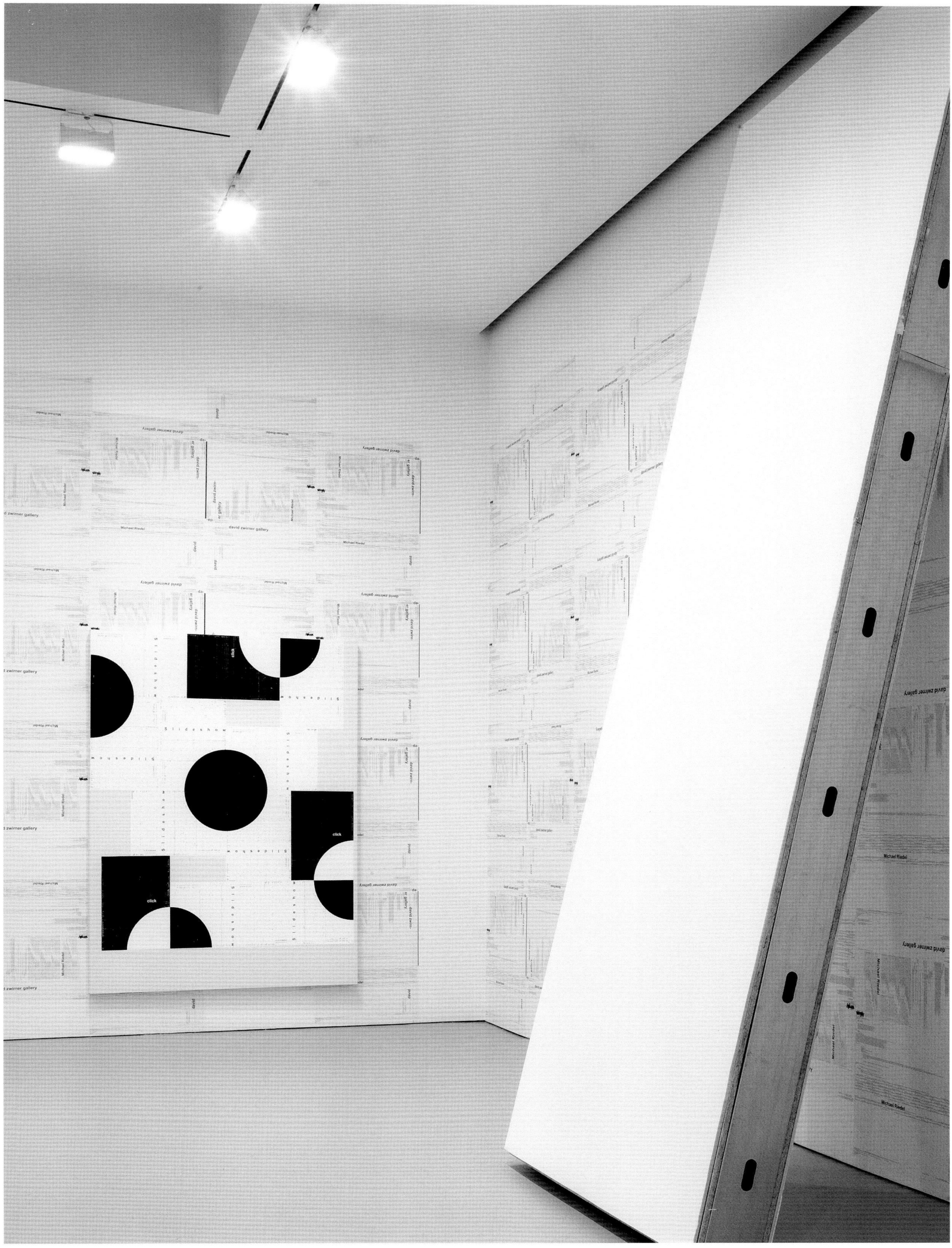
click
Slideshow
david zwirner gallery
Michael Riedel

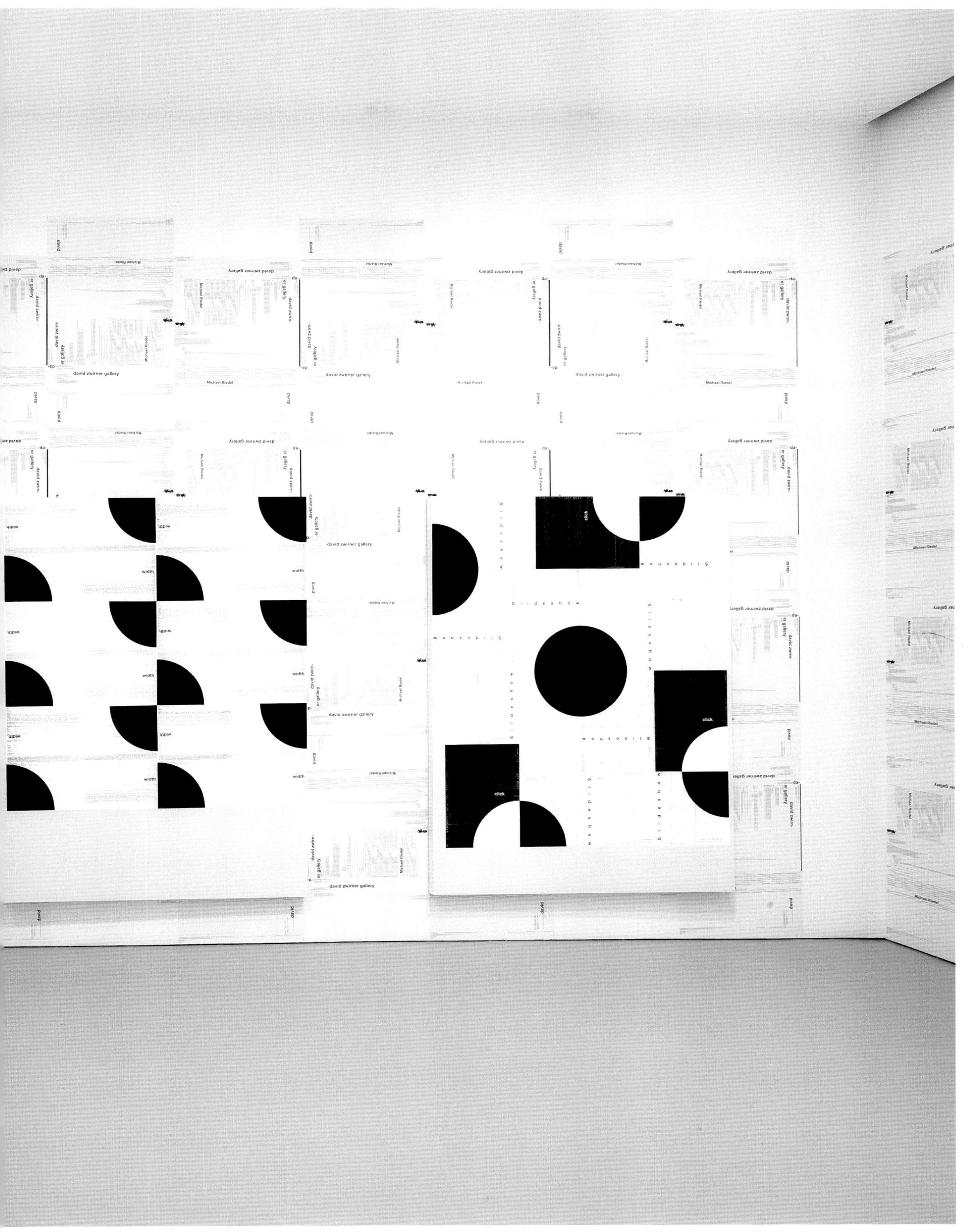
david zwirner gallery
Michael Riedel
width
Slideshow
click

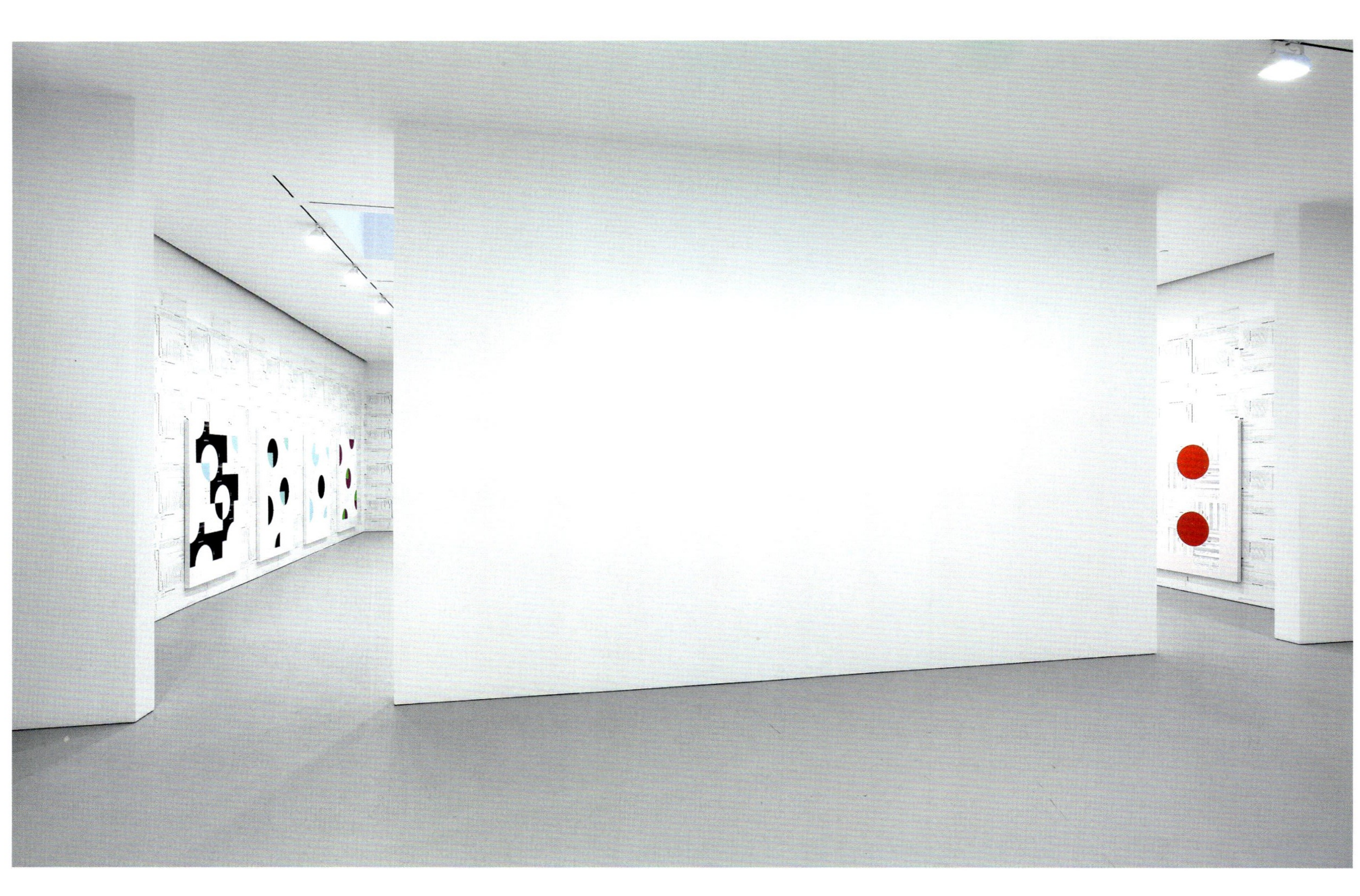

Installation view, *Michael Riedel: The quick brown fox jumps over the lazy dog*
David Zwirner, New York, 2011

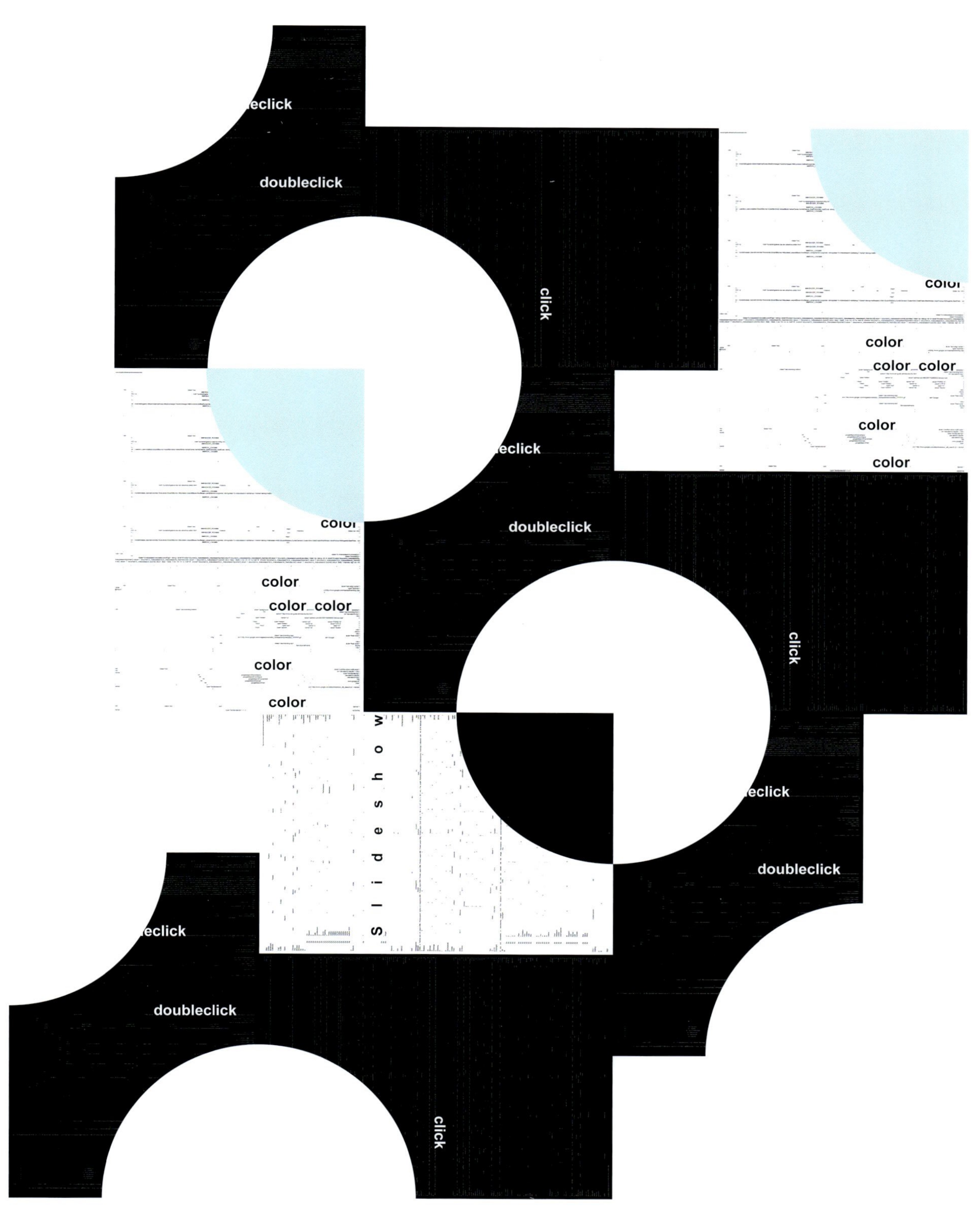

Untitled (doubleclick; click 1; color, light blue; Slideshow), 2011
Silkscreen on linen
90 1/2 x 67 x 2 1/4 inches
(229.9 x 170.2 x 5.7 cm)

Following pages:
Installation views, *Michael Riedel: The quick brown fox jumps over the lazy dog*
David Zwirner, New York, 2011

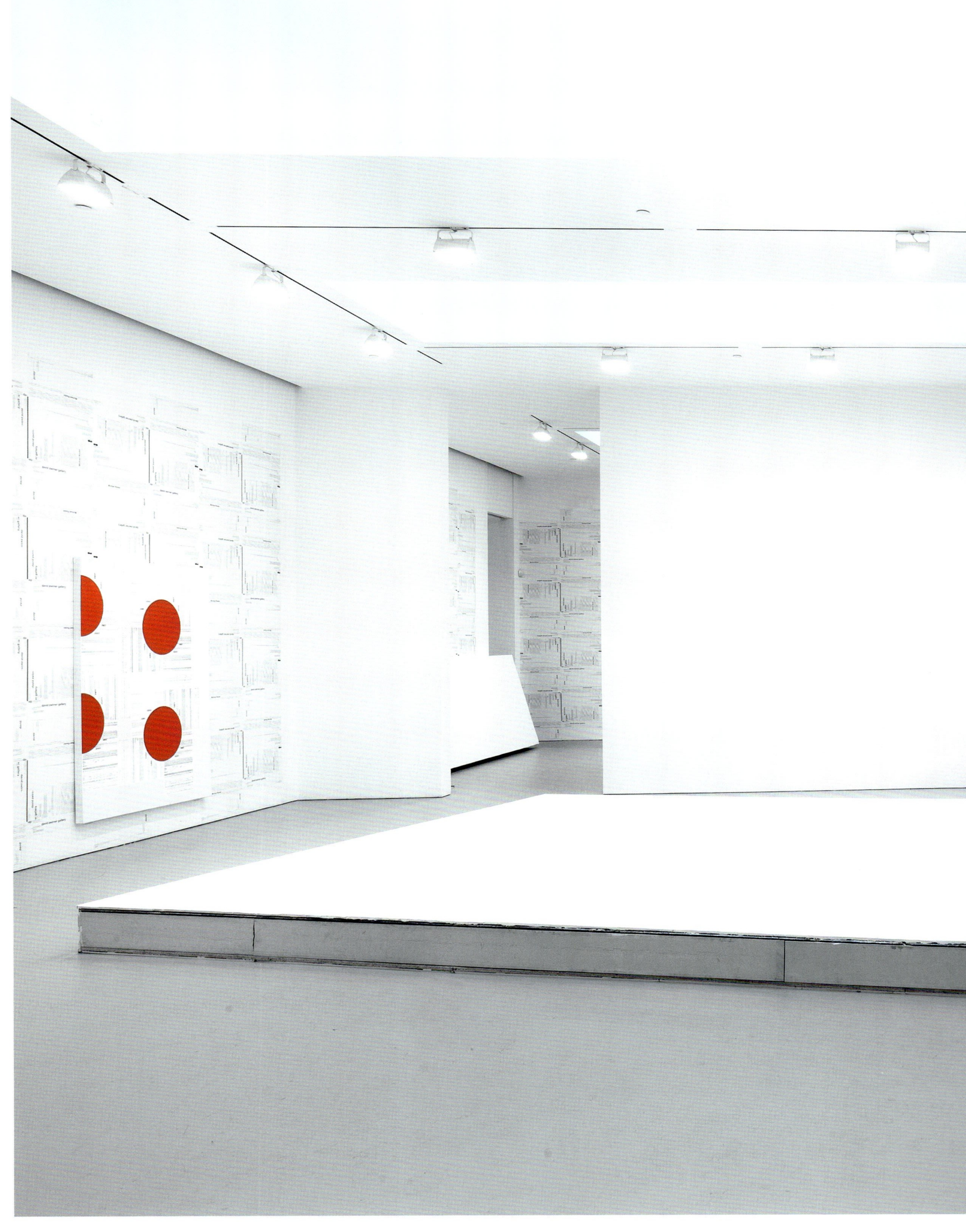

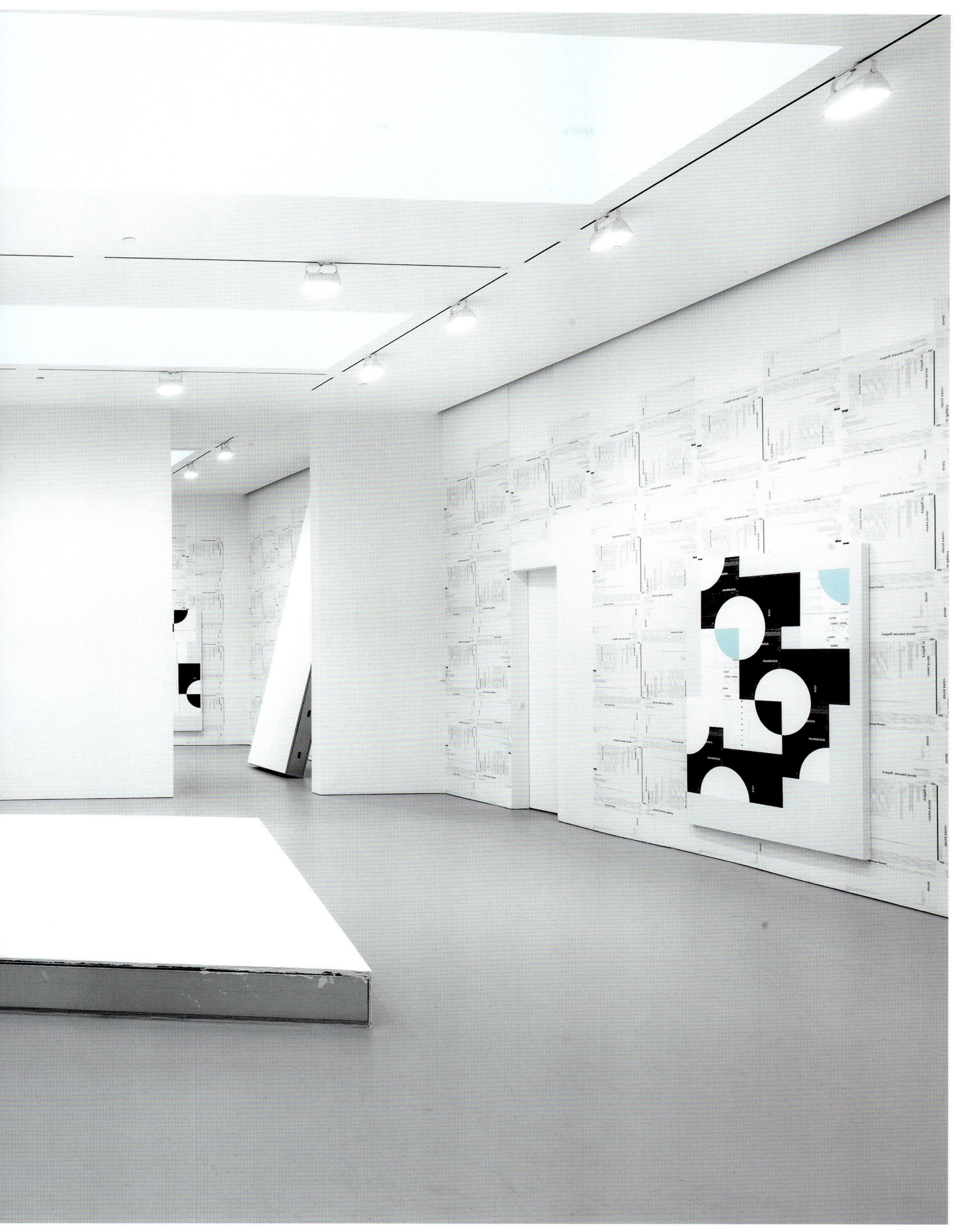

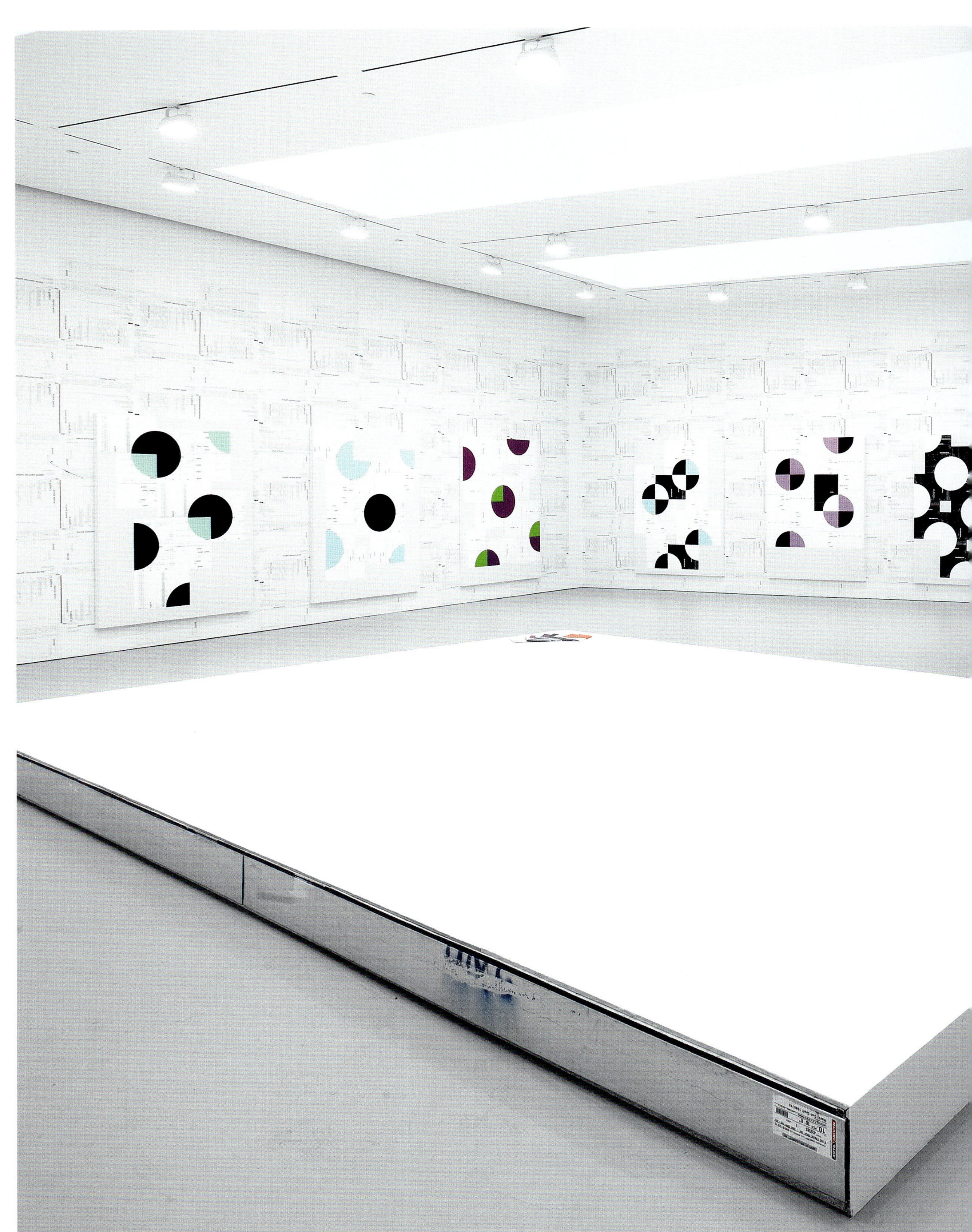

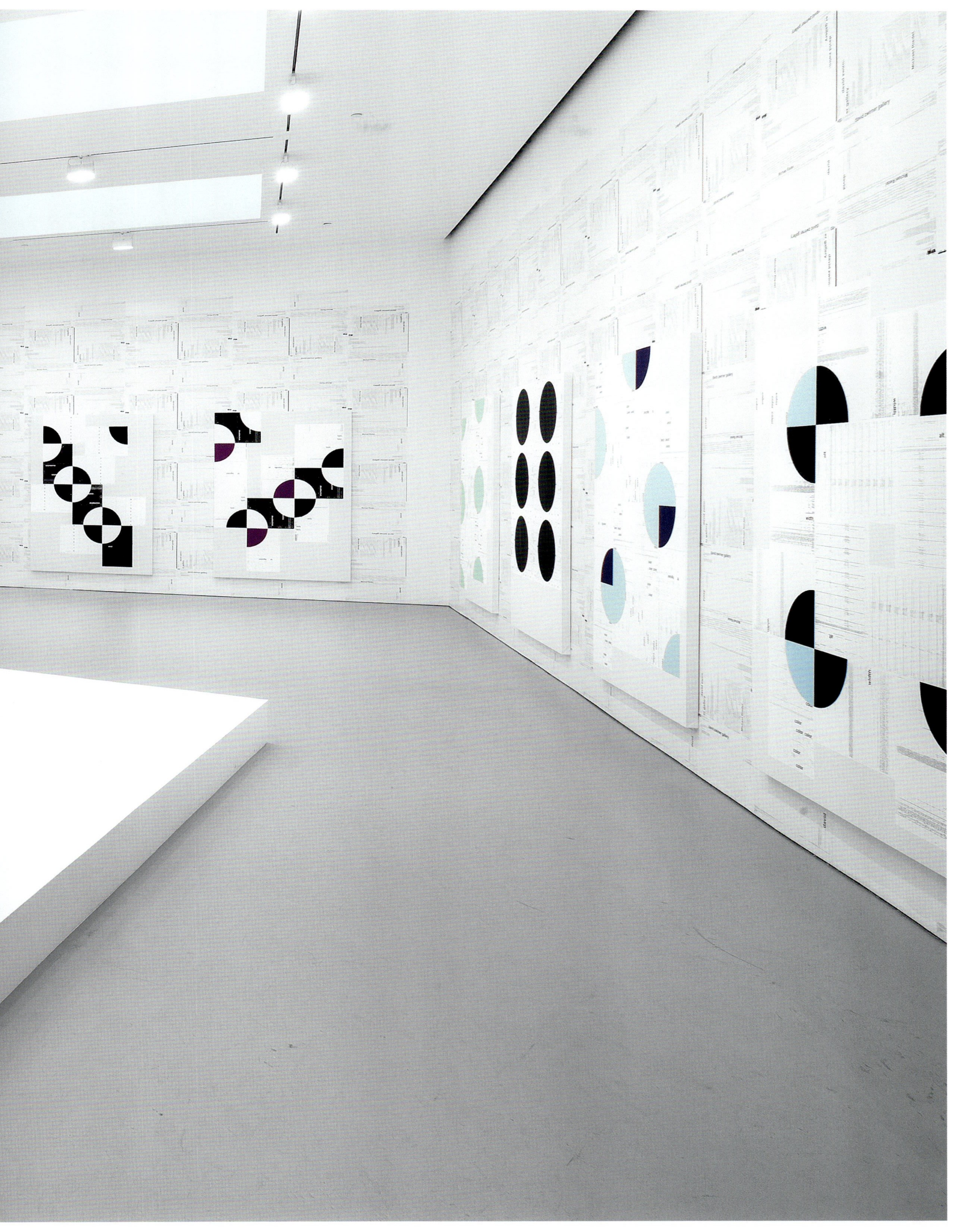

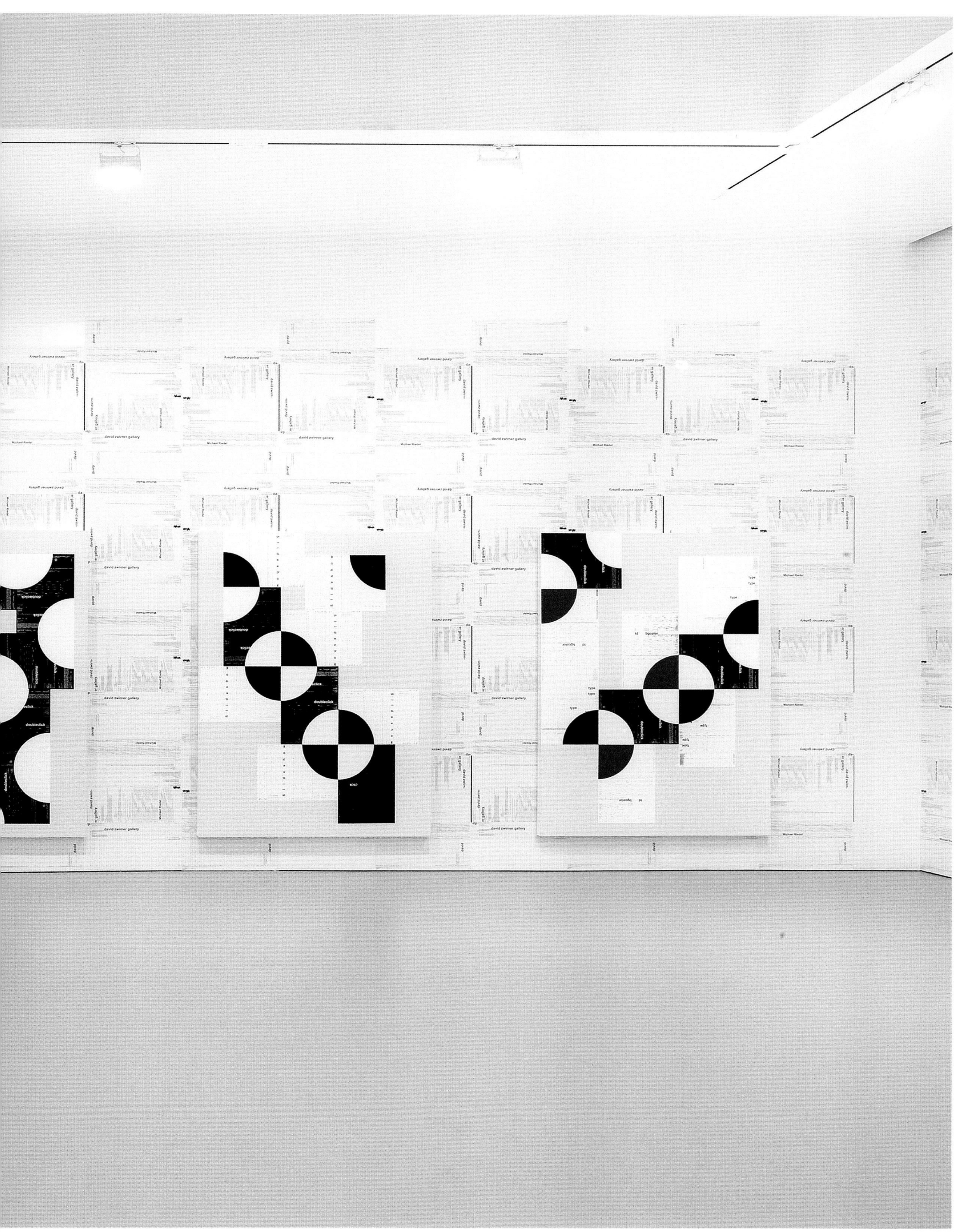
david zwirner gallery
Michael Riedel
doubleclick
type
td bgcolor
click

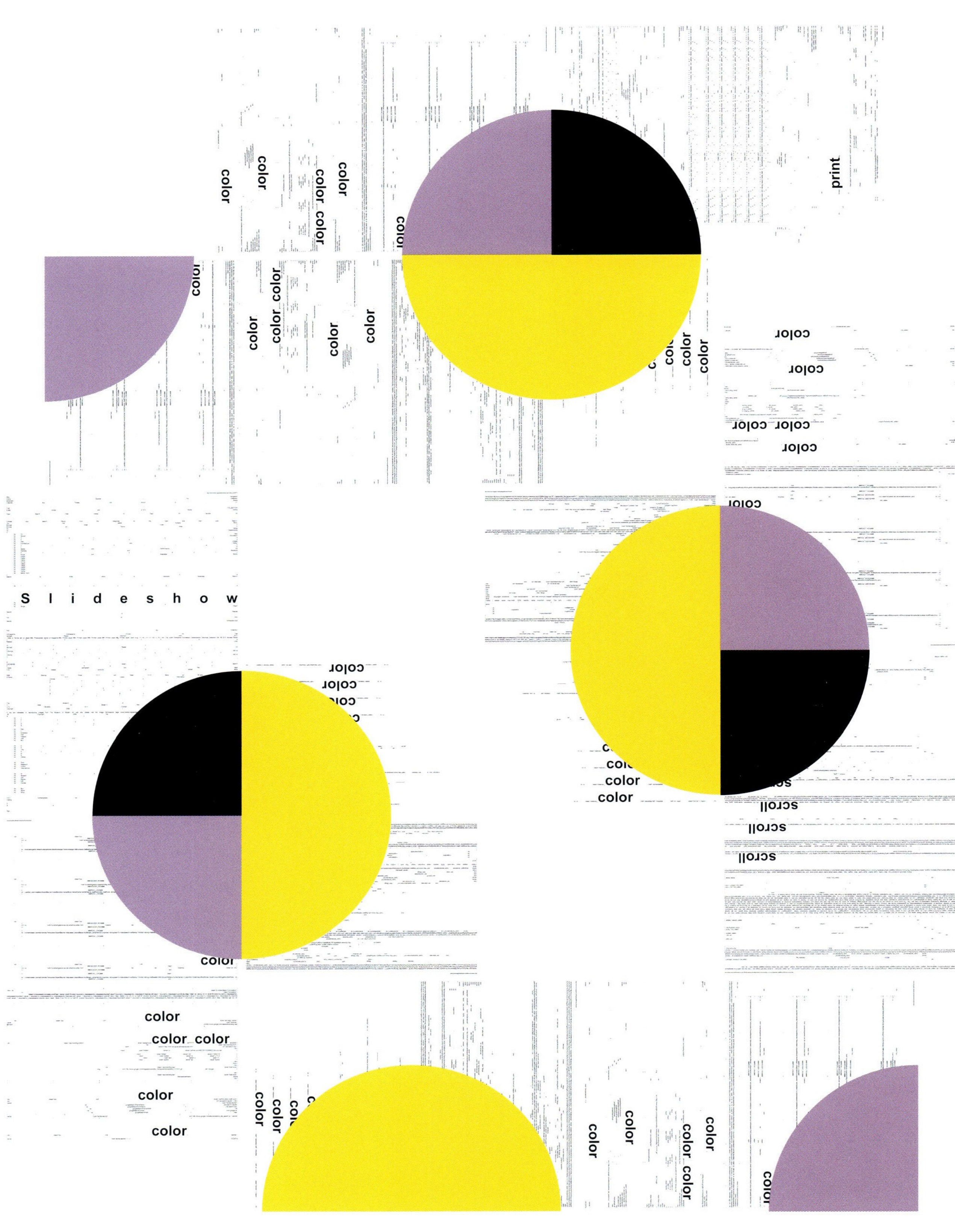

Untitled (color, yellow; color, light purple; Slideshow; print; scroll), 2013
Silkscreen on linen
90 1/2 x 67 x 2 1/4 inches
(229.9 x 170.2 x 5.7 cm)

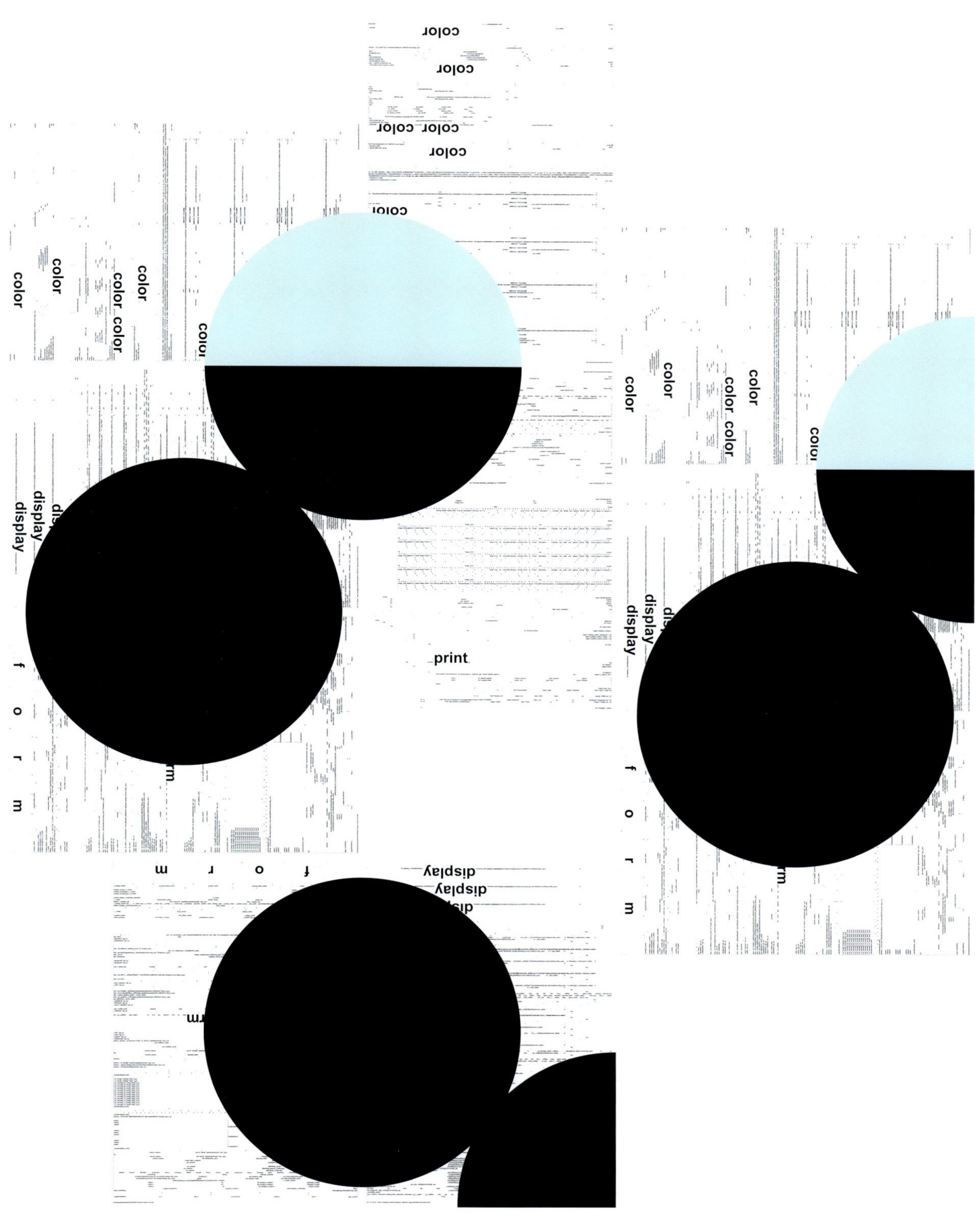

Untitled (color, light blue; display 2; form; print), 2013
Silkscreen on linen
90 1/2 x 67 x 2 1/4 inches
(229.9 x 170.2 x 5.7 cm)

Detail of *Untitled (color, light blue; display 2; form; print)*, 2013
Silkscreen on linen
90 1/2 x 67 x 2 1/4 inches
(229.9 x 170.2 x 5.7 cm)

Following pages:
Detail of *Untitled (doubleclick)*, 2011
Silkscreen on linen
90 1/2 x 67 x 2 1/4 inches
(229.9 x 170.2 x 5.7 cm)

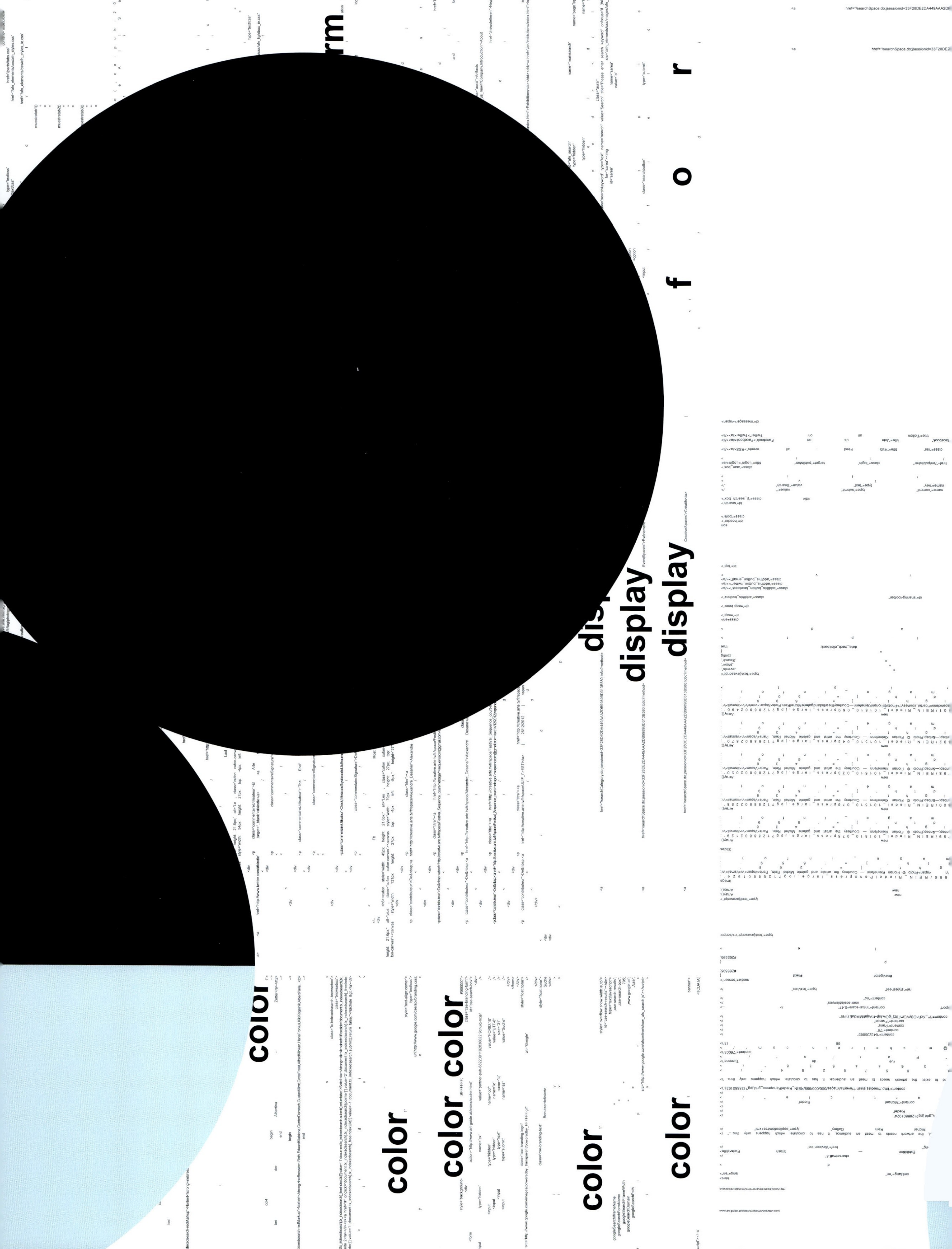

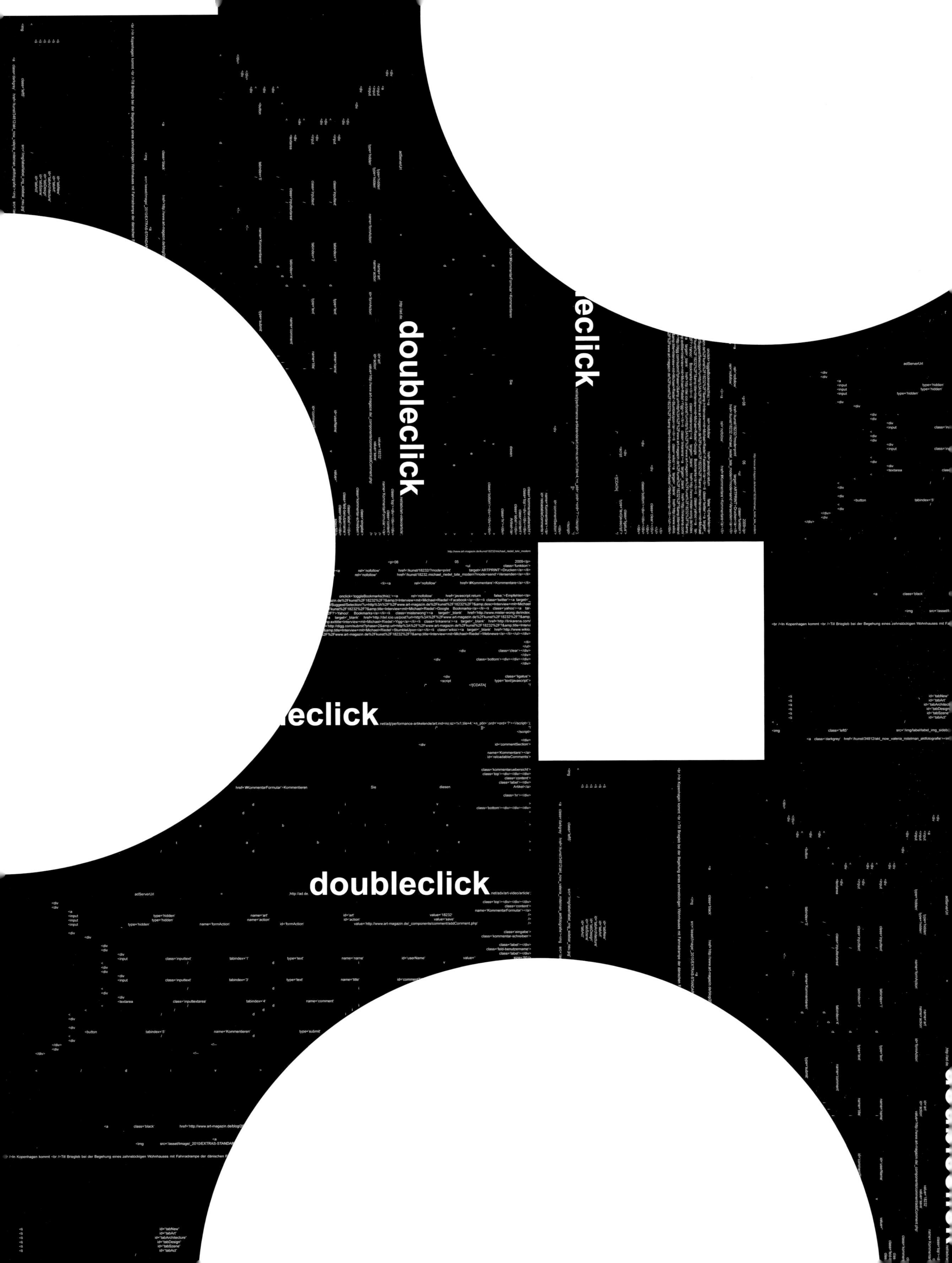
doubleclick
eclick
leclick
doubleclick

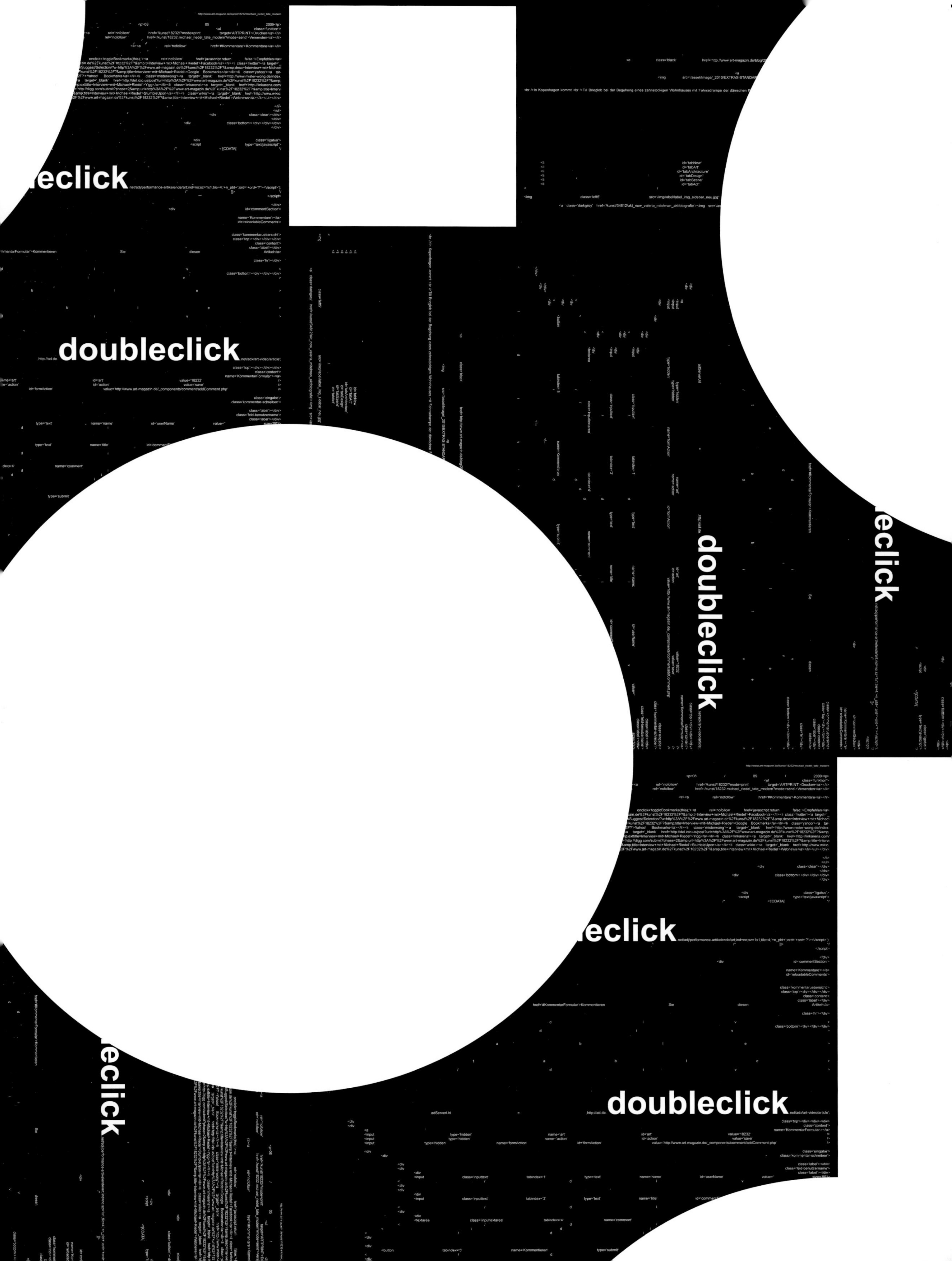
doubleclick
doubleclick
doubleclick
doubleclick

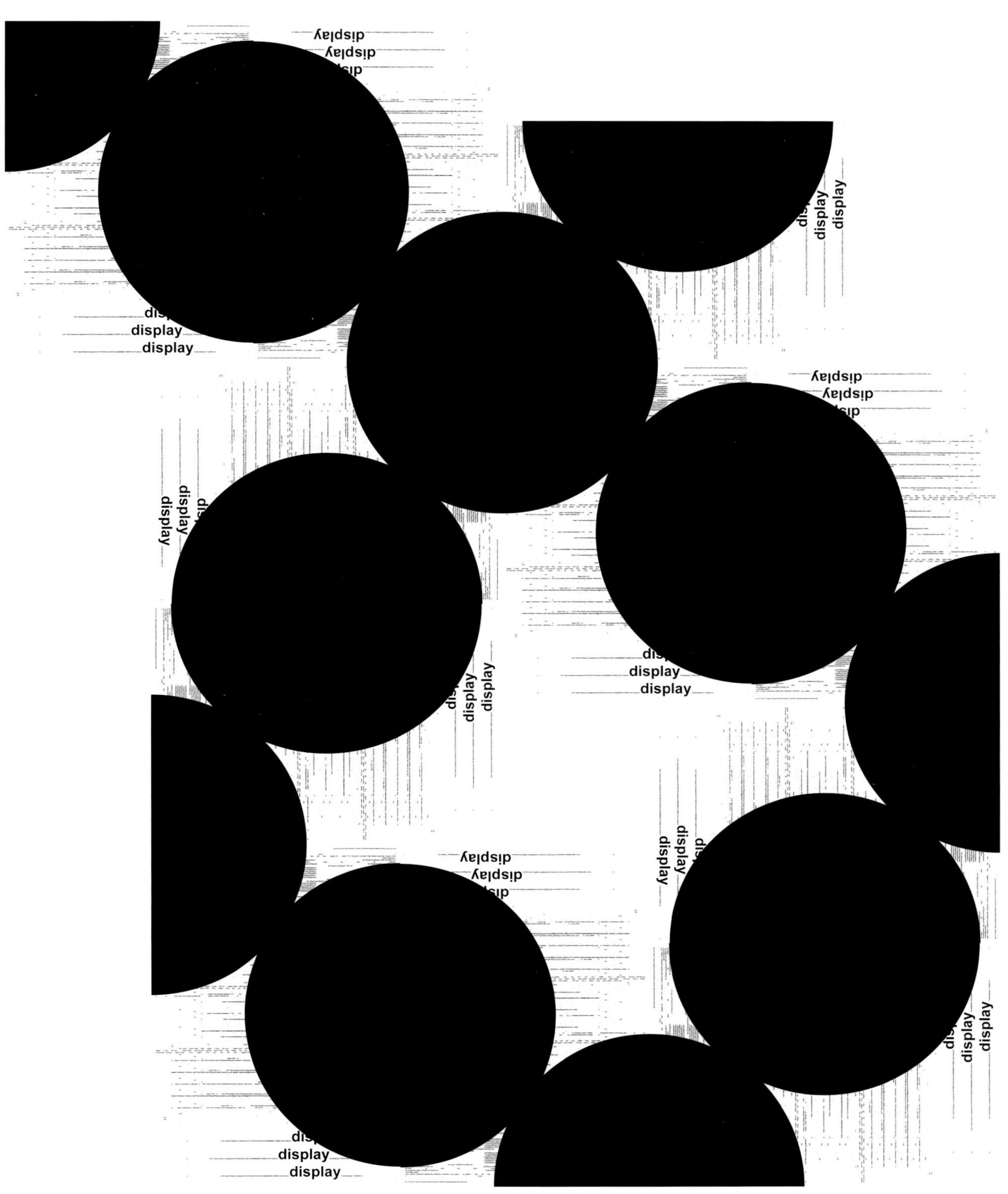

Untitled (display 2), 2013
Silkscreen on linen
90 1/2 x 67 x 2 1/4 inches
(229.9 x 170.2 x 5.7 cm)

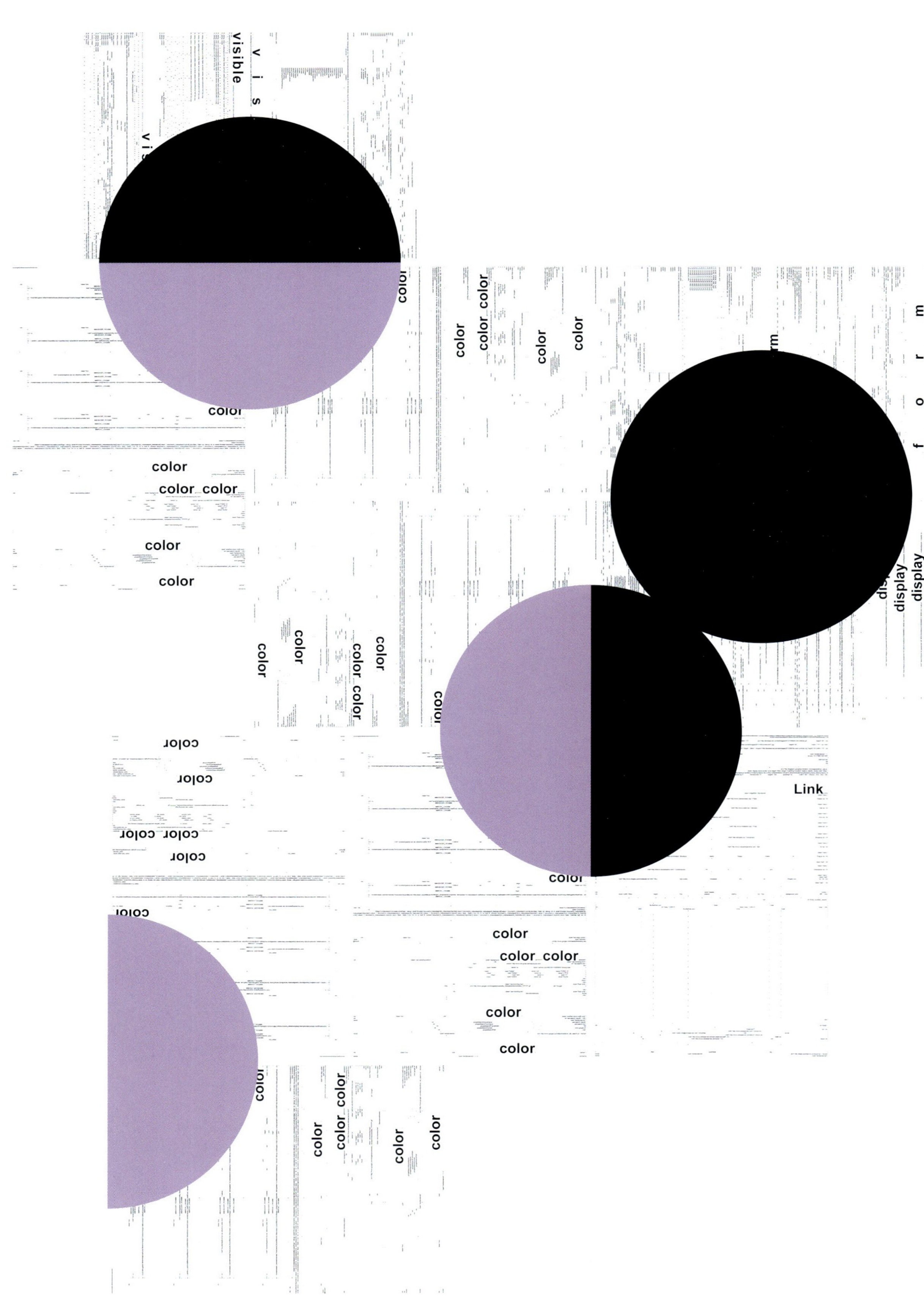

Untitled (form; Link; visible; display 2; color, light purple), 2014
Silkscreen on linen
90 1/2 x 67 x 2 1/4 inches
(229.9 x 170.2 x 5.7 cm)

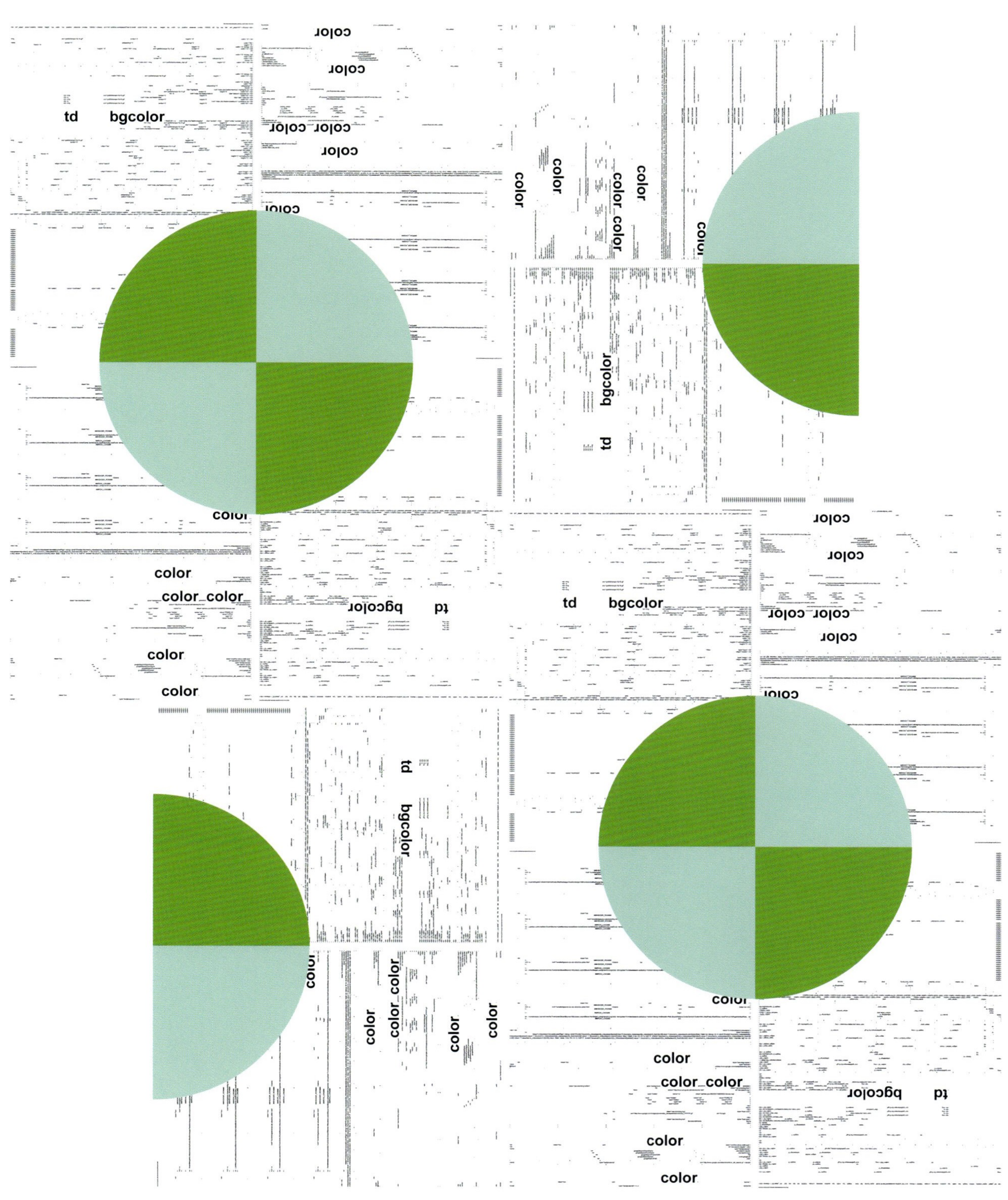

Untitled (td bgcolor, green; color, light green), 2013
Silkscreen on linen
90 1/2 x 67 x 2 1/4 inches
(229.9 x 170.2 x 5.7 cm)

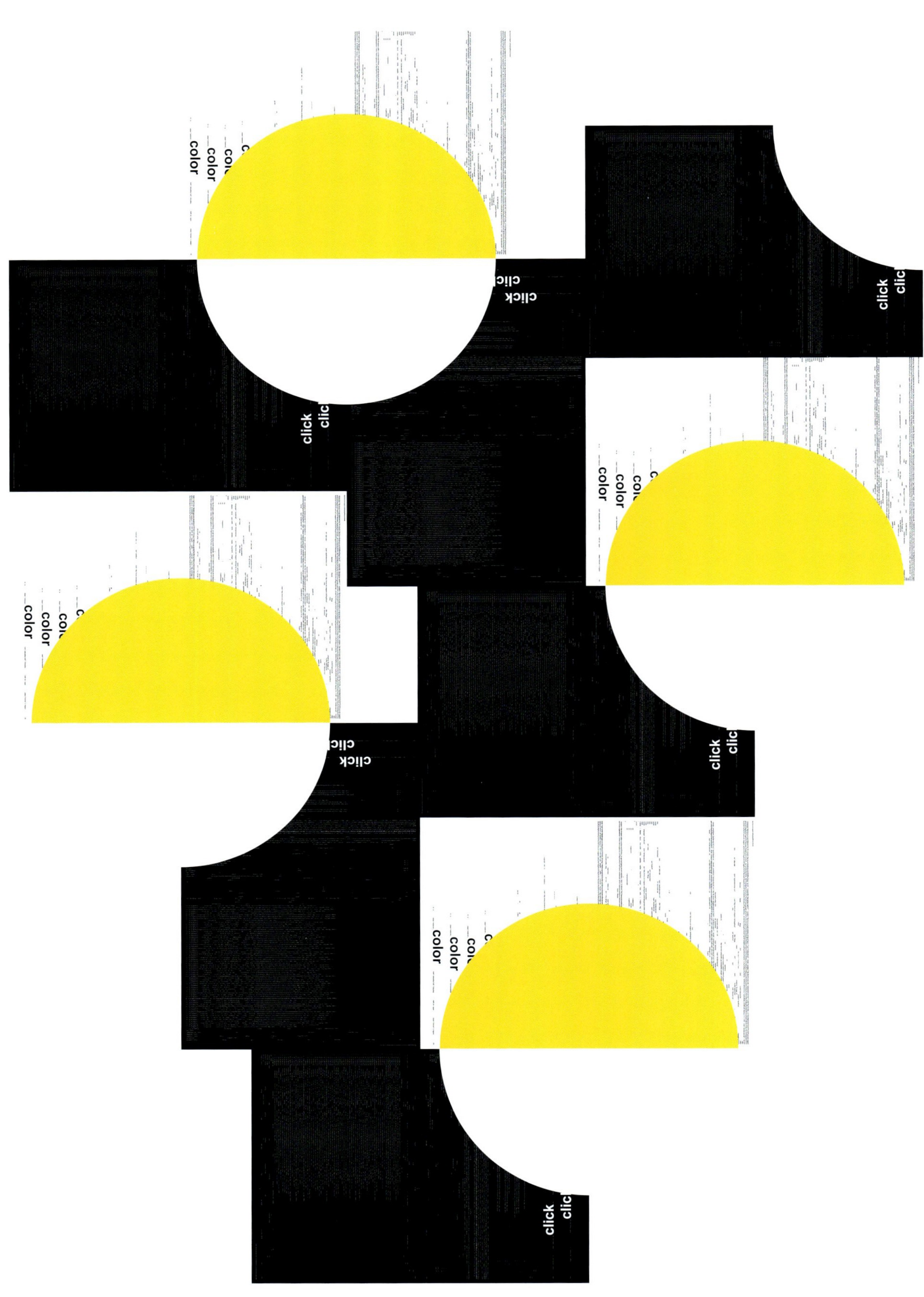

Untitled (color, yellow; click 2), 2013
Silkscreen on linen
90 1/2 x 67 x 2 1/4 inches
(229.9 x 170.2 x 5.7 cm)

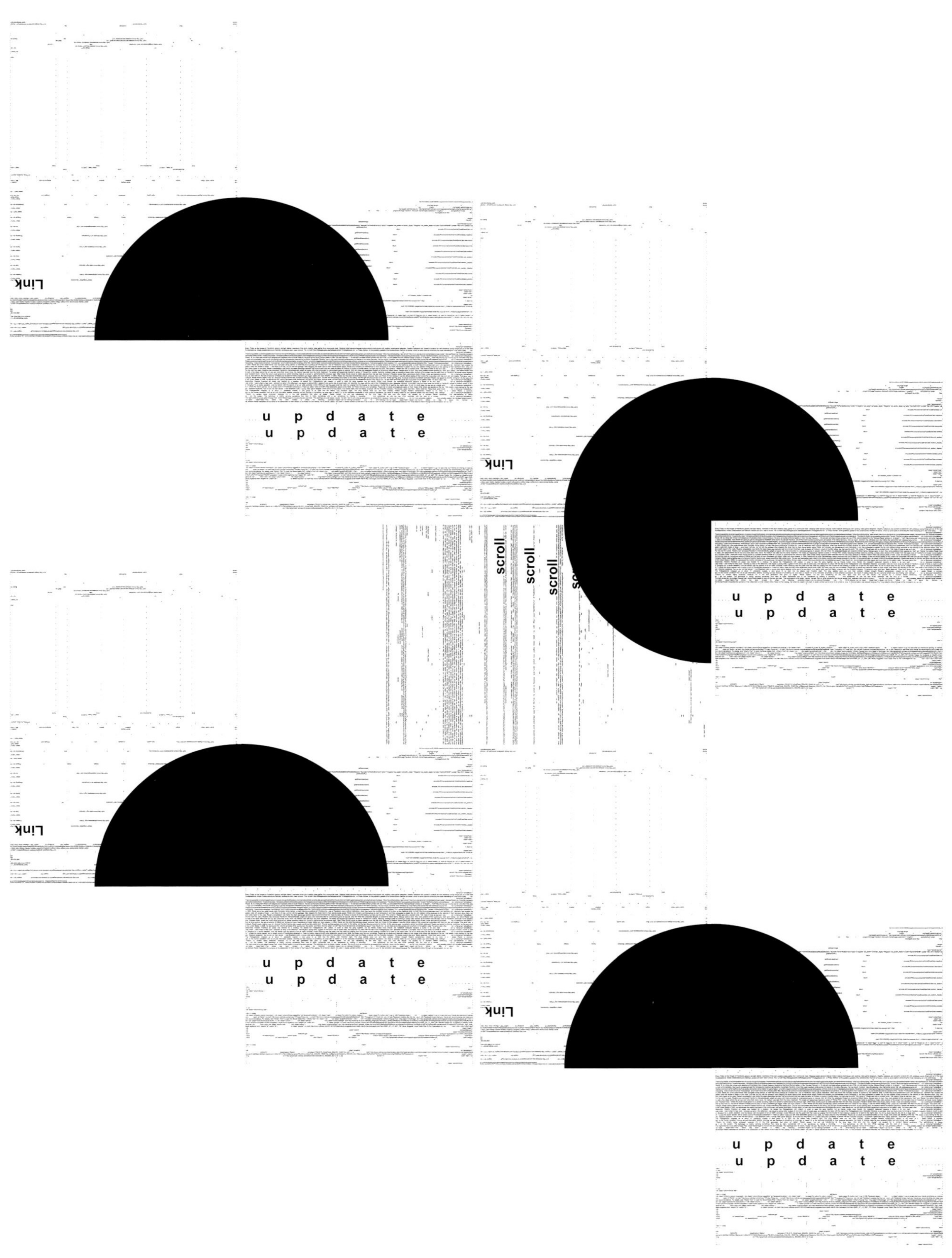

Untitled (update; Link; scroll), 2013
Silkscreen on linen
90 1/2 x 67 x 2 1/4 inches
(229.9 x 170.2 x 5.7 cm)

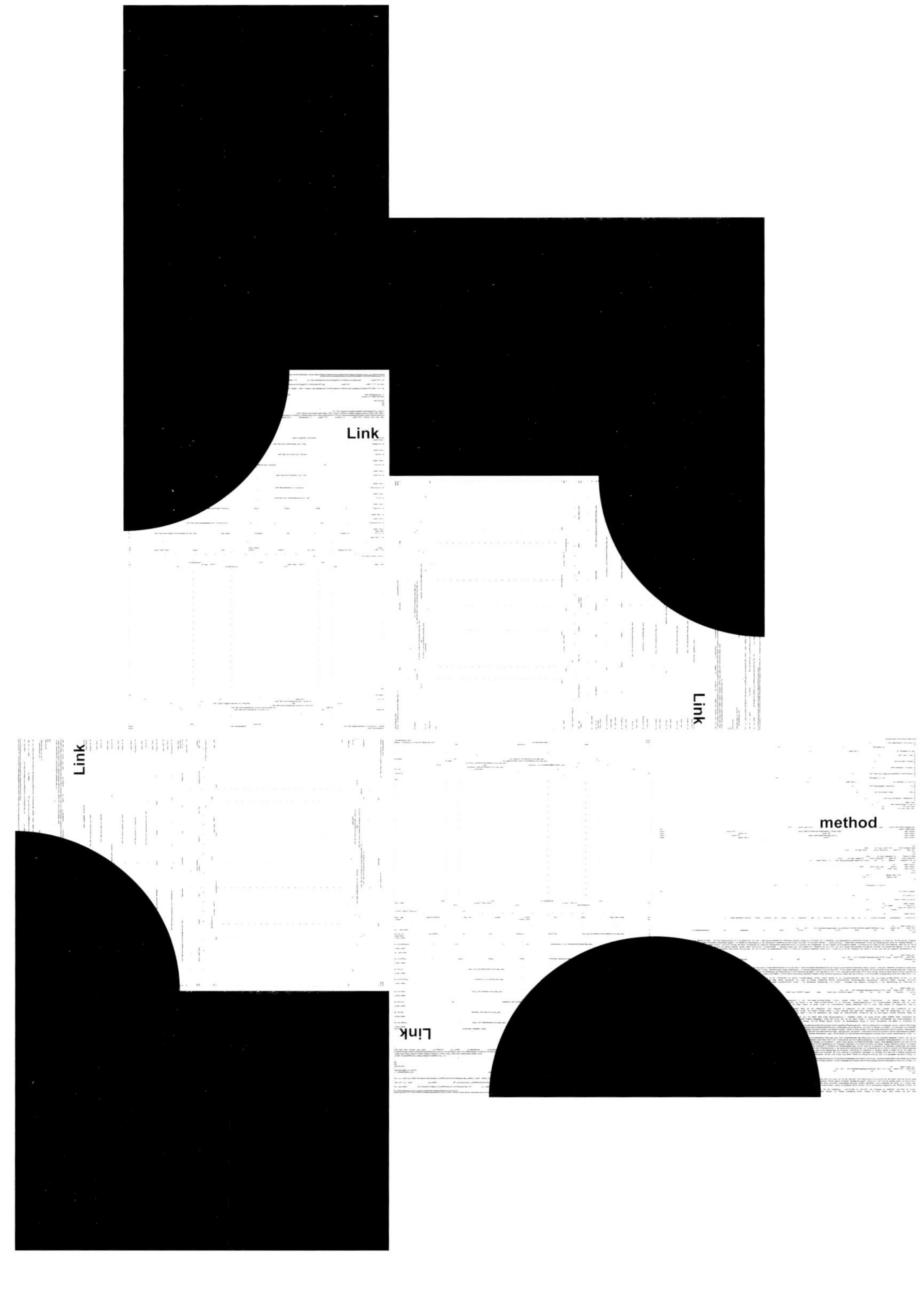

Untitled (Link; method; solid black), 2014
Silkscreen on linen
90 1/2 x 67 x 2 1/4 inches
(229.9 x 170.2 x 5.7 cm)

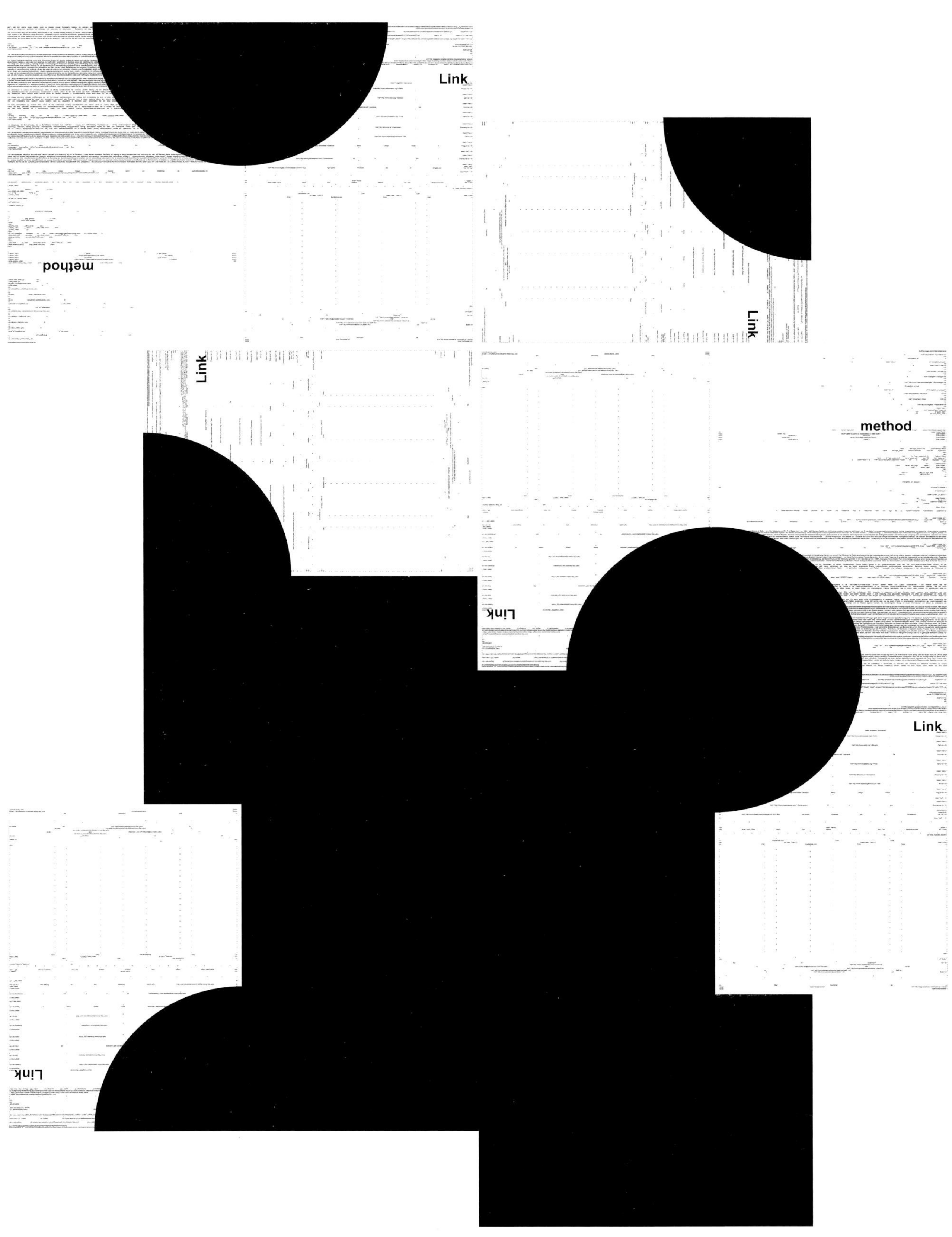

Untitled (Link; method; solid black), 2014
Silkscreen on linen
90 1/2 x 67 x 2 1/4 inches
(229.9 x 170.2 x 5.7 cm)

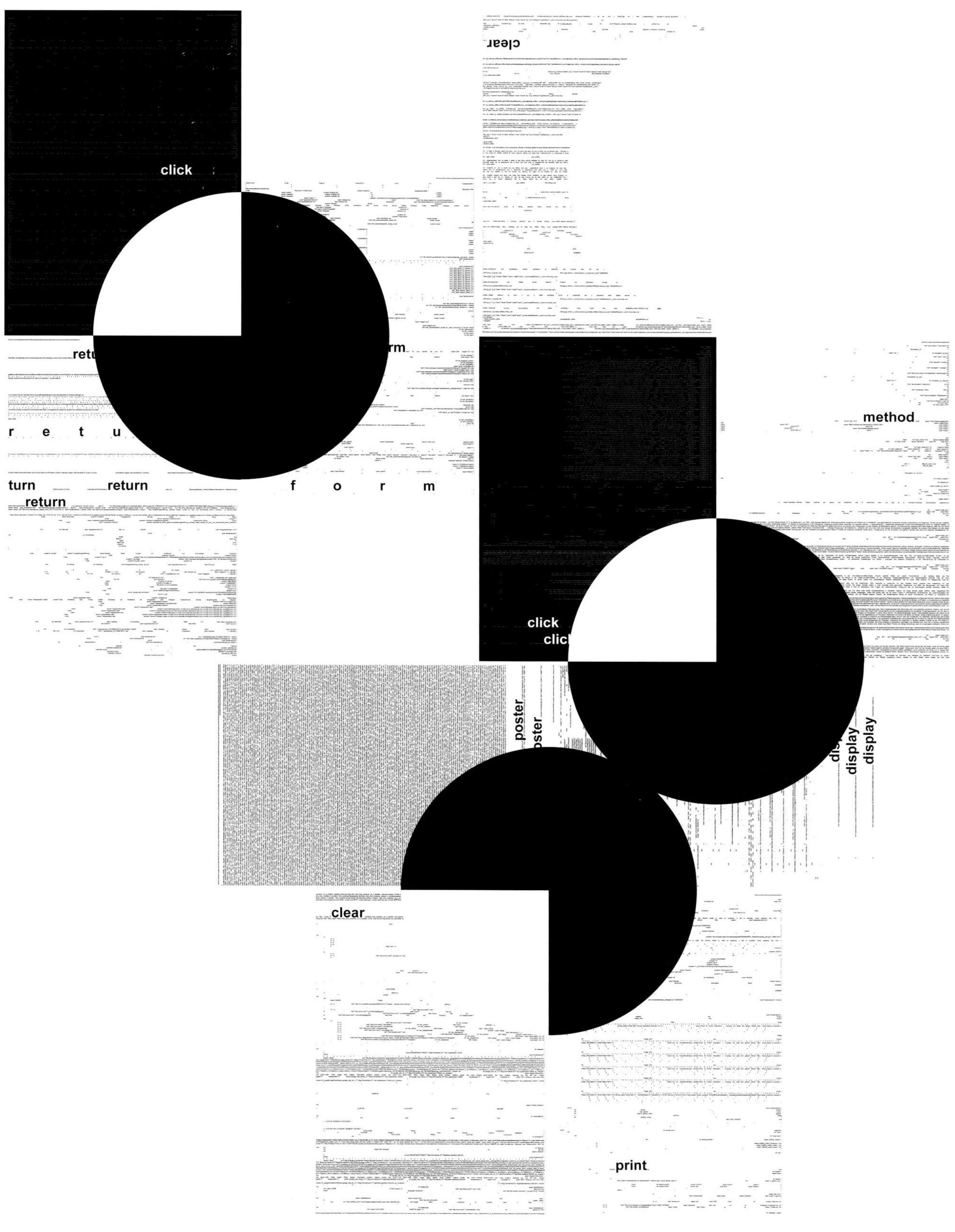
clear
click
retu
rm
r e t u
turn
return
return
f o r m
method
click
clic
poster
poster
disp
display
display
clear
print

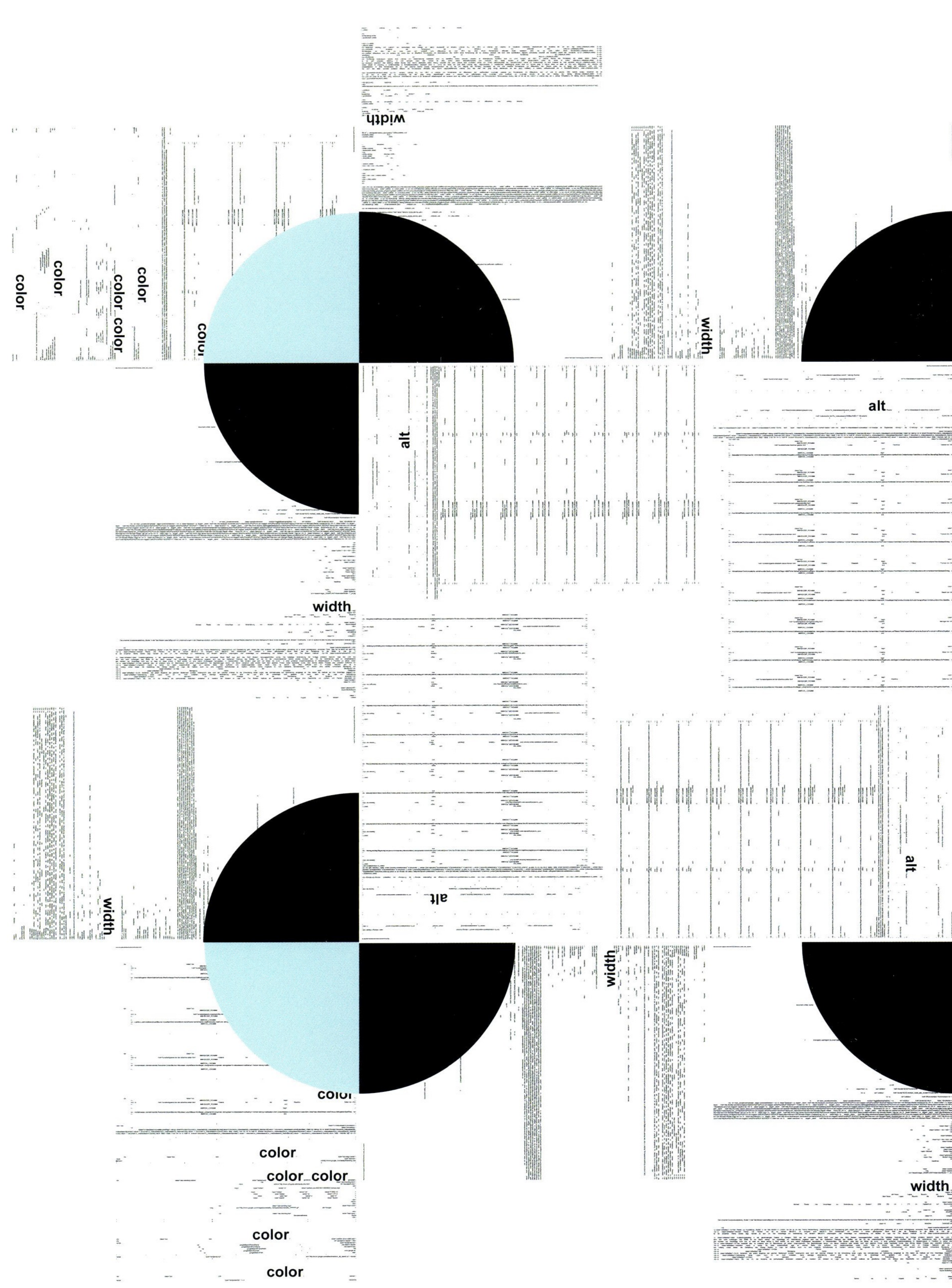

Untitled (color, light blue; width; alt), 2011
Silkscreen on linen
90 1/2 x 67 x 2 1/4 inches
(229.9 x 170.2 x 5.7 cm)

Installation view, *Michael Riedel: The quick brown fox jumps over the lazy dog*
David Zwirner, New York, 2011

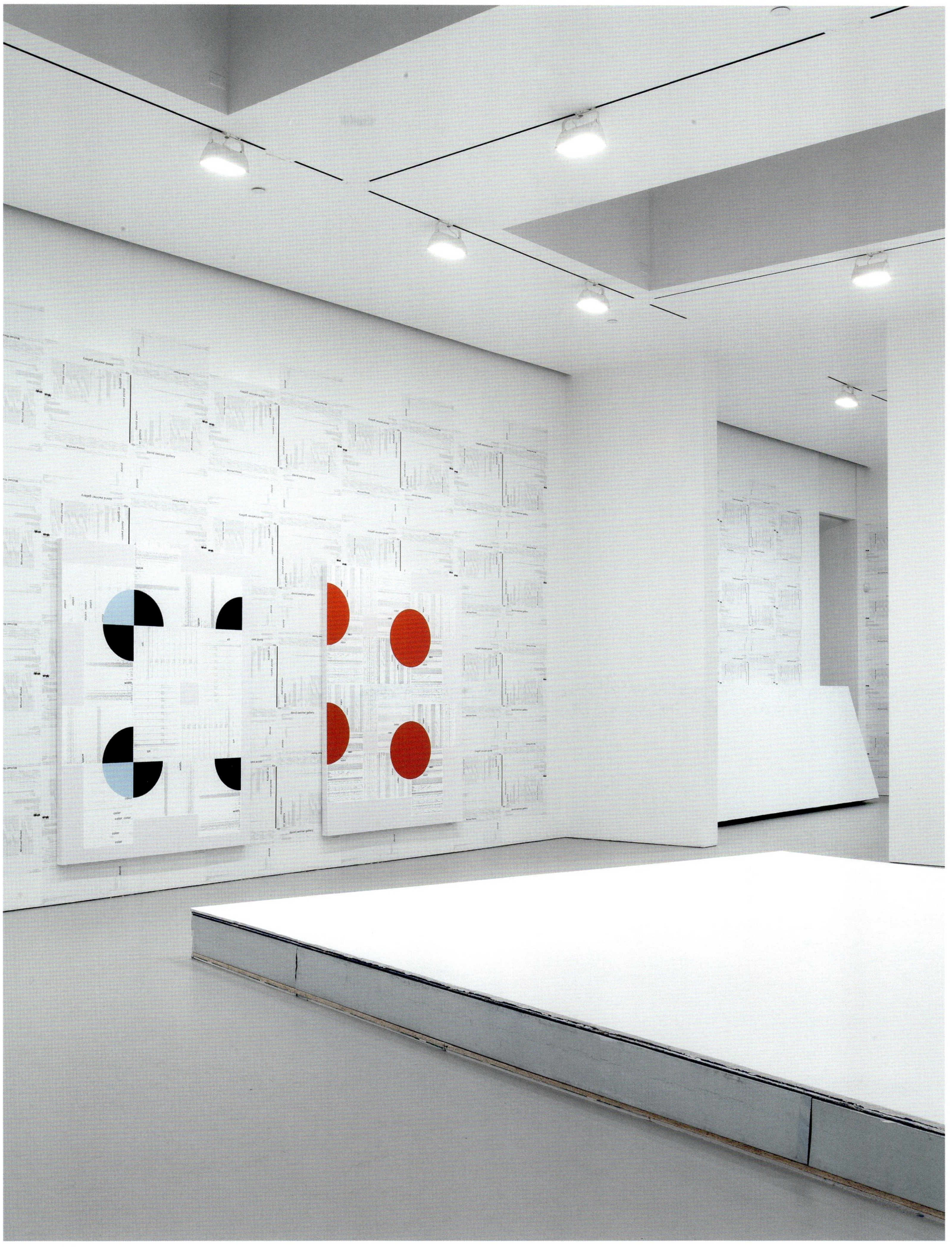

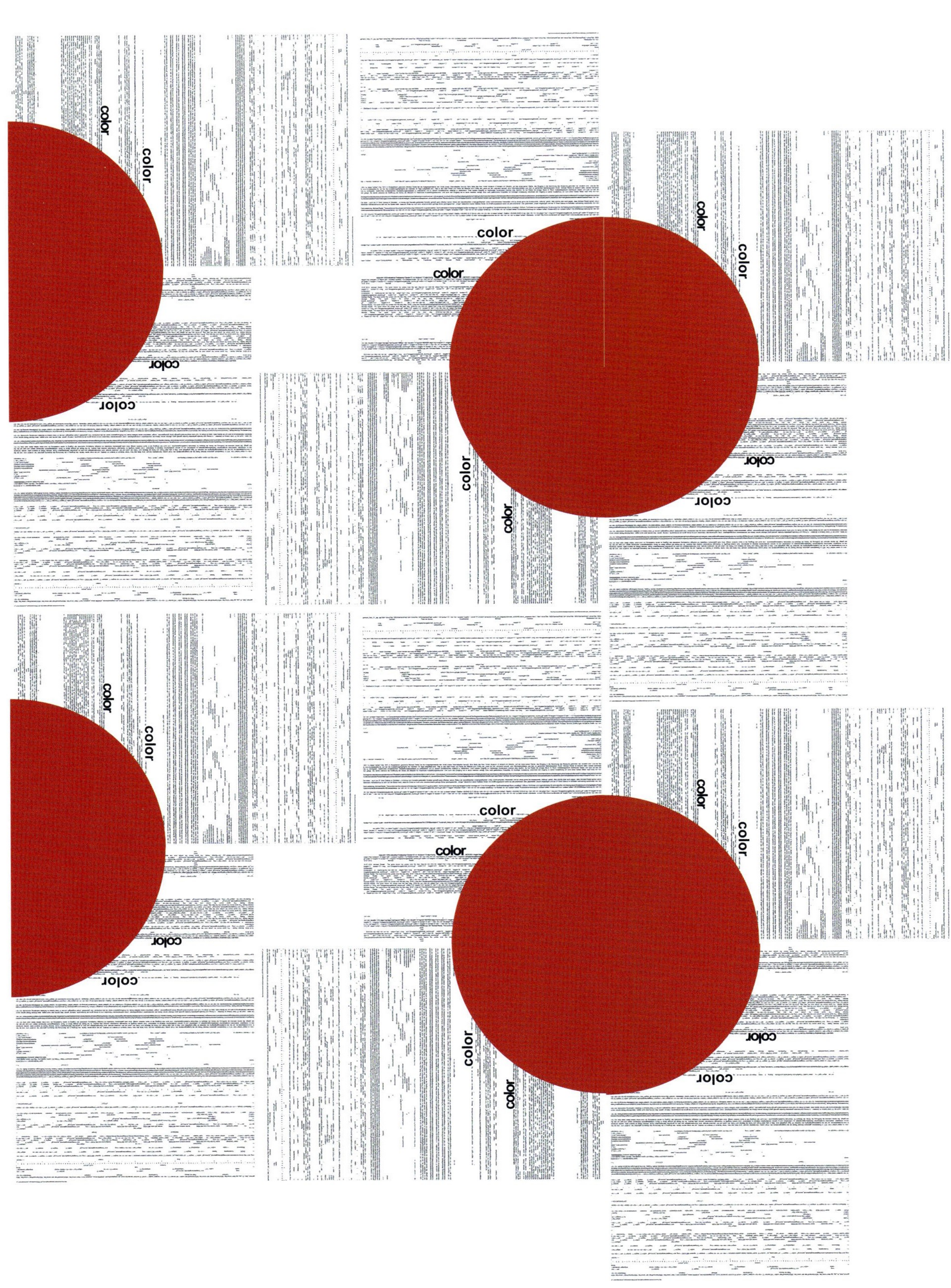

Untitled (color, red), 2011
Silkscreen on linen
90 1/2 x 67 x 2 1/4 inches
(229.9 x 170.2 x 5.7 cm)

The booklet contains all the posters required to make the Poster Painting *Untitled (color, red)*.

Booklet Untitled (color, red)
The quick brown fox jumps over the lazy dog [David Zwirner, 2011], 2011
1 of 17 booklets, 96 pages; offset print
11 5/8 x 8 1/4 inches
(29.5 x 21 cm)

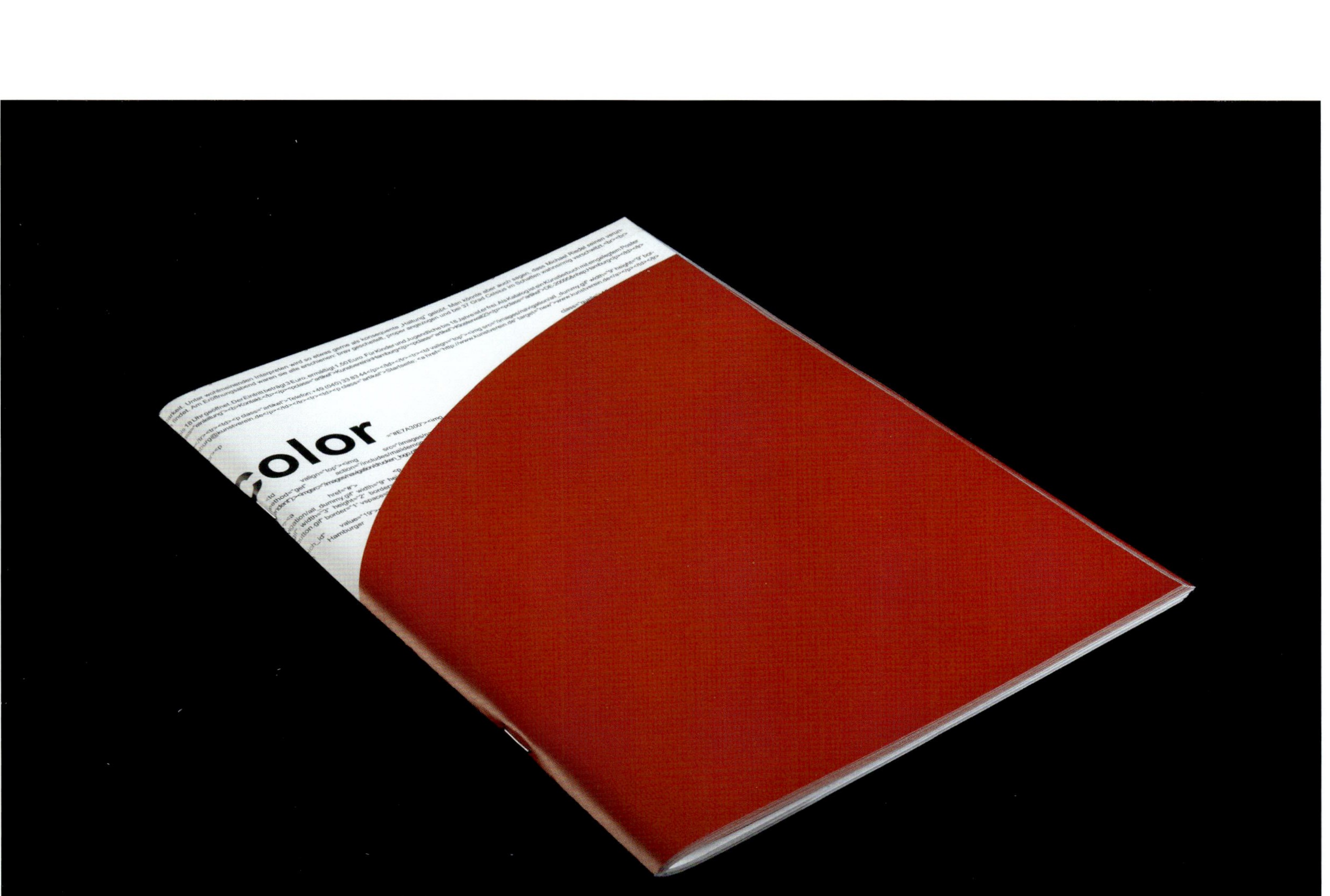

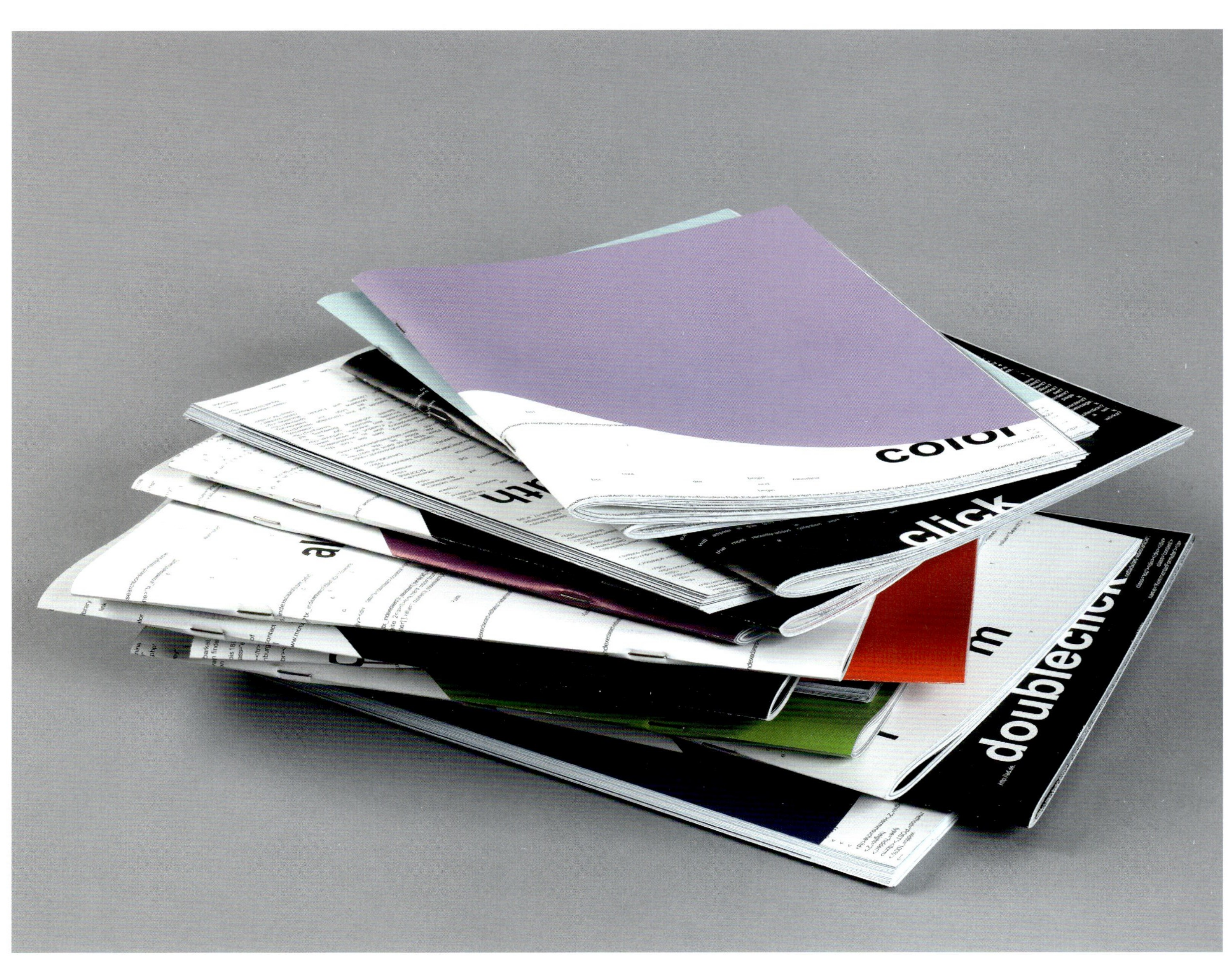

Each booklet contains all the posters required to make an individual Poster Painting.

Booklets for Poster Paintings
The quick brown fox jumps over the lazy dog [David Zwirner, 2011], 2011
17 booklets, each: 96 pages; offset print
Each: 11 5/8 x 8 1/4 inches
(29.5 x 21 cm)

text

http://www.papermag.com/2011/03/michael_riedel.php
(Accessed March 30, 2011)

```
<html lang="en"><head>
  <link href="http://fonts.googleapis.com/css?family=Open+Sans:300italic,400italic,700italic,400,300,700" rel="stylesheet" type="text/css">

  <meta charset="utf-8">
  <meta http-equiv="Content-Type" content="text/html; charset=utf-8">

  <meta http-equiv="Content-Style-Type" content="text/css">

  <meta http-equiv="Content-Script-Type" content="text/javascript">
  <meta name="viewport" content="width=device-width, initial-scale=1.0">
  <meta name="twitter:card" content="summary_large_image">
  <meta name="twitter:site" content="@papermagazine">
  <meta name="twitter:title" content="Michael Riedel's Internet-y Exhibit, &quot;The Quick Brown Fox Jumps Over The Lazy Dog&quot;">
  <meta name="twitter:description" content="<img alt=&quot;michaelriedel1.jpg&quot; src=&quot;../../uploaded_images/michaelriedel1.jpg&quot;

class=&quot;mt-image-center&quot; style=&quot;text-align: center; display: block; margin: 0pt auto 20px;&quot; width=&quot;320&quot; />">
  <meta name="twitter:image" content="http://cdn.papermag.com/uploaded_images/michaelriedel1.jpg">

  <script src="//cdn.viglink.com/api/vglnk.js" async="" type="text/javascript"></script><script async="" src="//cdn.linksmart.com/

linksmart_2.3.0.min.js"></script><script src="http://stats.g.doubleclick.net/dc.js" async="" type="text/javascript"></script><script src="//
connect.facebook.net/en_US/all.js#xfbml=1&amp;appId=139143962828899" id="facebook-jssdk"></script><script src="http://cdn.papermag.com/
article/js/jquery-1.7.1.js"></script>
  <script src="http://cdn.papermag.com/article/js/jquery.bxSlider.min.js" type="text/javascript"></script>

  <script src="http://cdn.papermag.com/article/js/lazy.js" type=text/javascript"></script>

  <script src="http://cdn.papermag.com/article/js/jquery.lazyload.js" type="text/javascript"></script>
  <script src="http://cdn.papermag.com/article/js/article_js.js?v=748"></script>
  <script src="http://cdn.papermag.com/article/js/ad-takeover.js?v=748"></script>

  <link rel="stylesheet" href="http://cdn.papermag.com/article/css/bootstrap.min.css">
  <link rel="stylesheet" href="http://cdn.papermag.com/article/css/styles.css?v=748">
  <link rel="stylesheet" href="http://cdn.papermag.com/article/css/takeover.css?v=748">
  <link rel="shortcut icon" href="http://cdn.papermag.com/article/css/images/favicon.ico?v2">

  <title>PAPERMAG: Michael Riedel's Internet-y Exhibit, „The Quick Brown Fox Jumps Over The Lazy Dog"
</title>
 <style type="text/css">.fb_hidden{position:absolute;top:-10000px;z-index:10001}.fb_invisible{display:none}.fb_reset{background:none;
border:0;border-spacing:0;color:#000;cursor:auto;direction:ltr;font-family:"lucida grande", tahoma, verdana, arial, sans-serif;font-size:11px;font-

style:normal;font-variant:normal;font-weight:normal;letter-spacing:normal;line-height:1;margin:0;overflow:visible;padding:0;text-

align:left;text-decoration:none;text-indent:0;text-shadow:none;text-transform:none;visibility:visible;white-space:normal;word-
spacing:normal}.fb_reset>div{overflow:hidden}.fb_link img{border:none}
.fb_dialog{background:rgba(82, 82, 82, .7);position:absolute;top:-10000px;z-index:10001}.fb_reset .fb_dialog_legacy{overflow:visible}.fb_dialog_
advanced{padding:10px;-moz-border-radius:8px;-webkit-border-radius:8px;border-radius:8px}.fb_dialog_content{background:#fff;color:#333}.
fb_dialog_close_icon{background:url(http://static.ak.fbcdn.net/rsrc.php/v2/yq/r/IE9JII6Z1Ys.png) no-repeat scroll 0 0 transparent;_background-
image:url(http://static.ak.fbcdn.net/rsrc.php/v2/yL/r/s816eWC-2sl.gif);cursor:pointer;display:block;height:15px;position:absolute;right:18px;top:17p
x;width:15px}.fb_dialog_mobile .fb_dialog_close_icon{top:5px;left:5px;right:auto}.fb_dialog_padding{background-color:transparent;position:abso
lute;width:1px;z-index:-1}.fb_dialog_close_icon:hover{background:url(http://static.ak.fbcdn.net/rsrc.php/v2/yq/r/IE9JII6Z1Ys.png) no-repeat scroll
0 -15px transparent;_background-image:url(http://static.ak.fbcdn.net/rsrc.php/v2/yL/r/s816eWC-2sl.gif)}.fb_dialog_close_icon:active{background
:url(http://static.ak.fbcdn.net/rsrc.php/v2/yq/r/IE9JII6Z1Ys.png) no-repeat scroll 0 -30px transparent;_background-image:url(http://static.ak.fbcdn.
net/rsrc.php/v2/yL/r/s816eWC-2sl.gif)}.fb_dialog_loader{background-color:#f6f7f8;border:1px solid #606060;font-size:24px;padding:20px}.
fb_dialog_top_left,.fb_dialog_top_right,.fb_dialog_bottom_left,.fb_dialog_bottom_right{height:10px;width:10px;overflow:hidden;position:ab
solute}.fb_dialog_top_left{background:url(http://static.ak.fbcdn.net/rsrc.php/v2/ye/r/8YeTNIITZjm.png) no-repeat 0 0;left:-10px;top:-10px}.
fb_dialog_bottom_left{background:url(http://static.ak.fbcdn.net/rsrc.php/v2/ye/r/8YeTNIITZjm.png) no-repeat 0 -20px;bottom:-10px;left:-10px}.
fb_dialog_vert_left,.fb_dialog_vert_right,.fb_dialog_horiz_top,.fb_dialog_horiz_bottom{position:absolute;background:#525252;filter:alpha(op
acity=70);opacity:.7}.fb_dialog_vert_left,.fb_dialog_vert_right{width:10px;height:100%}.fb_dialog_vert_left{margin-left:-10px}.fb_dialog_vert_
right{right:0;margin-right:-10px}.fb_dialog_horiz_top,.fb_dialog_horiz_bottom{width:100%;height:10px}.fb_dialog_horiz_top{margin-top:-10px}.
fb_dialog_horiz_bottom{bottom:0;margin-bottom:-10px}.fb_dialog_iframe{line-height:0}.fb_dialog_content .dialog_title{background:#6d84b4;b
order:1px solid #3a5795;color:#fff;font-size:14px;font-weight:bold;margin:0}.fb_dialog_content .dialog_title>span{background:url(http://static.
ak.fbcdn.net/rsrc.php/v2/yd/r/Cou7n-nqK52.gif) no-repeat 5px 50%;float:left;padding:5px 0 7px 26px}body.fb_hidden{-webkit-transform:none;he
ight:100%;margin:0;overflow:visible;position:absolute;top:-10000px;left:0;width:100%}.fb_dialog.fb_dialog_mobile.loading{background:url(http://
static.ak.fbcdn.net/rsrc.php/v2/ya/r/3rhSv5V8j3o.gif) white no-repeat 50% 50%;min-height:100%;min-width:100%;overflow:hidden;position:absolu
te;top:0;z-index:10001}.fb_dialog.fb_dialog_mobile.loading.centered{max-height:590px;min-height:590px;max-width:500px;min-width:500px}#fb-
root #fb_dialog_ipad_overlay{background:rgba(0, 0, 0, .45);position:absolute;left:0;top:0;width:100%;min-height:100%;z-index:10000}#fb-root
#fb_dialog_ipad_overlay.hidden{display:none}.fb_dialog.fb_dialog_mobile.loading iframe{visibility:hidden}.fb_dialog_content .dialog_header{-
webkit-box-shadow:white 0 1px 1px -1px inset;background:-webkit-gradient(linear, 0% 0%, 0% 100%, from(#738ABA), to(#2C4987));border-
```

```
the Internet? What drew you to use website texts in this exhibition?</b></i><br><br>I belong to the first generation that digested the
Internet. It‘s not a fascination; it‘s everyday life.<br> <br><i><b>The exhibition‘s title is a „pangram“ containing each letter of the
English alphabet at least once. How did you come up with „The Quick Brown Fox Jumps Over The Lazy Dog?“</b></i><br><br>A friend told
me about this phrase. And I liked the fact that it‘s meaning is about how it was written.<br> <br><i><b>What‘s your thought process
behind using materials in your artwork, such as the Internet pages containing information, that are already an established product? </b></
i><br> <br>Reproduction must be read as production and not as a product anymore. With this change, the artwork became another
artwork that‘s marking a distance from where it originally began. This might be seen as unusual material in contrast to other cultural efforts, but
the material I work with represents the „nature“ that‘s surrounding me.<br><br> 

    </div><!-- end post-body -->

    <div style=“margin-left: 75px; width: 700px;“ class=“post-bottom“>
    <div class=“row post-bottom-section post-meta“>
      <div class=“post-note pull-left“>
      This story was published on March 11, 2011  9:36 AM
        </div>

    <div class=“post-actions big span pull-right“>
      <a href=“http://twitter.com/share?url=http://www.papermag.com/2011/03/michael_riedel.php&amp;text=PAPERMAG: Michael
Riedel‘s Internet-y Exhibit, „ the=““ quick=““ brown=““ fox=““ jumps=““ over=““ lazy=““ dog““=““ class=“twitter-share“ target=“_blank“>twitter</a>
      <a href=“http://pinterest.com/pin/create/button/?url=http://www.papermag.com/2011/03/michael_riedel.php
&amp;media=http://www.papermag.com/uploaded_images/michaelriedel1.jpg
&amp;description=PAPERMAG: Michael Riedel‘s Internet-y Exhibit, „ the=““ quick=““ brown=““ fox=““ jumps=““ over=““ lazy=““ dog““=““ class=“pin-
share“ target=“_blank“>pinterest</a>
      <a href=“https://www.facebook.com/sharer.php?u=http://www.papermag.com/2011/03/michael_riedel.php&amp;t=PAPERMAG: Michael
Riedel‘s Internet-y Exhibit, „ the=““ quick=““ brown=““ fox=““ jumps=““ over=““ lazy=““ dog““=““ class=“facebook-share“ target=“_blank“>facebook</
a>
      <a href=“mailto:?subject=PAPERMAG: Michael Riedel‘s Internet-y Exhibit, „ the=““ quick=““ brown=““ fox=““ jumps=““ over=““ lazy=““
dog“&body=“http://www.papermag.com/2011/03/michael_riedel.php&quot;“ class=“email-share“ target=“_blank“>email</a>
    </div><!-- post-actions -->
  </div>

  <div class=“row“>
    <div class=“post-tags“>
Tags: <a href=“http://www.papermag.com/tag/David Zwirner“>David Zwirner</a>, <a href=“http://www.papermag.com/tag/Michael
Riedel“>Michael Riedel</a>       </div>
  </div>

          <div style=“display: none;“ class=“row post-bottom-section mobile-ad-widget“>
                    <div class=“mobile-ad“>
                    <script language=“javascript“><!--
document.write(‚<scr‘+‘ipt language=“javascript1.1“ src=“http://adserver.adtechus.com/addyn/3.0/5151/855808/0/170/ADTECH;loc=100;target=_
blank;key=key1+key2+key3+key4;grp=311;misc=‘+new Date().getTime()+‘“></scri‘+‘pt>‘);
//-->
</script><script language=“javascript1.1“ src=“http://adserver.adtechus.com/addyn/3.0/5151/855808/0/170/ADTECH;loc=100;target=_blank;key
=key1+key2+key3+key4;grp=311;misc=1433324957436“></script><a href=“http://adserver.adtechus.com/?adlink/5151/855808/0/170/AdId=695
0939;BnId=1;itime=324957788;key=key1%2Bkey2%2Bkey3%2Bkey4;“ target=“_blank“><img src=“http://aka-cdn-ns.adtechus.com/images/27/
Ad6950939St1Sz170Sq24392847V0Id1.png“ alt=“click here“ height=“250“ border=“0“ width=“300“></a><noscript><a href=“http://adserver.
adtechus.com/adlink/3.0/5151/855808/0/170/ADTECH;loc=300;key=key1+key2+key3+key4;grp=311“ target=“_blank“><img src=“http://adserver.
adtechus.com/adserv/3.0/5151/855808/0/170/ADTECH;loc=300;key=key1+key2+key3+key4;grp=311“ border=“0“ width=“300“ height=“250“></
a></noscript>
                    </div>
          </div>

    <div class=“row post-bottom-section“>
    <div class=“related-stories“>
      <div class=“post-bottom-title“>
                                  more stories...
                              </div>


                                  <div class=“related-story bottom pull-left“>
                                    <div class=“thumbnail pull-left“><a href=“http://www.papermag.com/2012/07/curator_james_morrill_
on_his_n.php“><img style=“display: inline;“ src=“http://cdn.papermag.com/assets_c/2012/07/Screen shot 2012-07-25 at 2.59.59 PM-thumb-
150xauto-100377.png“ class=“lazy“ greg=“1“ data-original=“http://cdn.papermag.com/assets_c/2012/07/Screen shot 2012-07-25 at 2.59.59 PM-
thumb-150xauto-100377.png“ alt=““ height=“150“ width=“150“></a></div>

              <div class=“related-story-description pull-left“>
                <div class=“related-story-title“>

                    <a href=“http://www.papermag.com/tag/gallery“>gallery</a>
                </div>
                <div class=“related-story-dek“><a href=“http://www.papermag.com/2012/07/curator_james_morrill_on_his_n.php“>Curator
James Morrill on His New David Zwirner Show, „People...</a></div>
              </div>
            </div>

  </div><!-- end related-stores -->
```

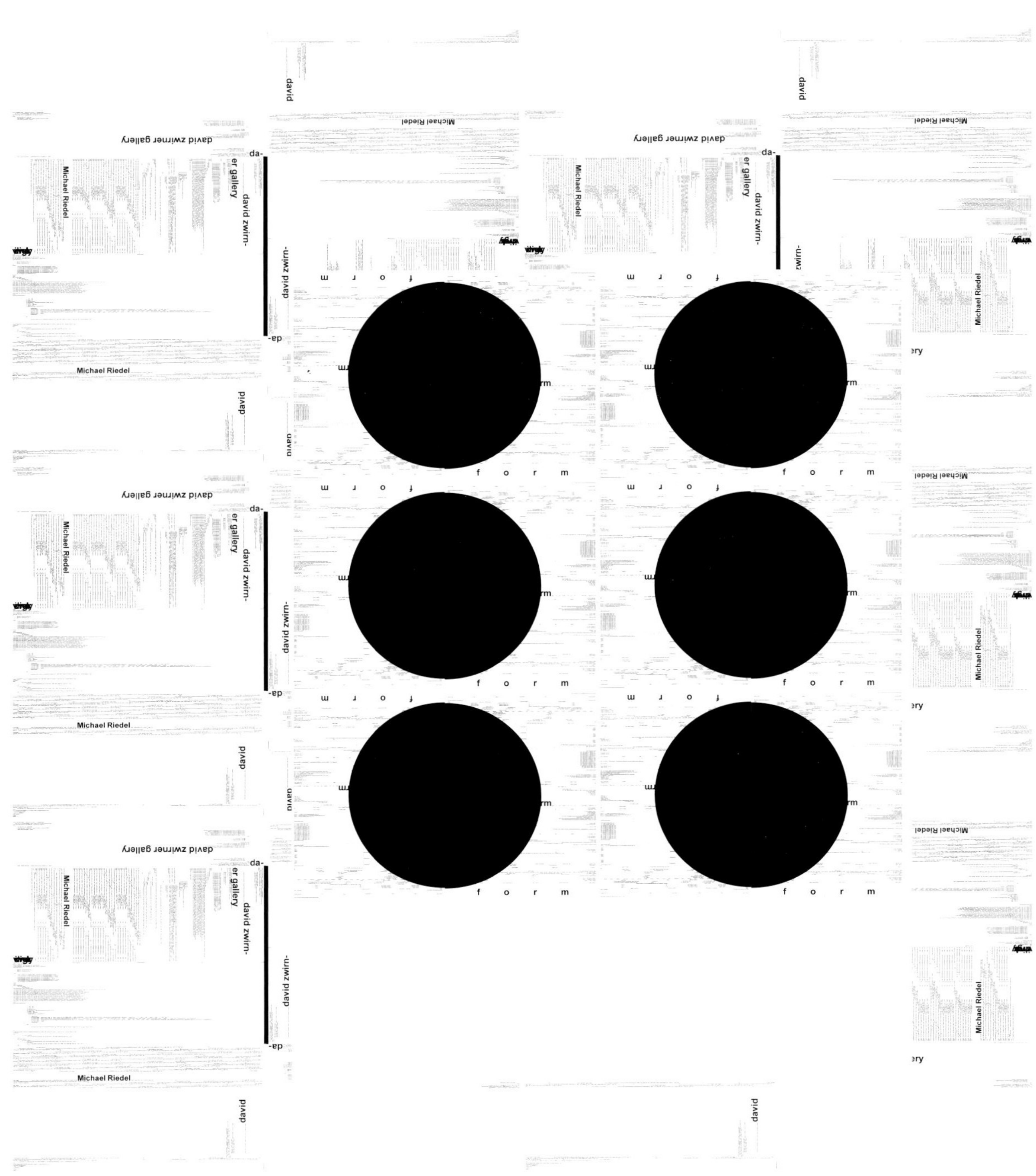

Untitled (17 invitation cards, The quick brown fox jumps over the lazy dog [David Zwirner]), 2011
1 of 17 invitation cards; offset print
8 1/8 x 8 1/8 inches
(20.6 x 20.6 cm)

Untitled (17 invitation cards, The quick brown fox jumps over the lazy dog [David Zwirner]), 2011
Installation view, *Michael Riedel: PowerPoint*
David Zwirner, New York, 2013

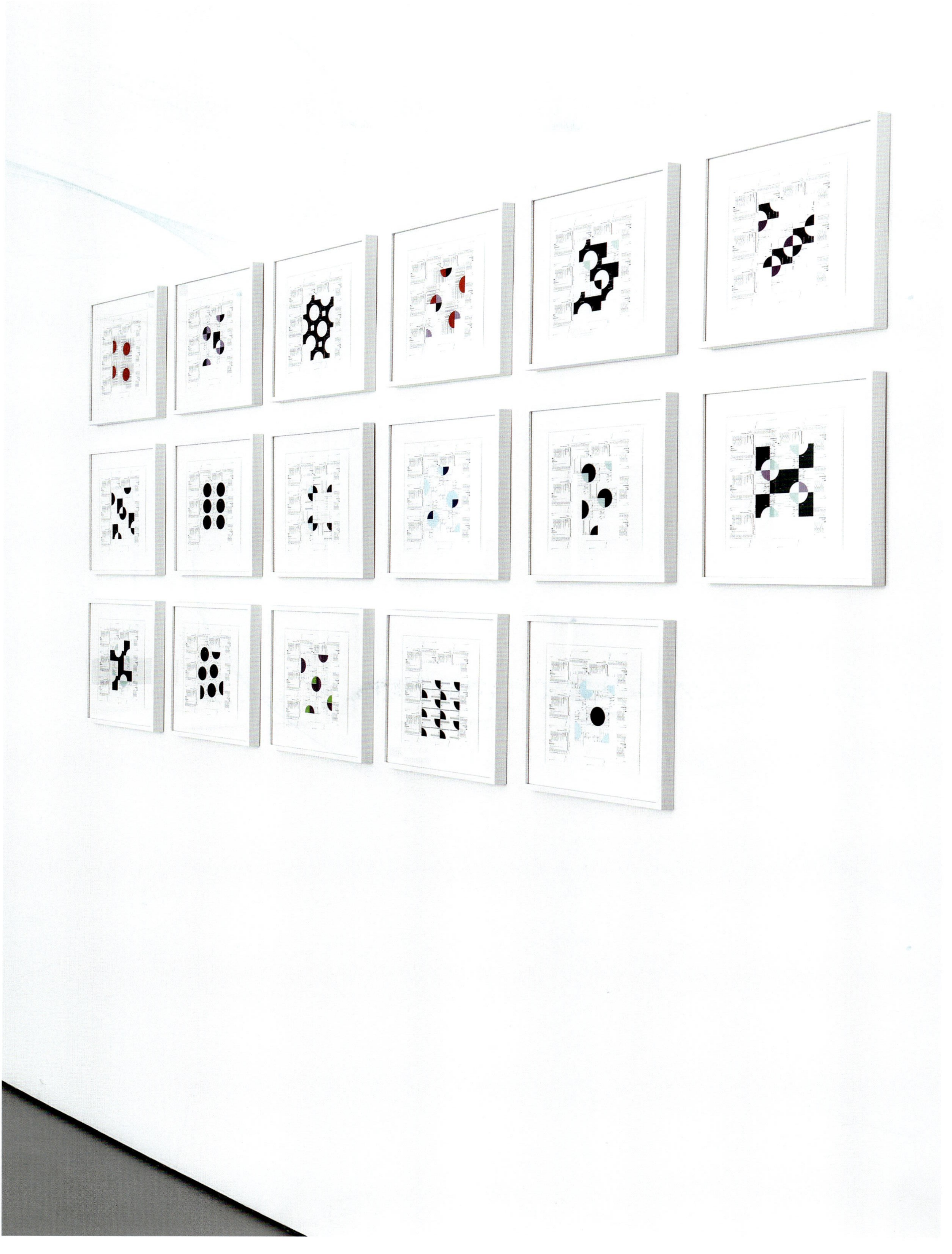

```
        </div>

        <div class="row post-bottom-section">
          <div class="post-bottom-title">Comments...</div>
          <div fb-xfbml-state="rendered" class="fb-comments fb_iframe_widget" data-href="http://www.papermag.com/2011/03/michael_riedel.php"
data-num-posts="2" data-width="700"><span style="height: 108px; width: 700px;"><iframe src="https://www.facebook.com/plugins/comments.
php?api_key=139143962828899&amp;channel_url=http%3A%2F%2Fstatic.ak.facebook.com%2Fconnect%2Fxd_arbiter%2F1ldYU13brY_.js%
3Fversion%3D41%23cb%3Df29f802b081993e%26domain%3Dwww.papermag.com%26origin%3Dhttp%253A%252F%252Fwww.papermag.co
m%252Ff11f24bb7b1f876%26relation%3Dparent.parent&amp;href=http%3A%2F%2Fwww.papermag.com%2F2011%2F03%2Fmichael_riedel.
php&amp;locale=en_US&amp;numposts=2&amp;sdk=joey&amp;width=700" class="fb_ltr" title="Facebook Social Plugin" style="border: medium
none; overflow: hidden; height: 108px; width: 700px;" scrolling="no" name="f37aa300d0bdb68" id="f269cb2f343c2b2"></iframe></span></div>
        </div>
        </div><!-- post-bottom-->

    </div><!-- end post -->

</div><!-- end main -->


<div style="position: static; top: auto;" class="side span">
     <div style="position: static; top: auto;" class="side-ad widget"><script language="javascript"><!--
document.write(,<scr'+'ipt language="javascript1.1" src="http://adserver.adtechus.com/addyn/3.0/5151/2030111/0/529/ADTECH;loc=100;target=_
blank;key=key1+key2+key3+key4;grp=311;misc='+new Date().getTime()+'"></scri'+'pt>');
//-->
</script><script language="javascript1.1" src="http://adserver.adtechus.com/addyn/3.0/5151/2030111/0/529/ADTECH;loc=100;target=_blank;ke
y=key1+key2+key3+key4;grp=311;misc=1433324957644"></script><a href="http://adserver.adtechus.com/?adlink/5151/2030111/0/529/AdId=69
50938;BnId=1;itime=324957929;key=key1%2Bkey2%2Bkey3%2Bkey4;" target="_blank"><img src="http://aka-cdn-ns.adtechus.com/images/26/
Ad6950938St1Sz529Sq24392841V0Id1.png" alt="click here" height="600" border="0" width="300"></a><noscript><a href="http://adserver.
adtechus.com/adlink/3.0/5151/2030111/0/529/ADTECH;loc=300;key=key1+key2+key3+key4;grp=311" target="_blank"><img src="http://adserver.
adtechus.com/adserv/3.0/5151/2030111/0/529/ADTECH;loc=300;key=key1+key2+key3+key4;grp=311" border="0" width="300" height="600"></
a></noscript></div>


     <div class="featured-stories widget">
        <div class="widget-title">Editor's Picks...</div>


        <div class="featured-story right">
           <div class="thumbnail pull-left"><a href="http://www.papermag.com/2015/04/chloe_sevigny_photo_book.php"><img style="display:
inline;" src="http://cdn.papermag.com/assets_c/2015/04/chloesevignybook8-thumb-150xauto-132365.jpg" class="lazy" data-original="http://cdn.
papermag.com/assets_c/2015/04/chloesevignybook8-thumb-150xauto-132365.jpg" alt="" height="150" width="150"></a></div>
           <div class="featured-story-description pull-left">
              <div class="featured-story-title">
              </div>
              <div class="featured-story-dek"><a href="http://www.papermag.com/2015/04/chloe_sevigny_photo_book.php">"I Was Always on the
Periphery, Watching Everyone Else:"...</a></div>
           </div>
        </div>


        <div class="featured-story left">
             <div class="featured-story-description pull-left">


                <div class="featured-story-title">
                </div>
                <div class="featured-story-dek"><a href="http://www.papermag.com/2015/04/babycore_kidcore_is_a_thing.php">25 Is the New 8:
Why Babycore (Or, Rather, Kidcore) Is...</a></div>
             </div>


             <div class="thumbnail pull-left"><a href="http://www.papermag.com/2015/04/babycore_kidcore_is_a_thing.php"><img style="display:
inline;" src="http://cdn.papermag.com/assets_c/2015/04/Screen Shot 2015-04-10 at 4.15.02 PM-thumb-150xauto-132227.png" class="lazy" data-
original="http://cdn.papermag.com/assets_c/2015/04/Screen Shot 2015-04-10 at 4.15.02 PM-thumb-150xauto-132227.png" alt="" height="150"
width="150"></a></div>
          </div>
     </div><!-- end featured-stories-widget -->

  text-align: center;
  padding: 20px 0;
  margin-bottom: 20px;
 }
 .bbb:hover {
  text-decoration: none;
 }
 </style>
```

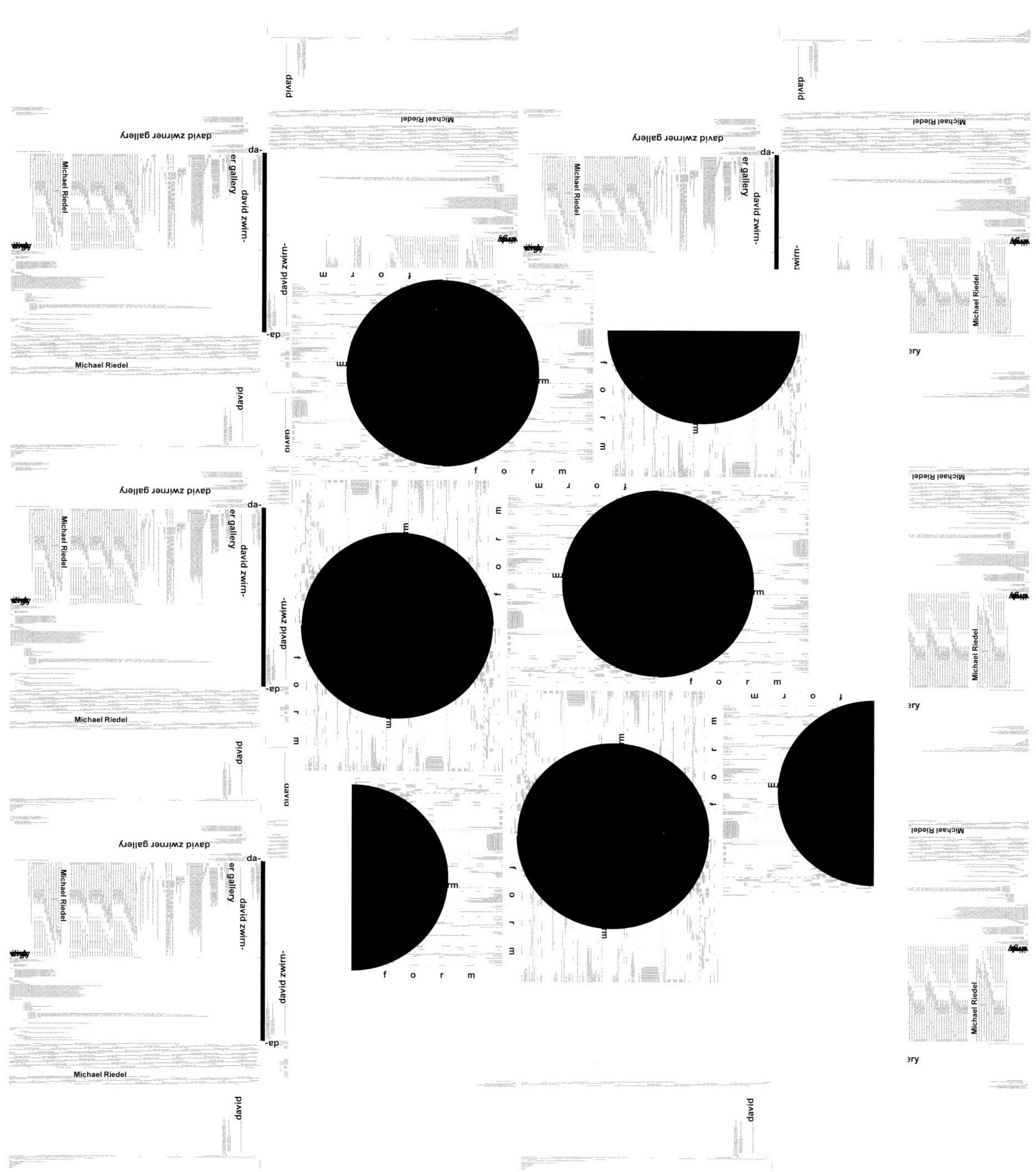

Untitled (17 invitation cards, The quick brown fox jumps over the lazy dog [David Zwirner]), 2011
1 of 17 invitation cards; offset print
8 1/8 x 8 1/8 inches
(20.6 x 20.6 cm)

```
 <a class="bbb" href="https://www.cambeywest.com/subscribe/?p=pap&amp;f=paid">SUBSCRIBE TO PAPER</a>
 <a class="bbb" style="padding: 10px 0;" href="http://visitor.r20.constantcontact.com/manage/optin/ea?v=001GEtTiJRQgs1GBjPn61VeFw%3D%
3D">SUBSCRIBE TO<br>OUR EMAIL</a>
</div>


  </div><!-- end side-->


      </div><!-- end row-->


    </div><!-- end container -->


<script type="text/javascript">
 var _gaq = _gaq || [];
 _gaq.push([‚_setAccount‘, ‚UA-1556053-2‘]);
 _gaq.push([‚_trackPageview‘]);
 (function() {
  var ga = document.createElement(‚script‘); ga.type = ‚text/javascript‘; ga.async = true;
  ga.src = (‚https:‘ == document.location.protocol ? ‚https://‘ : ‚http://‘) + ‚stats.g.doubleclick.net/dc.js‘;
  var s = document.getElementsByTagName(‚script‘)[0]; s.parentNode.insertBefore(ga, s);
 })();
</script>

                <script type="text/javascript">

    var _sf_async_config={uid:28451,domain:"papermag.com"};

    (function(){
      function loadChartbeat() {
        window._sf_endpt=(new Date()).getTime();
        var e = document.createElement(‚script‘);
        e.setAttribute(‚language‘, ‚javascript‘);

        e.setAttribute(‚type‘, ‚text/javascript‘);
        e.setAttribute(‚src‘,
          ((„https:" == document.location.protocol) ? „https://a248.e.akamai.net/chartbeat.download.akamai.com/102508/" : „http://static.chartbeat.
com/") +
           „js/chartbeat.js");
        document.body.appendChild(e);
      }
      var oldonload = window.onload;
      window.onload = (typeof window.onload != ‚function‘) ?
         loadChartbeat : function() { oldonload(); loadChartbeat(); };
    })();

    </script>

    <script type="text/javascript">
    // <![CDATA[
    var _ls_pub_id = „238";
    (function(d, t){
    var mb = d.createElement(t), s = d.getElementsByTagName(t)[0];
    mb.async = mb.src = ‚//cdn.linksmart.com/linksmart_2.3.0.min.js‘;
    s.parentNode.insertBefore(mb, s);
    }(document, ‚script‘));
    // ]]>
    </script>

    <script>
      takeover.loadInterior();
    </script>

<script src="http://static.chartbeat.com/js/chartbeat.js" type="text/javascript" language="javascript"></script></body></html>

<div>
 <style>
  .bbb {
   font-weight: bold;
   font-size: 16px;
   display: inline-block;
   width: 300px;
   background: black;
   color: white;
```

Installation view, *Michael Riedel*
Le Box – Fonds M-ARCO, Marseille, France, 2015

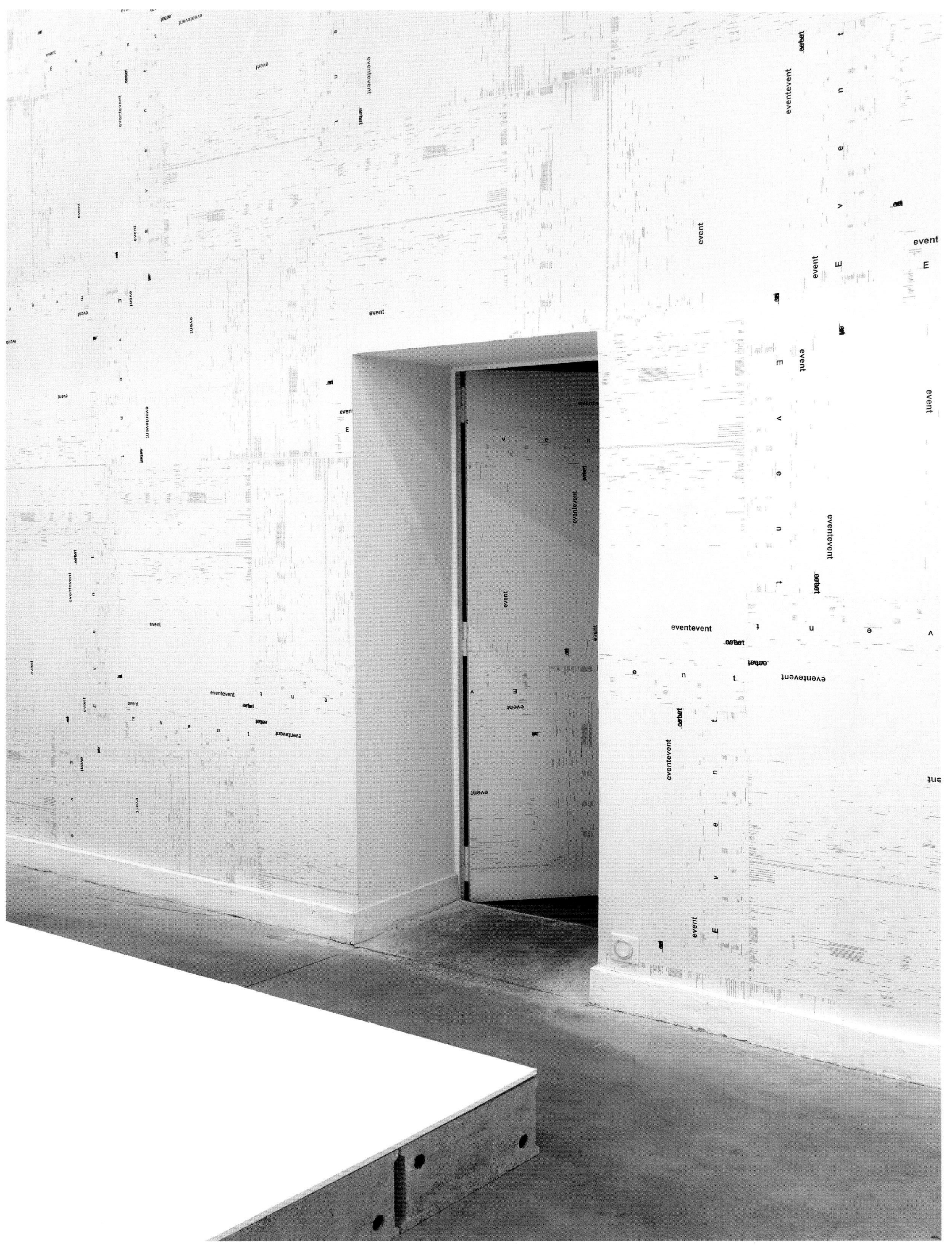
event
eventevent
event
eventevent

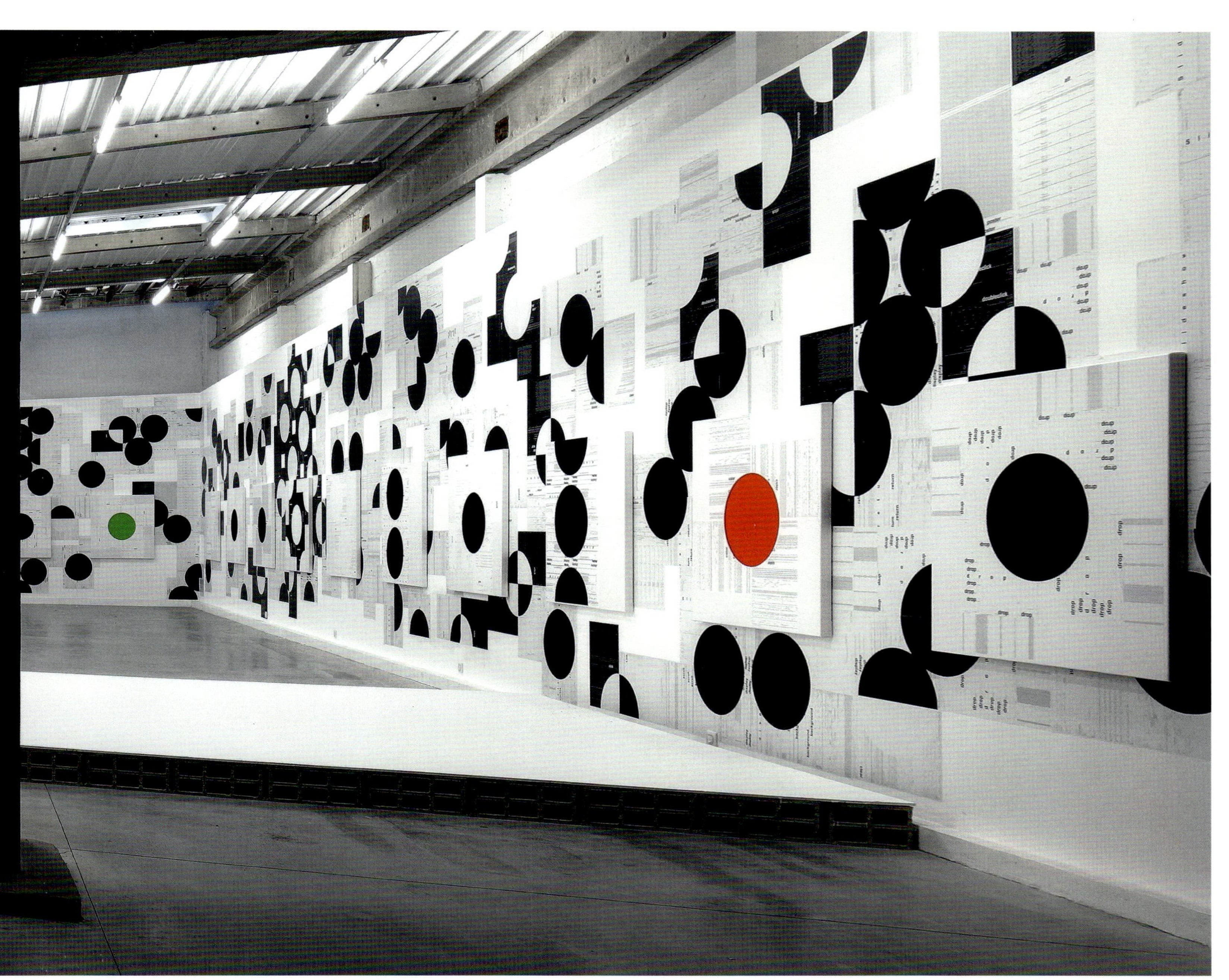

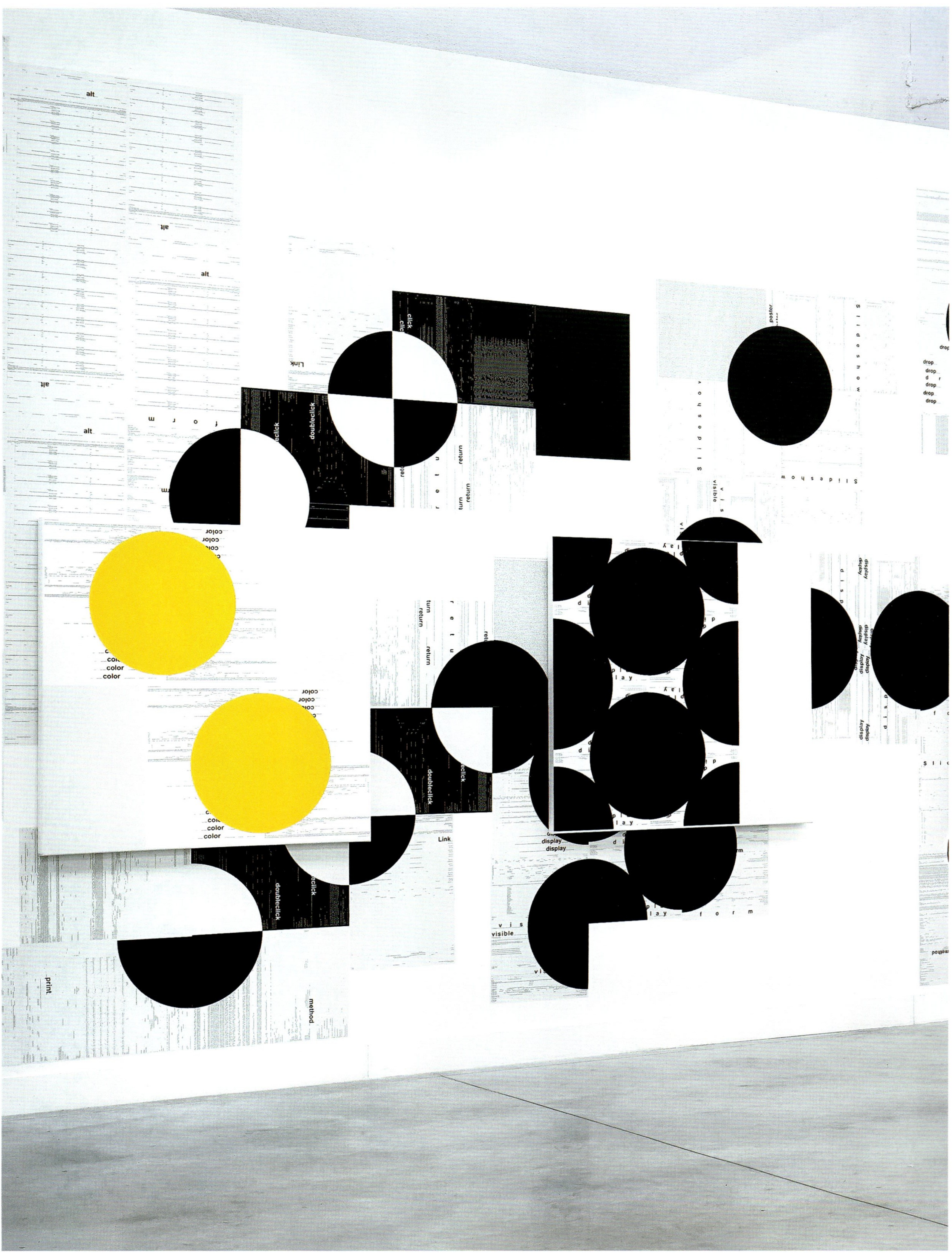
alt
alt
alt
alt
click
doubleclick
return
turn
color
color
color
color
color
poster
drop
drop
drop
drop
visible
display
display
display
Link
visible
print
method

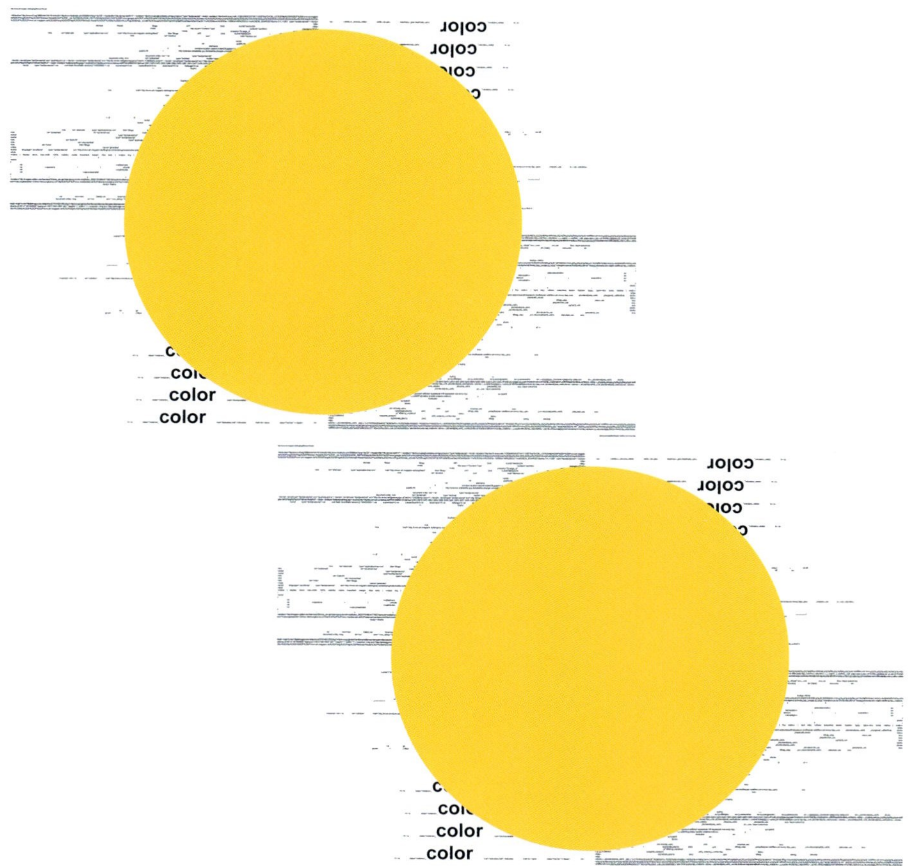

Installation view, *Michael Riedel*
Le Box – Fonds M-ARCO, Marseille, France, 2015

Untitled (color, yellow), 2013
Silkscreen on linen
47 1/4 x 47 1/4 inches
(120 x 120 cm)

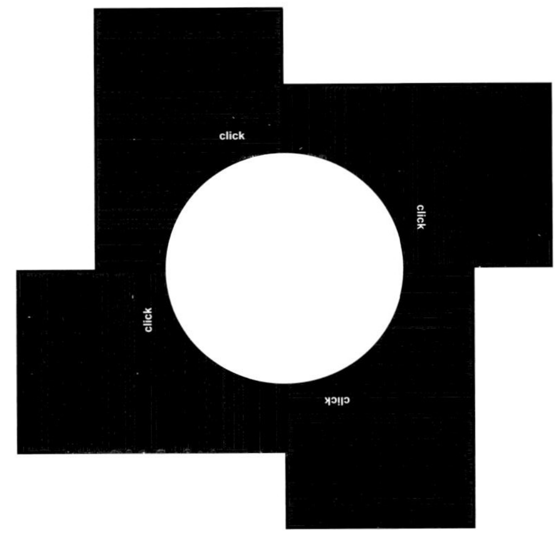

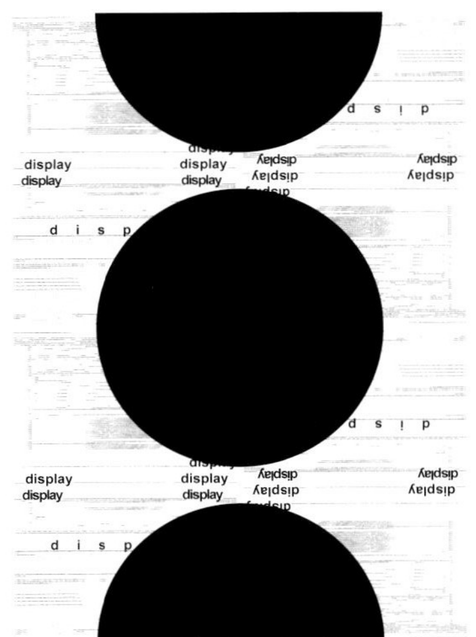

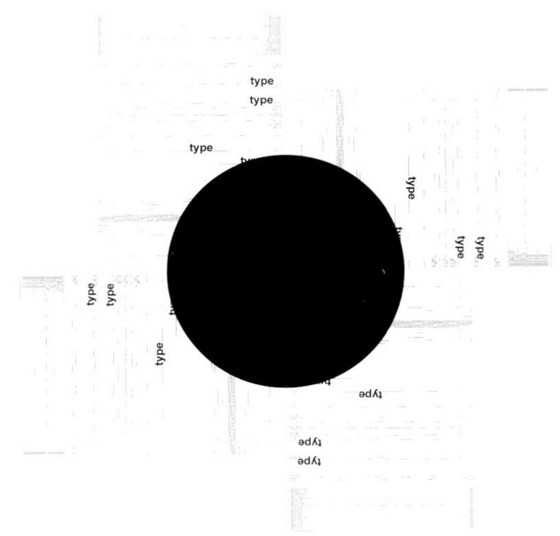

Untitled (click 1), *Untitled (update)*, *Untitled (solid black)*, *Untitled (alt)*, *Untitled (display 3)*, *Untitled (clear 1)*, *Untitled (drop)*, *Untitled (display 2)*, *Untitled (type)*, *Untitled (form)*, *Untitled (display 4)*, *Untitled (visible)*, 2013
Silkscreen on linen
Each: 47 1/4 x 47 1/4 inches
(120 x 120 cm)

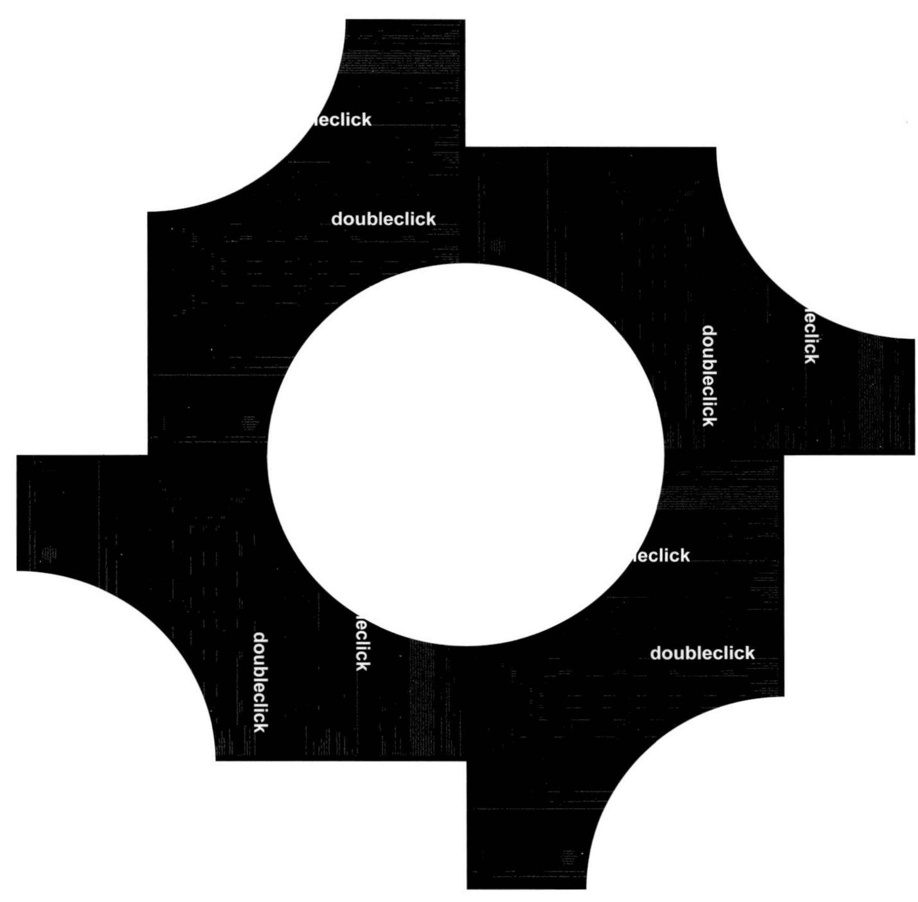

Untitled (doubleclick), 2013
Silkscreen on linen
47 1/4 x 47 1/4 inches
(120 x 120 cm)

Following pages:
Installation view, *Michael Riedel*
Le Box – Fonds M-ARCO, Marseille, France, 2015

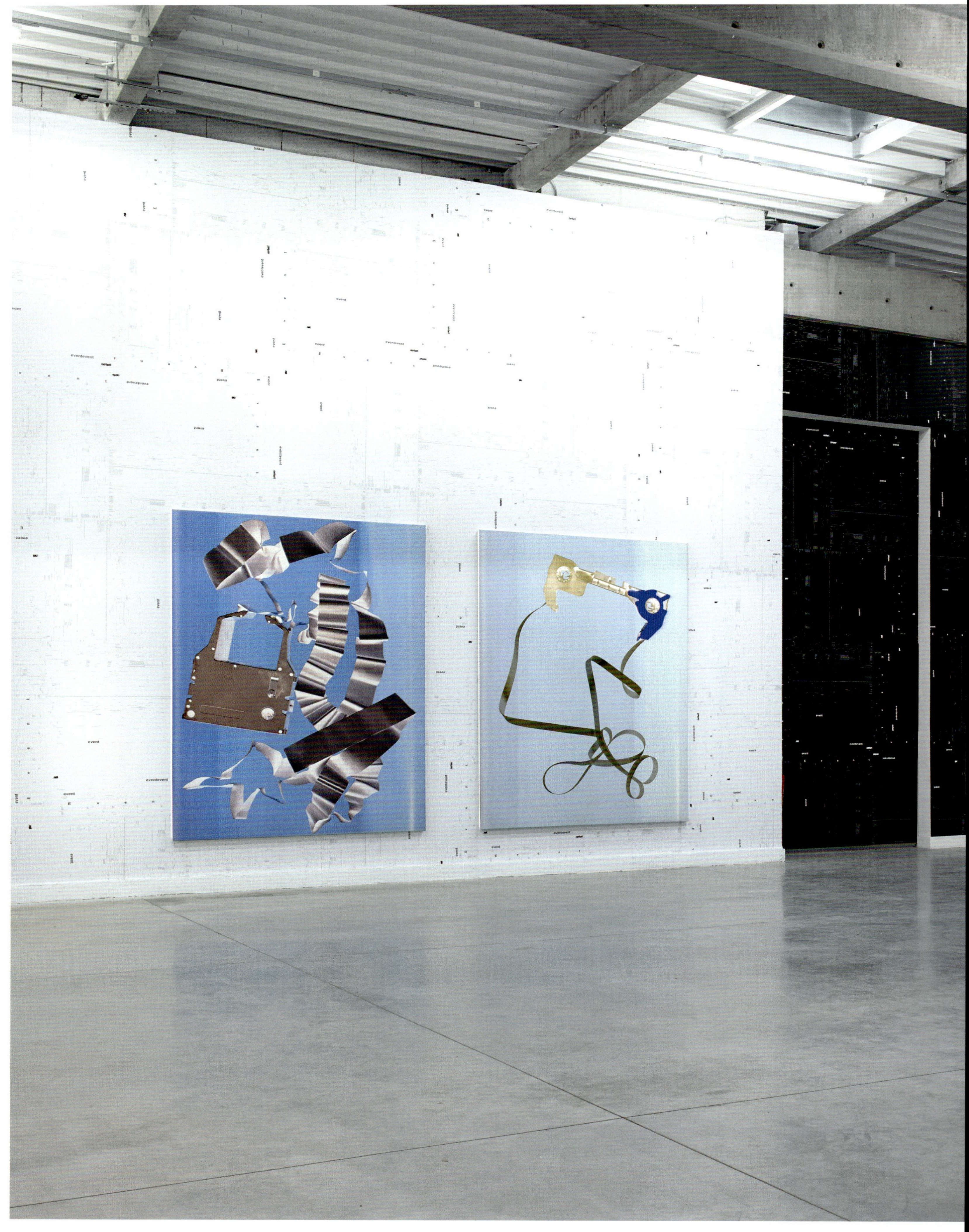

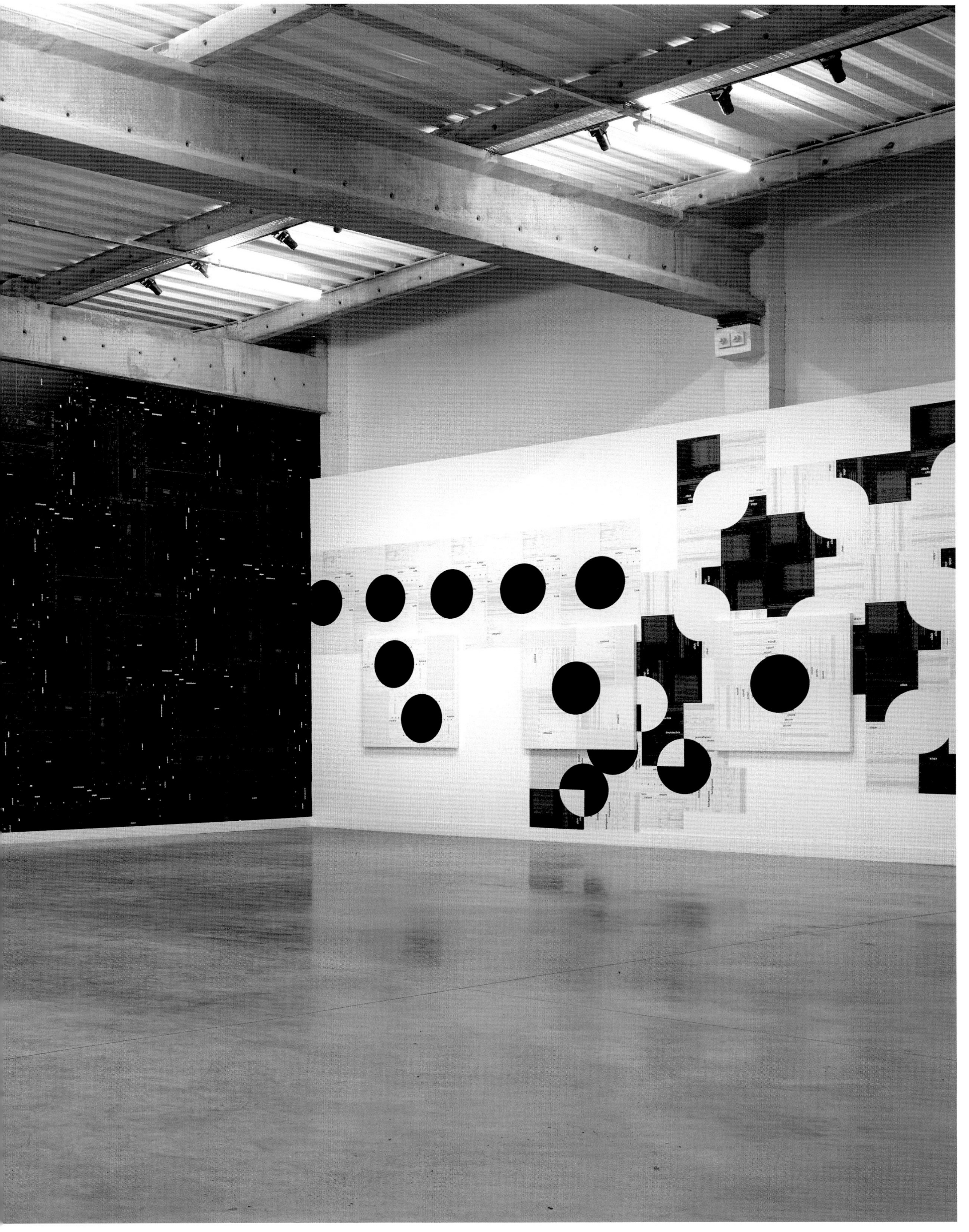

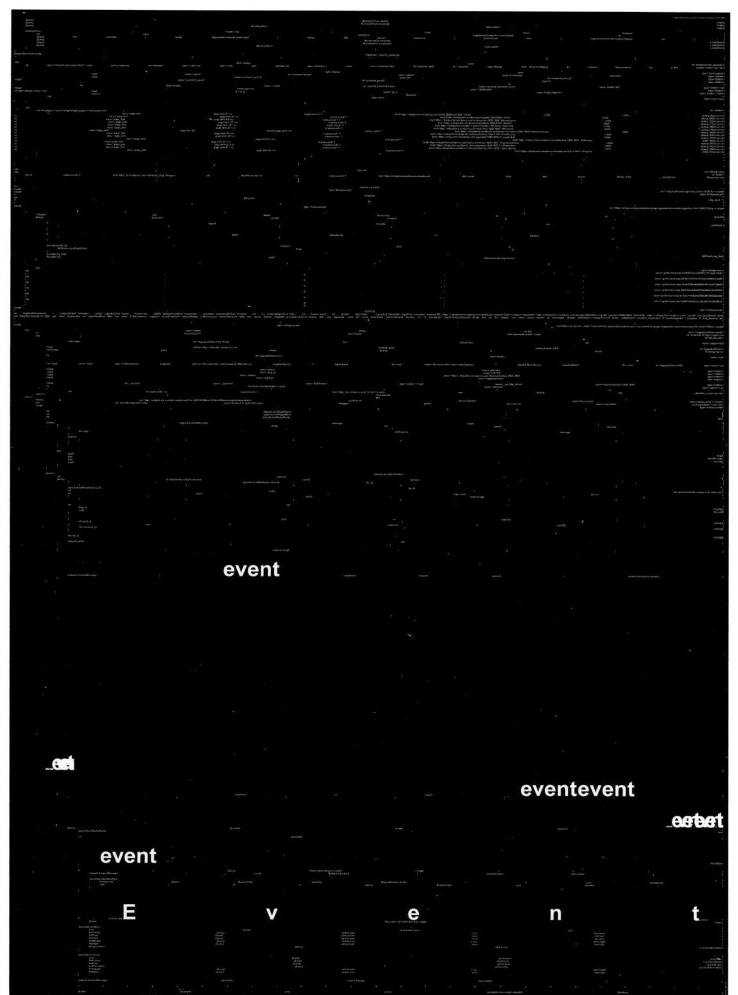

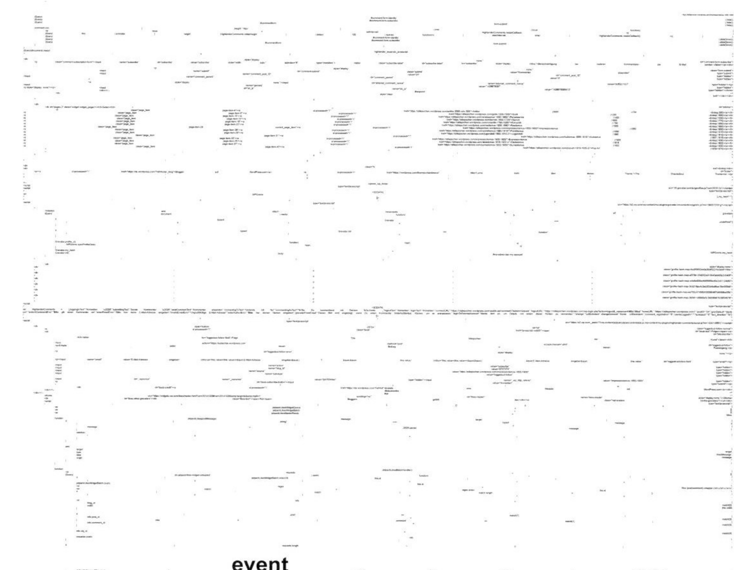

Untitled (Needle printer supplies for Facit E440), 2015
Digital print on linen
90 1/2 x 67 x 1 3/4 inches
(229.9 x 170.2 x 4.5 cm)

Untitled (event, black), 2015
Offset print
46 1/2 x 33 inches
(118.1 x 83.8 cm)

Untitled (event, white), 2015
Offset print
46 1/2 x 33 inches
(118.1 x 83.8 cm)

Presentation

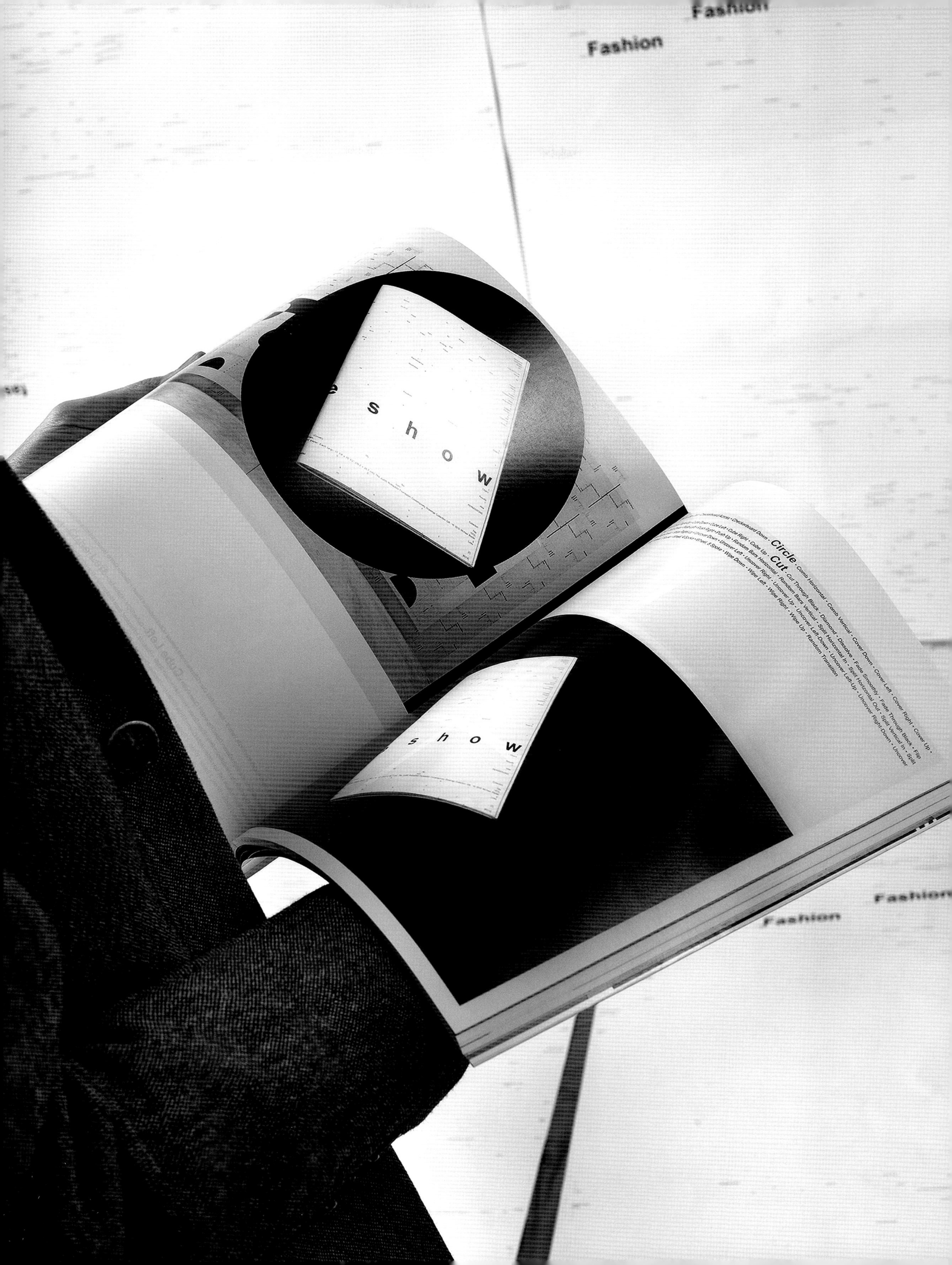
Fashion
Fashion
show
show
Circle
Cut
Fashion
Fashion

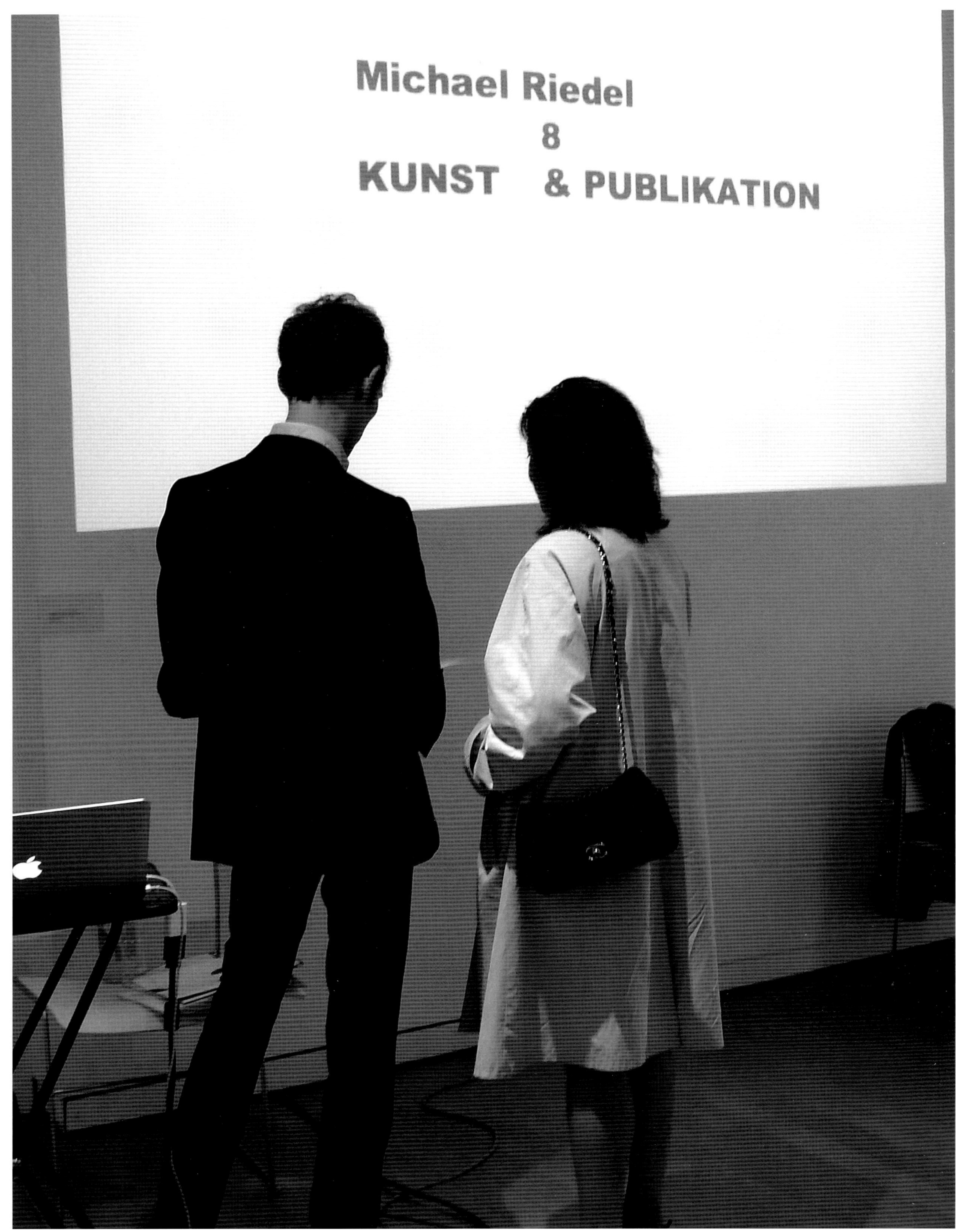
Michael Riedel
8
KUNST & PUBLIKATION

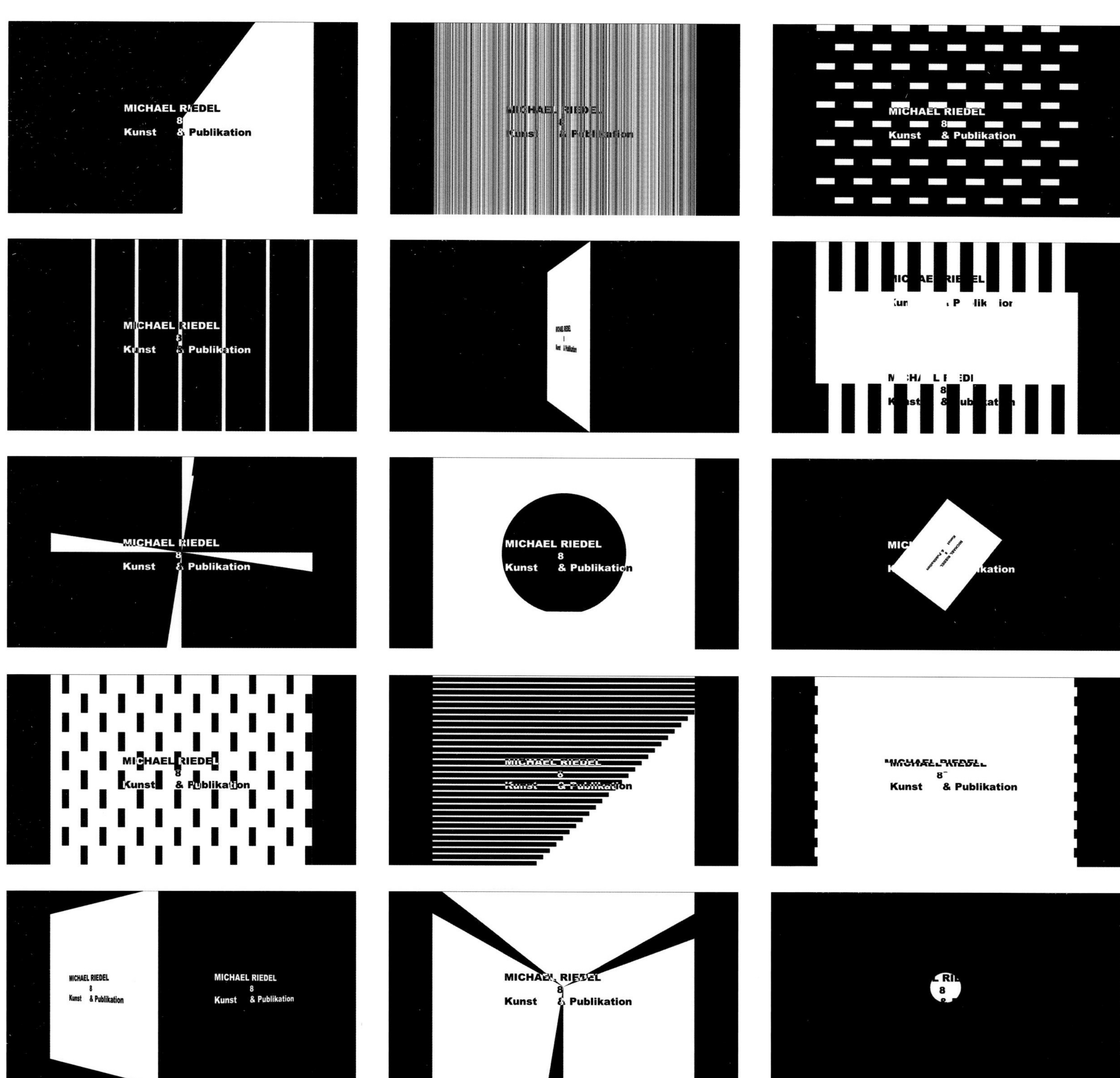

Screenshots of PowerPoint transition effects used for Riedel's artist talk "8 Kunst & Publikation" (ongoing since 2009)

Following pages:
Untitled (21 invitation cards, PowerPoint [David Zwirner]), 2013
Installation view, *Michael Riedel: PowerPoint*
David Zwirner, New York, 2013

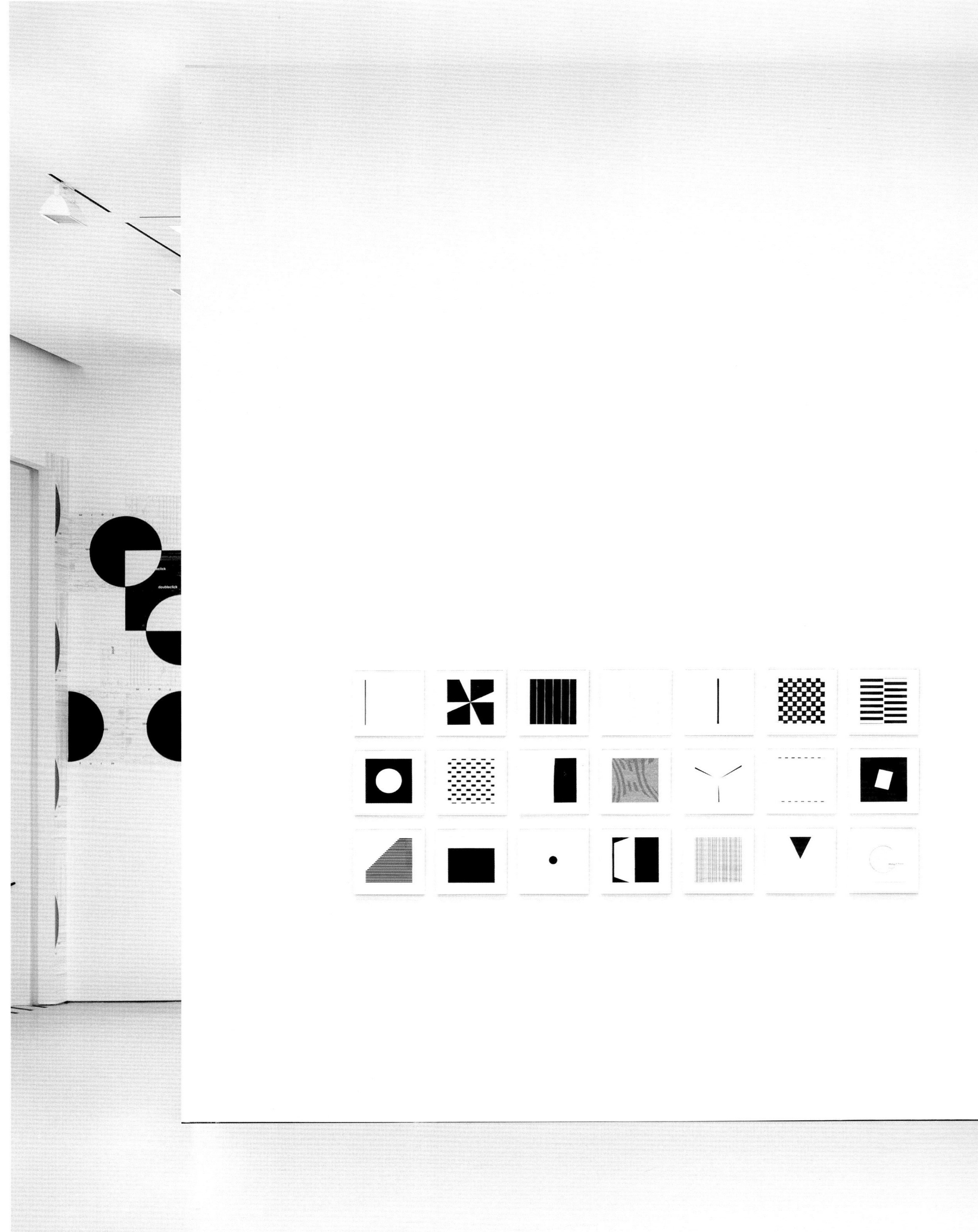
doubleclick

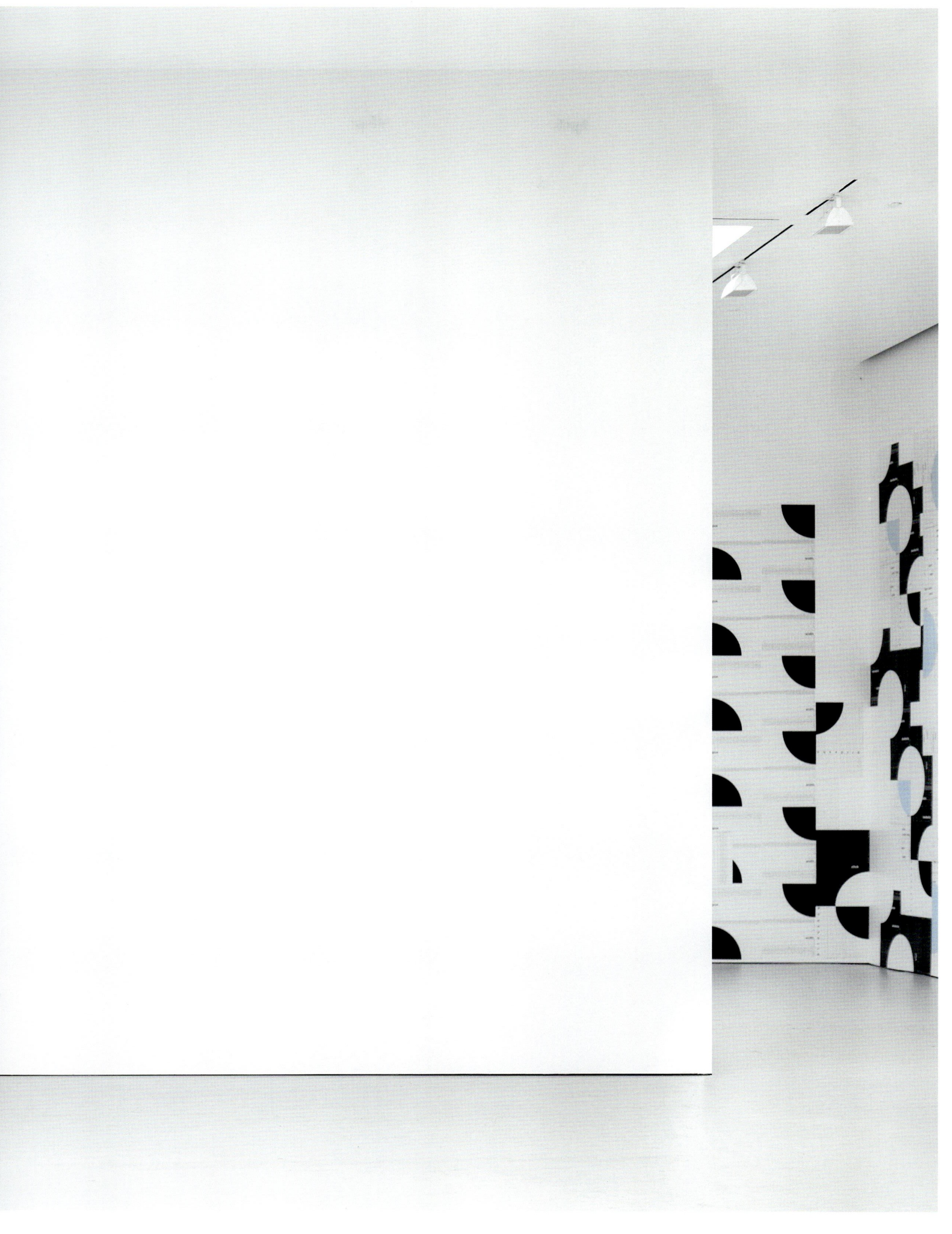

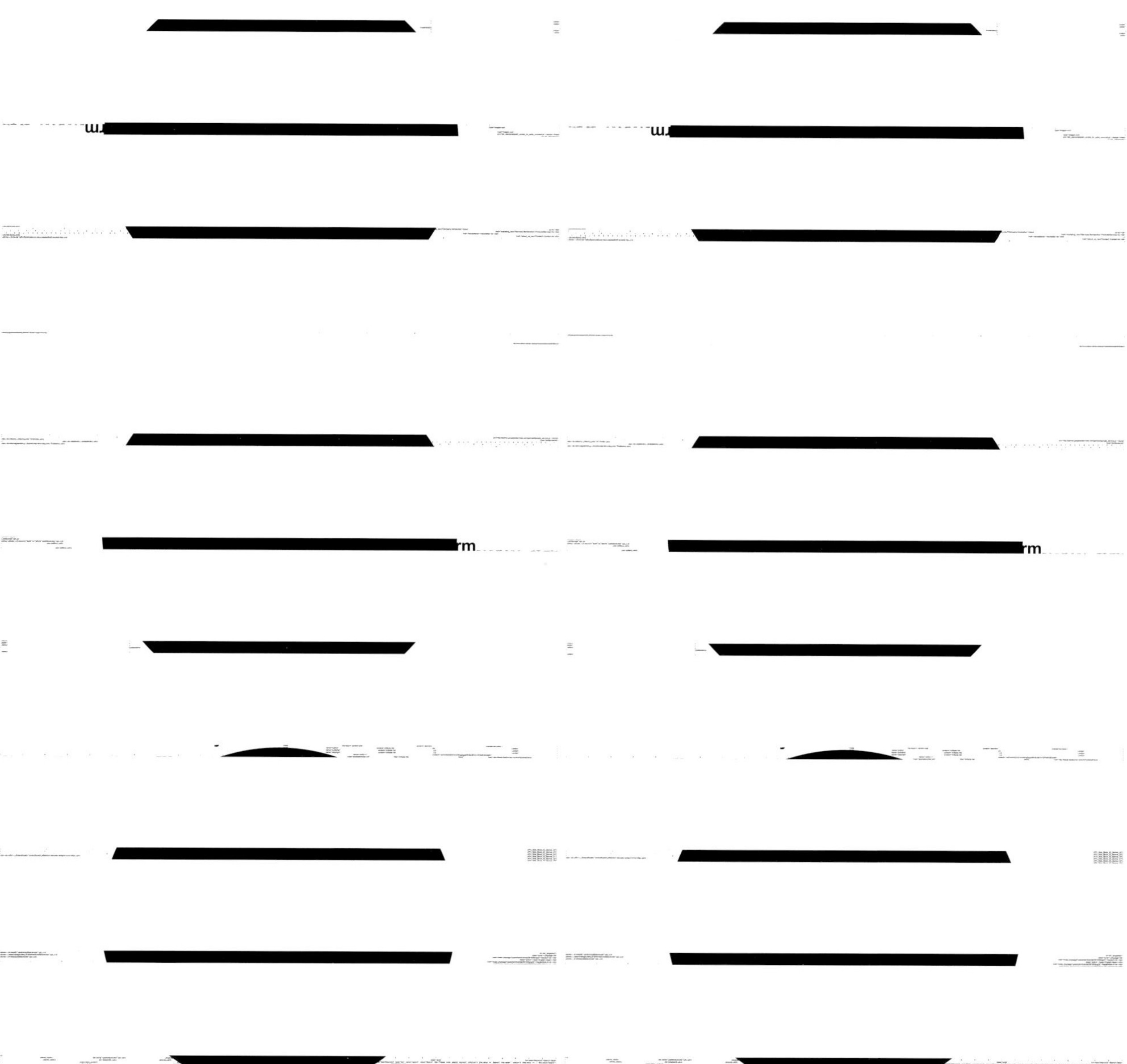

Untitled (Comb Horizontal), 2013
Silkscreen on linen
90 1/2 x 67 x 2 1/4 inches
(229.9 x 170.2 x 5.7 cm)

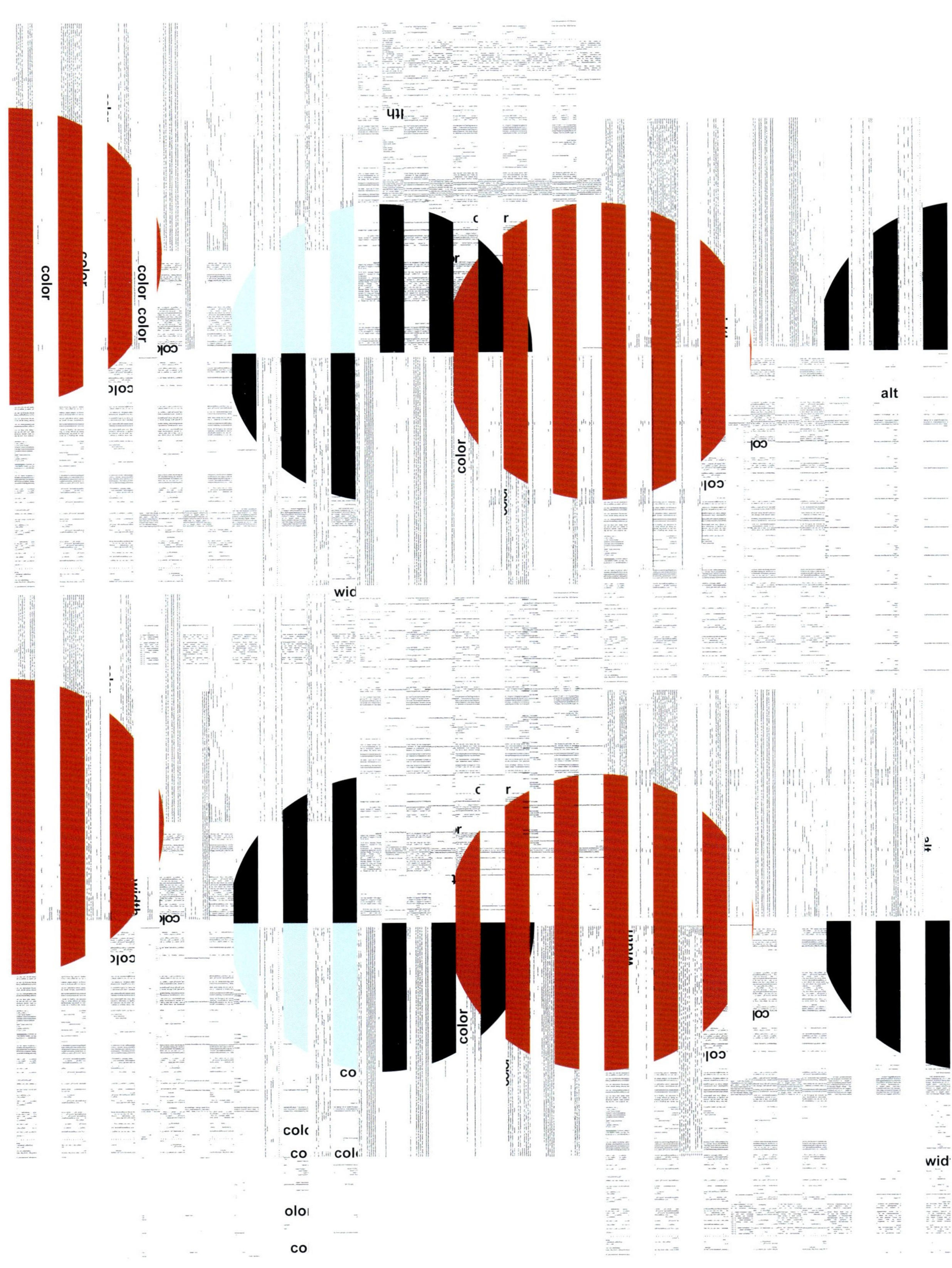

Untitled (Comb Vertical), 2013
Silkscreen on linen
90 1/2 x 67 x 2 1/4 inches
(229.9 x 170.2 x 5.7 cm)

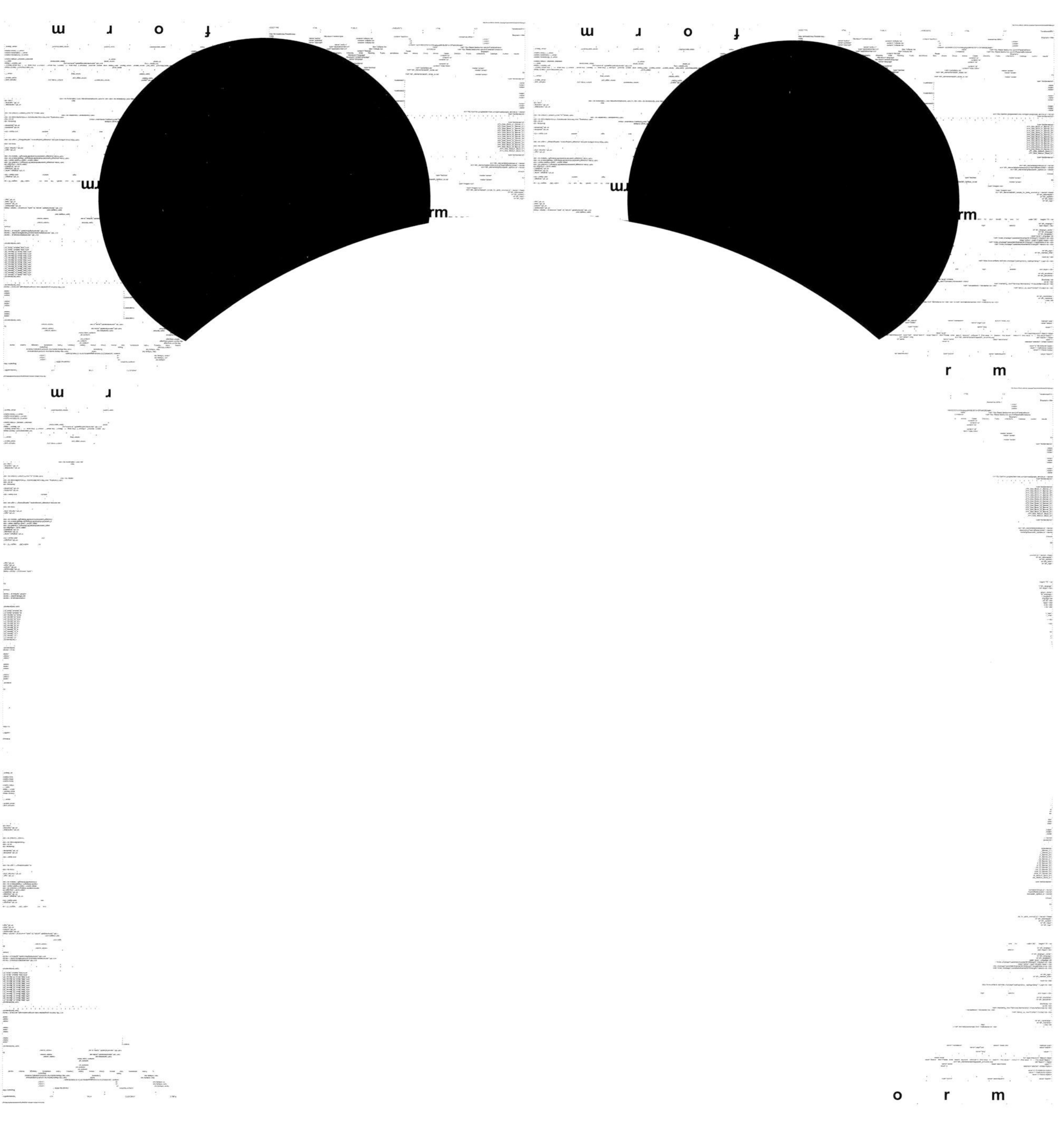

Untitled (Circle), 2013
Silkscreen on linen
90 1/2 x 67 x 2 1/4 inches
(229.9 x 170.2 x 5.7 cm)

Following pages:
Installation view, *Michael Riedel: PowerPoint*
David Zwirner, New York, 2013

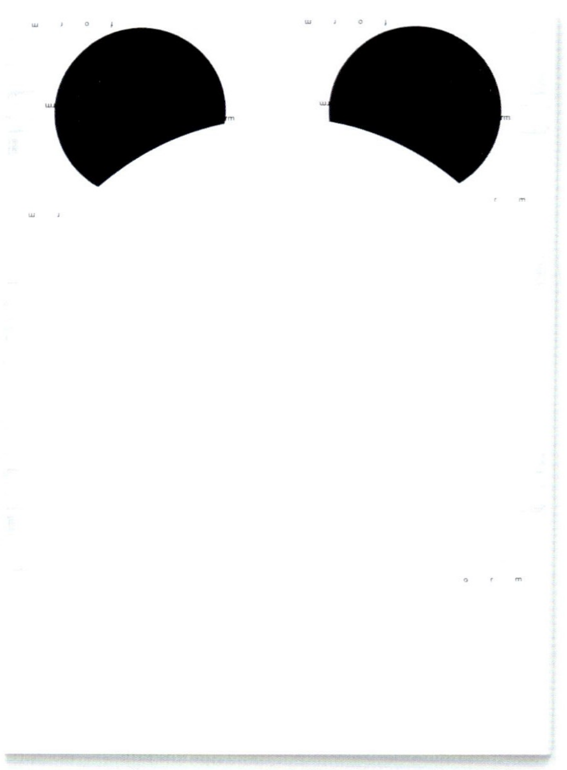

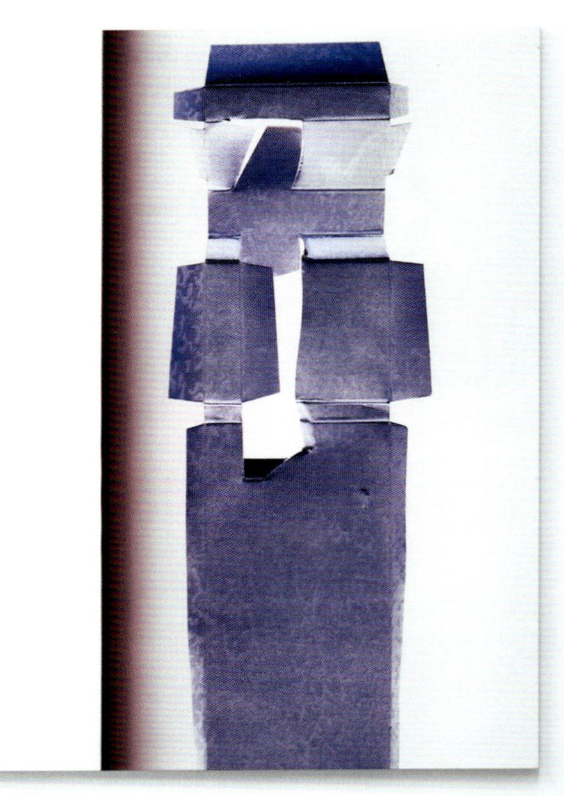

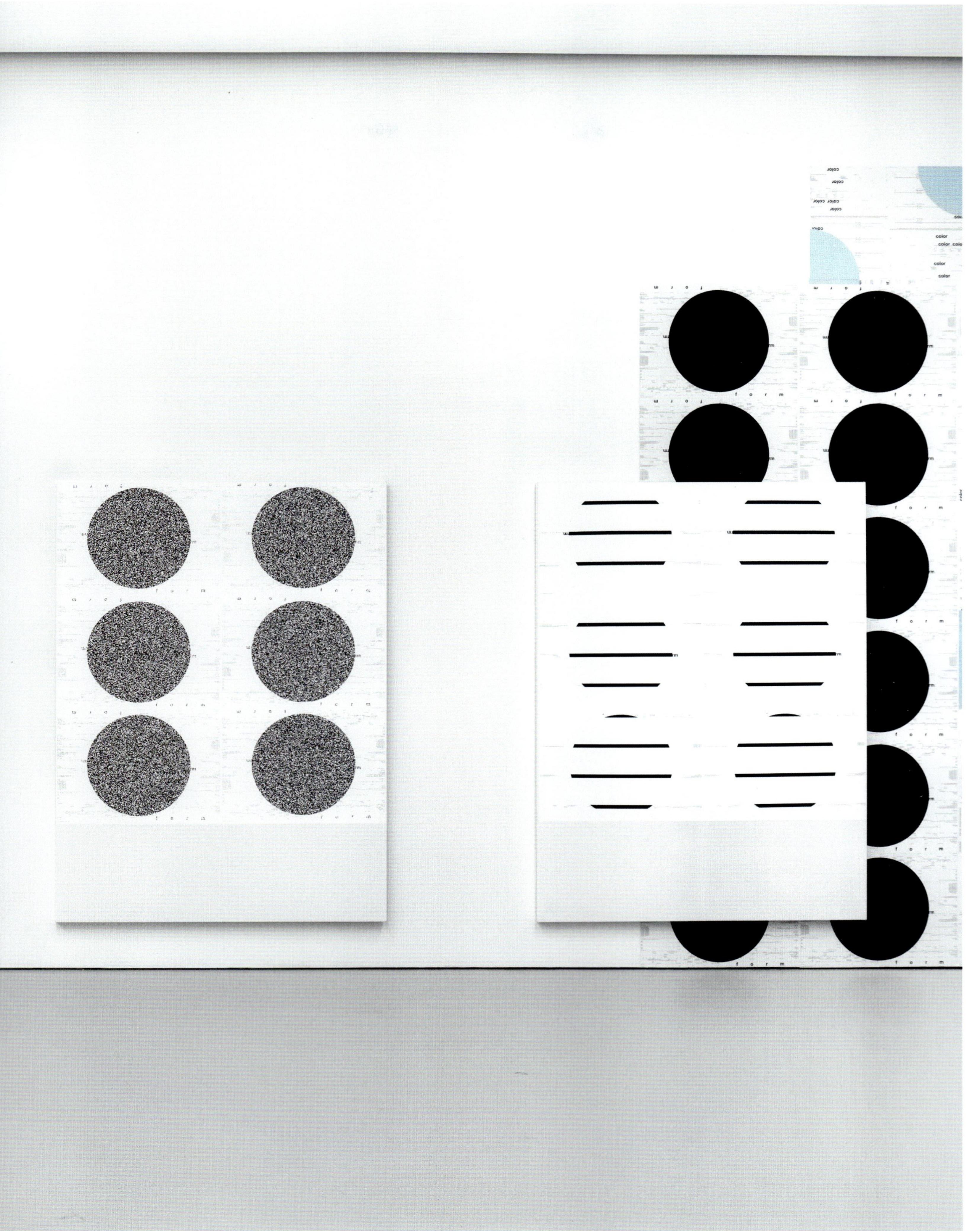

Untitled (Packing Material, violet), 2013
Digital print on linen
90 1/2 x 67 x 2 1/4 inches
(229.9 x 170.2 x 5.7 cm)

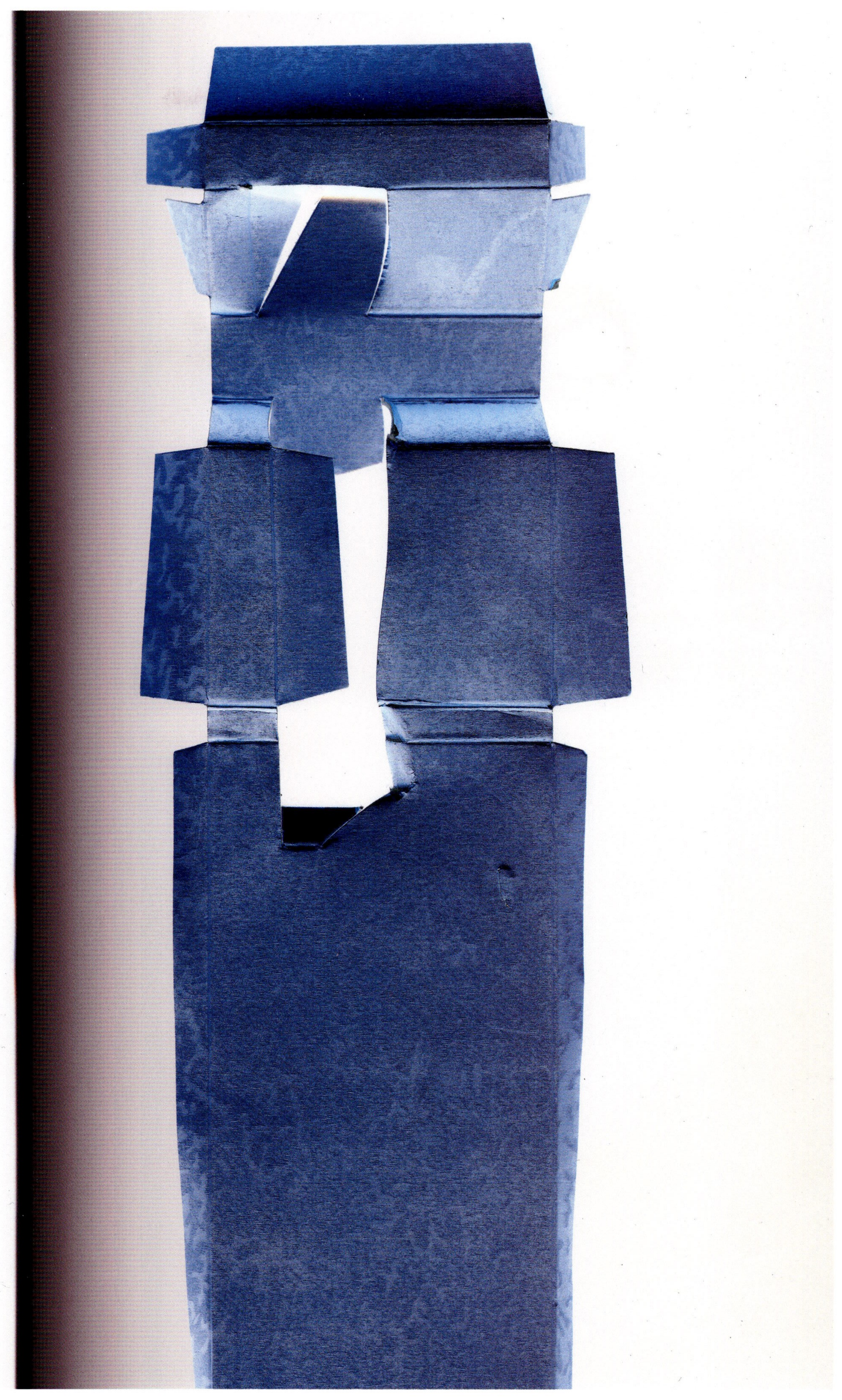

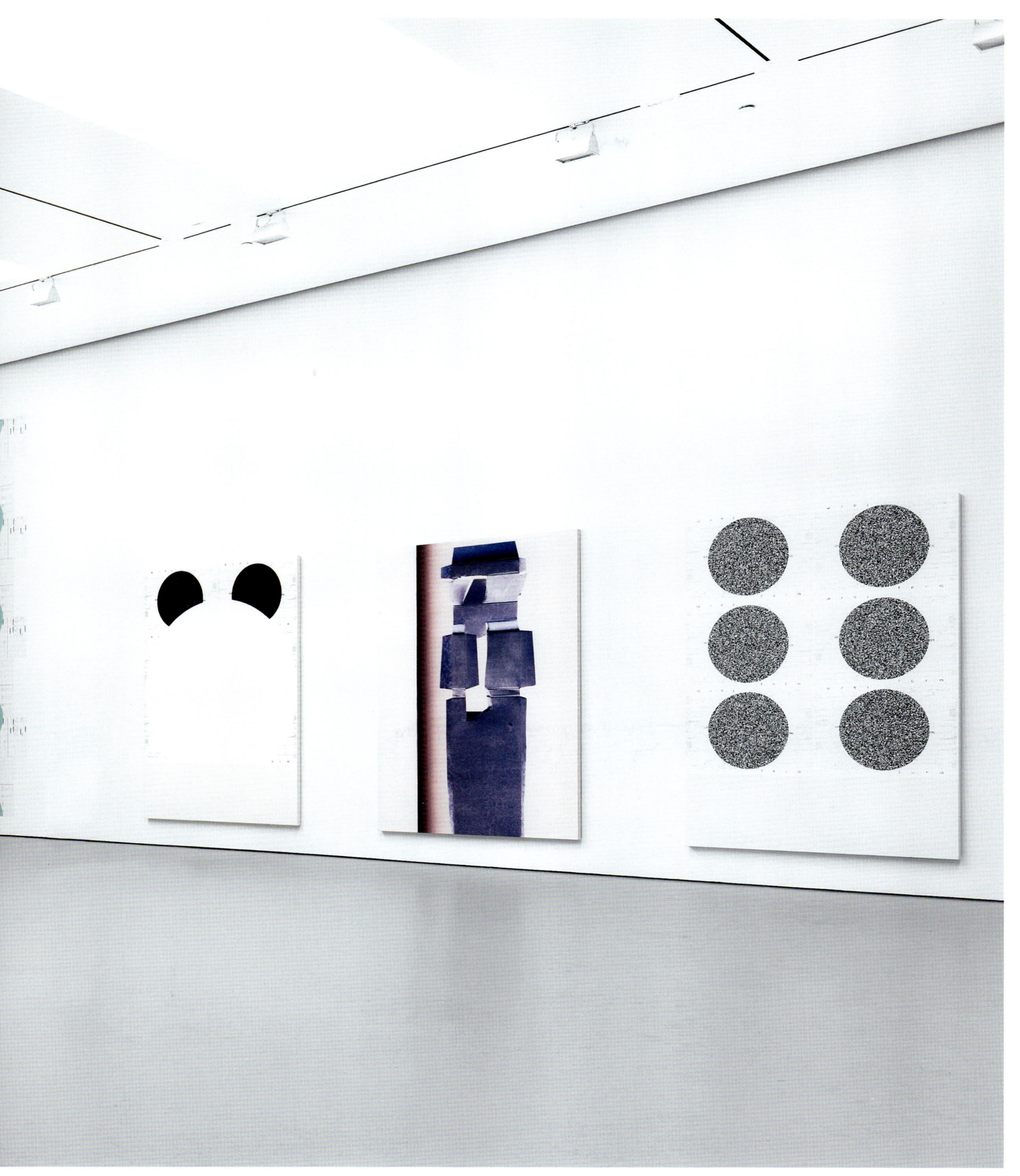

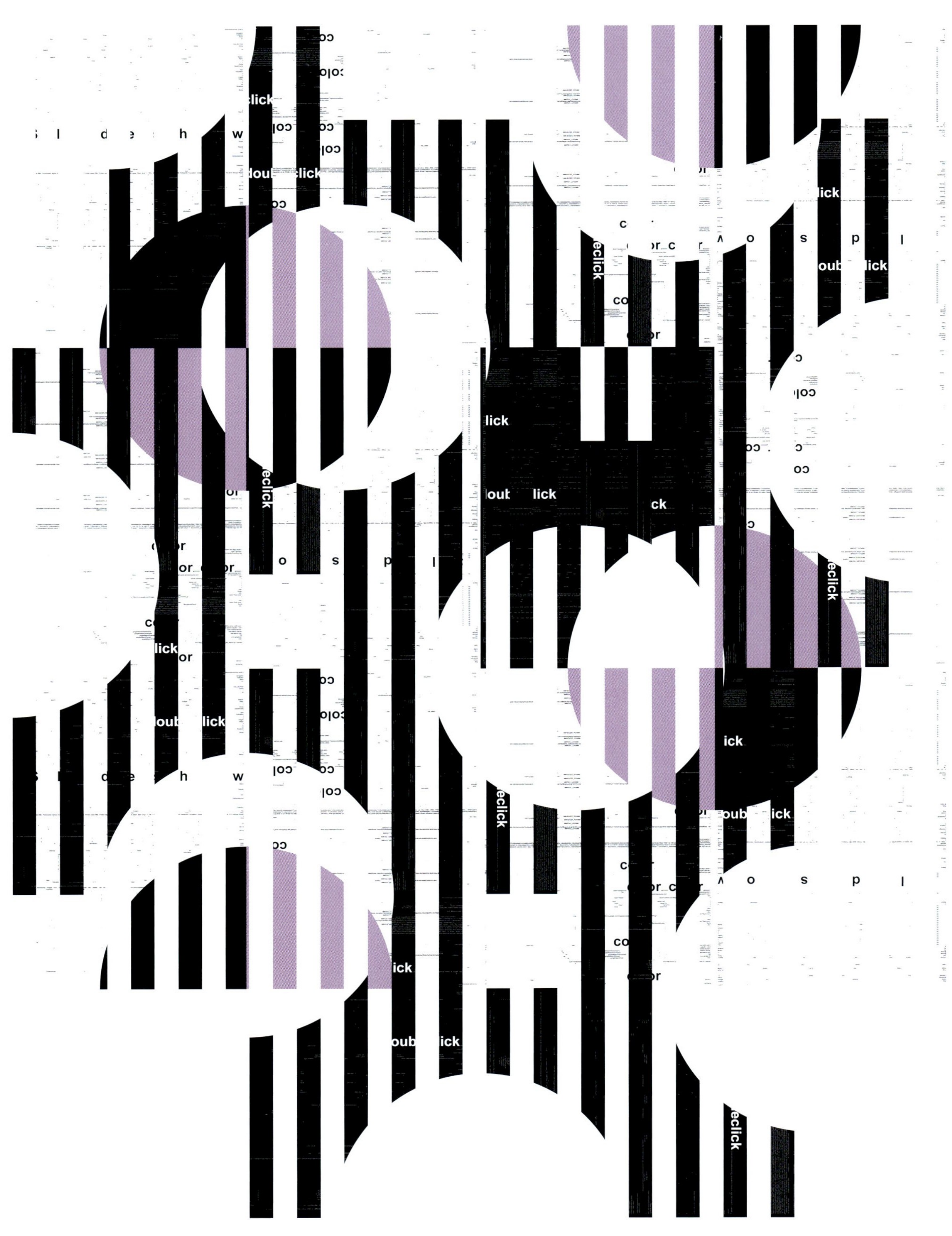

Untitled (Comb Vertical), 2013
Silkscreen on linen
90 1/2 x 67 x 2 1/4 inches
(229.9 x 170.2 x 5.7 cm)

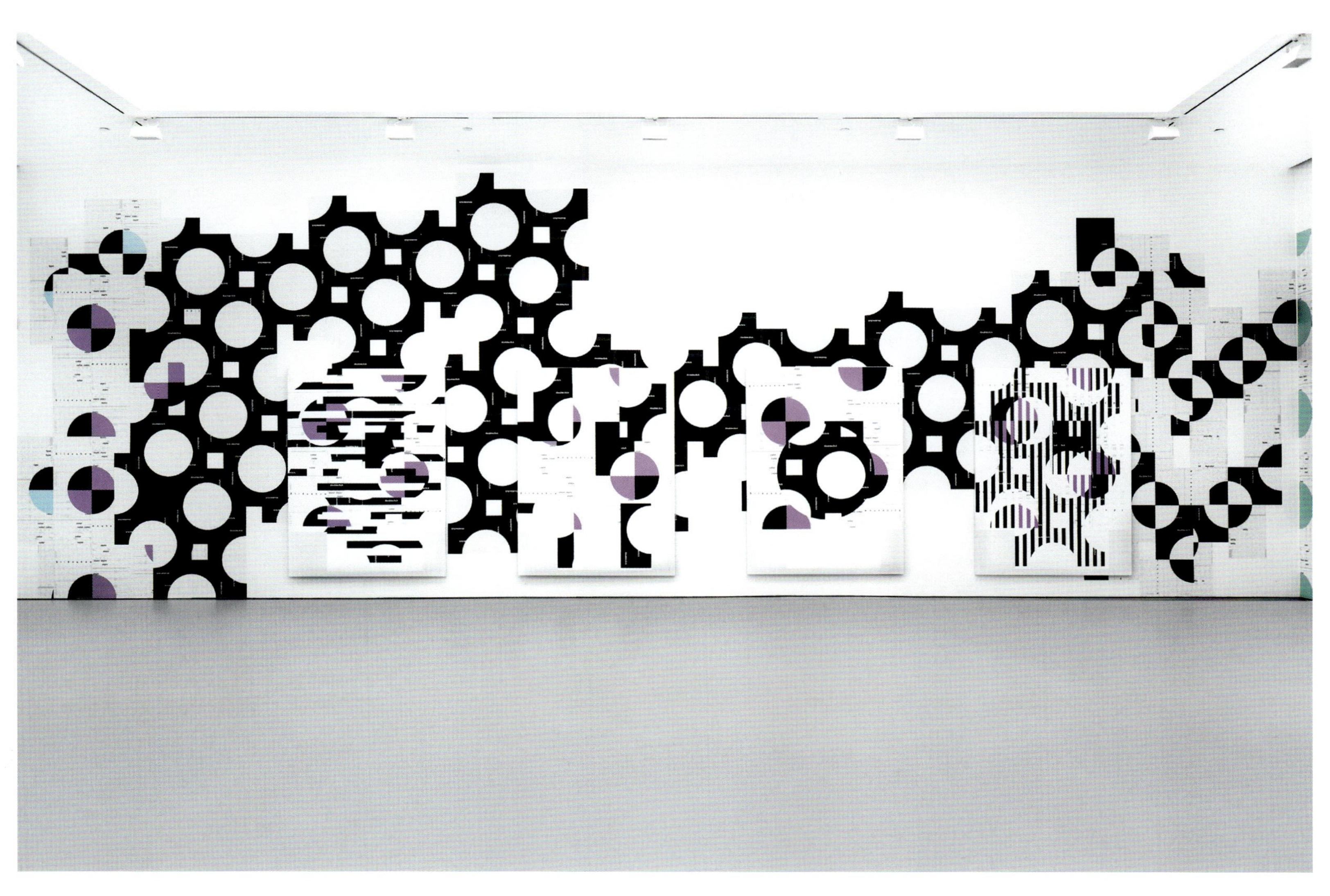

This page & following pages:
Installation views, *Michael Riedel: PowerPoint*
David Zwirner, New York, 2013

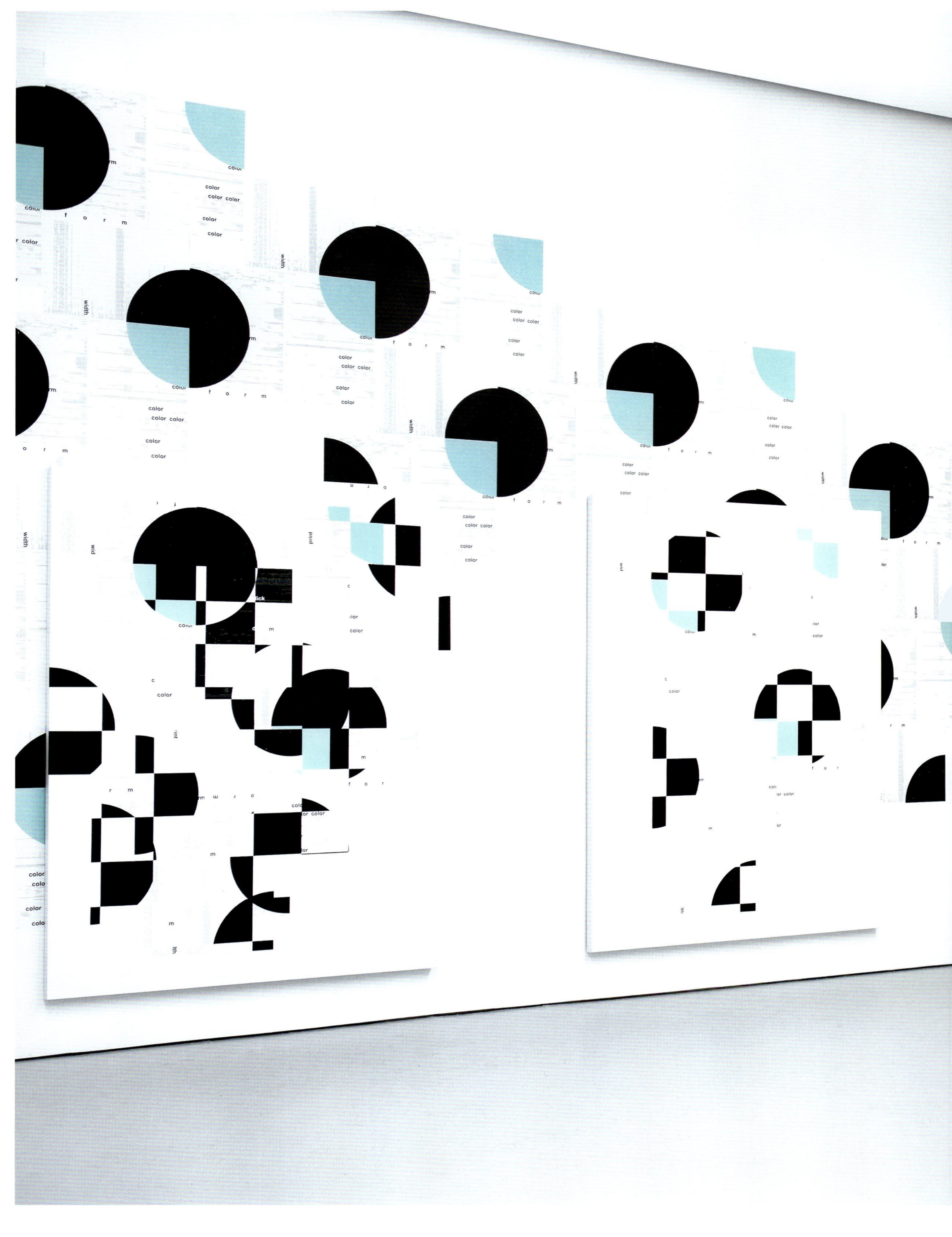
color
color color
color
color
f o r m
width
print

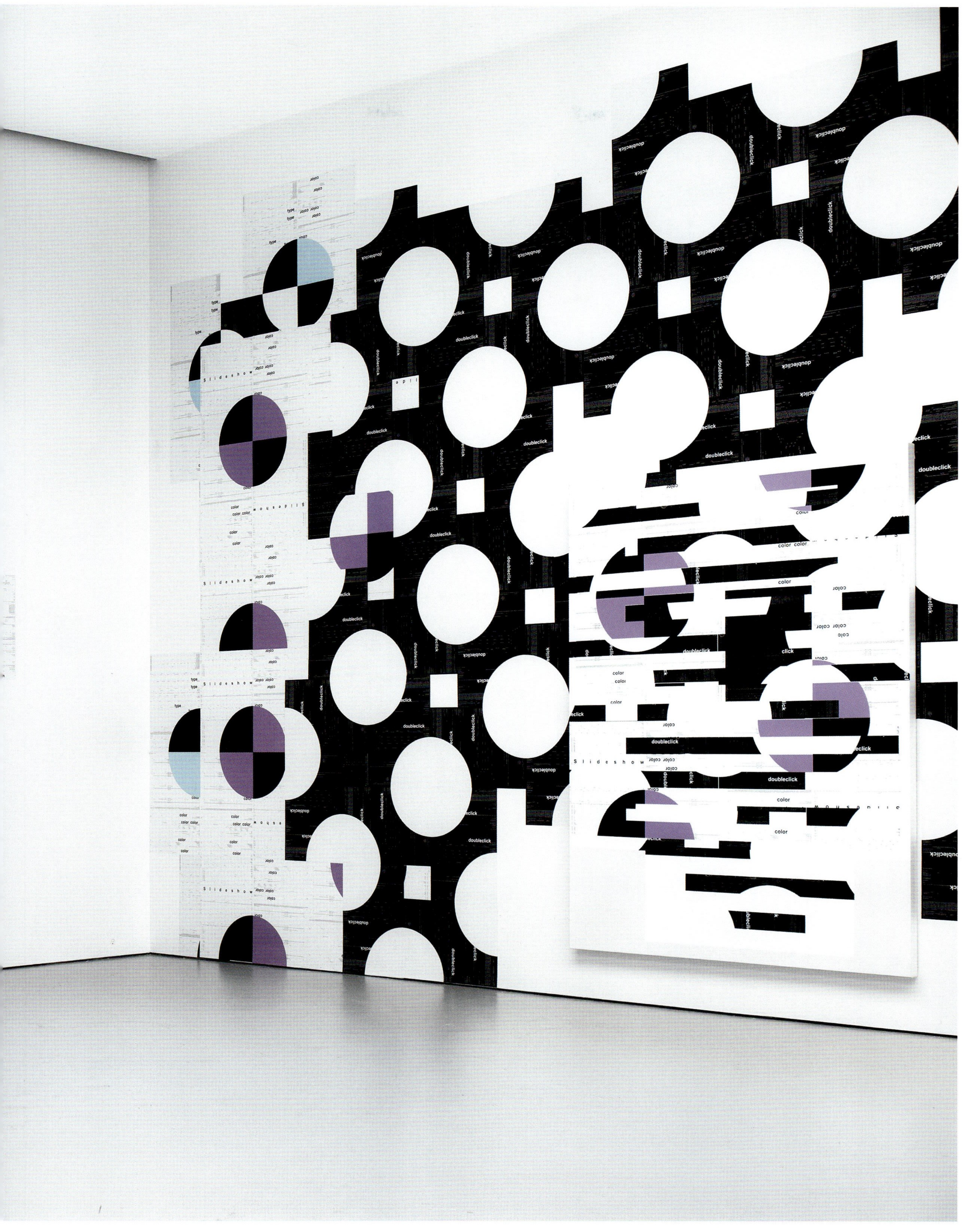
doubleclick
color
Slideshow
type

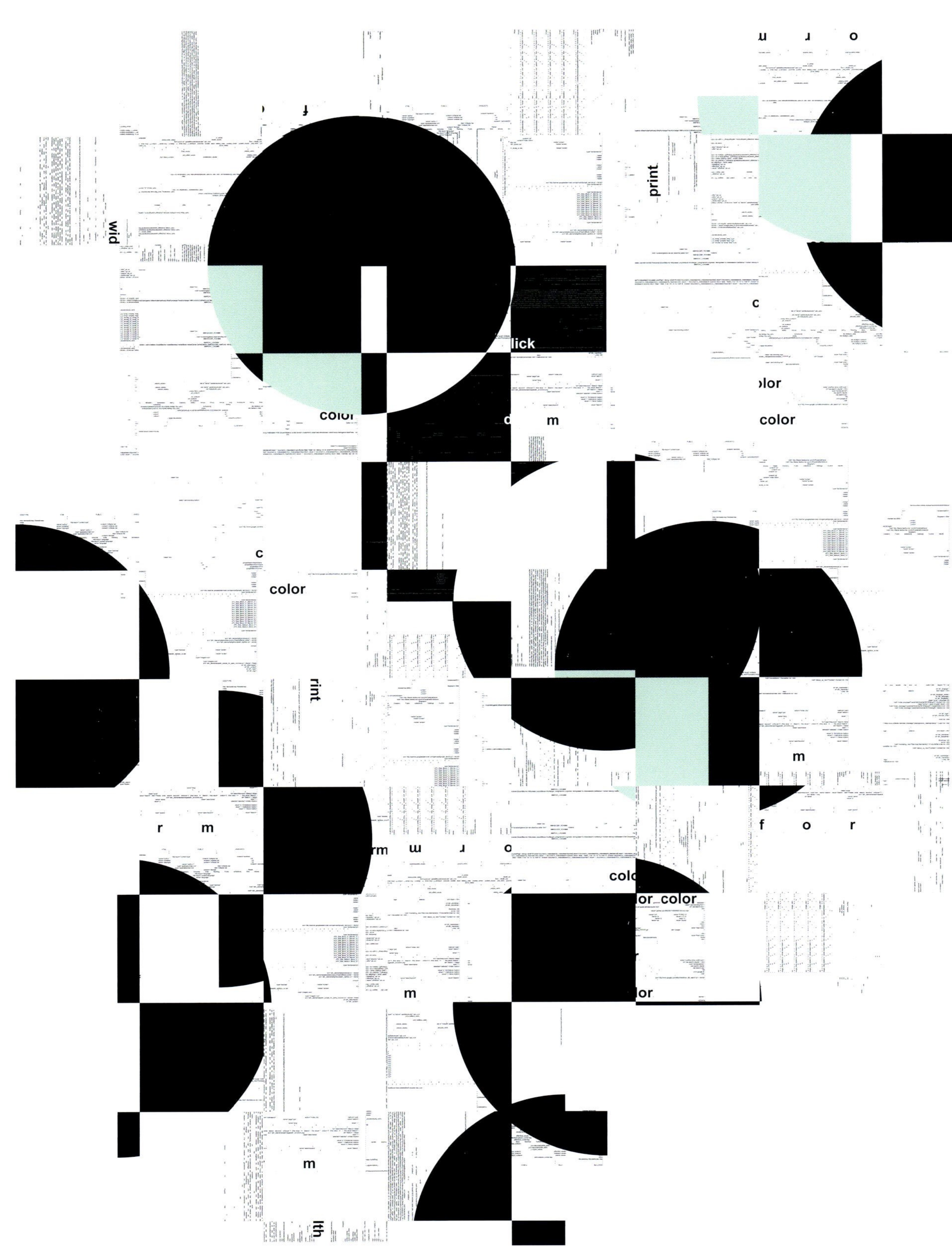

Untitled (Checkerboard Across), 2013
Silkscreen on linen
90 1/2 x 67 x 2 1/4 inches
(229.9 x 170.2 x 5.7 cm)

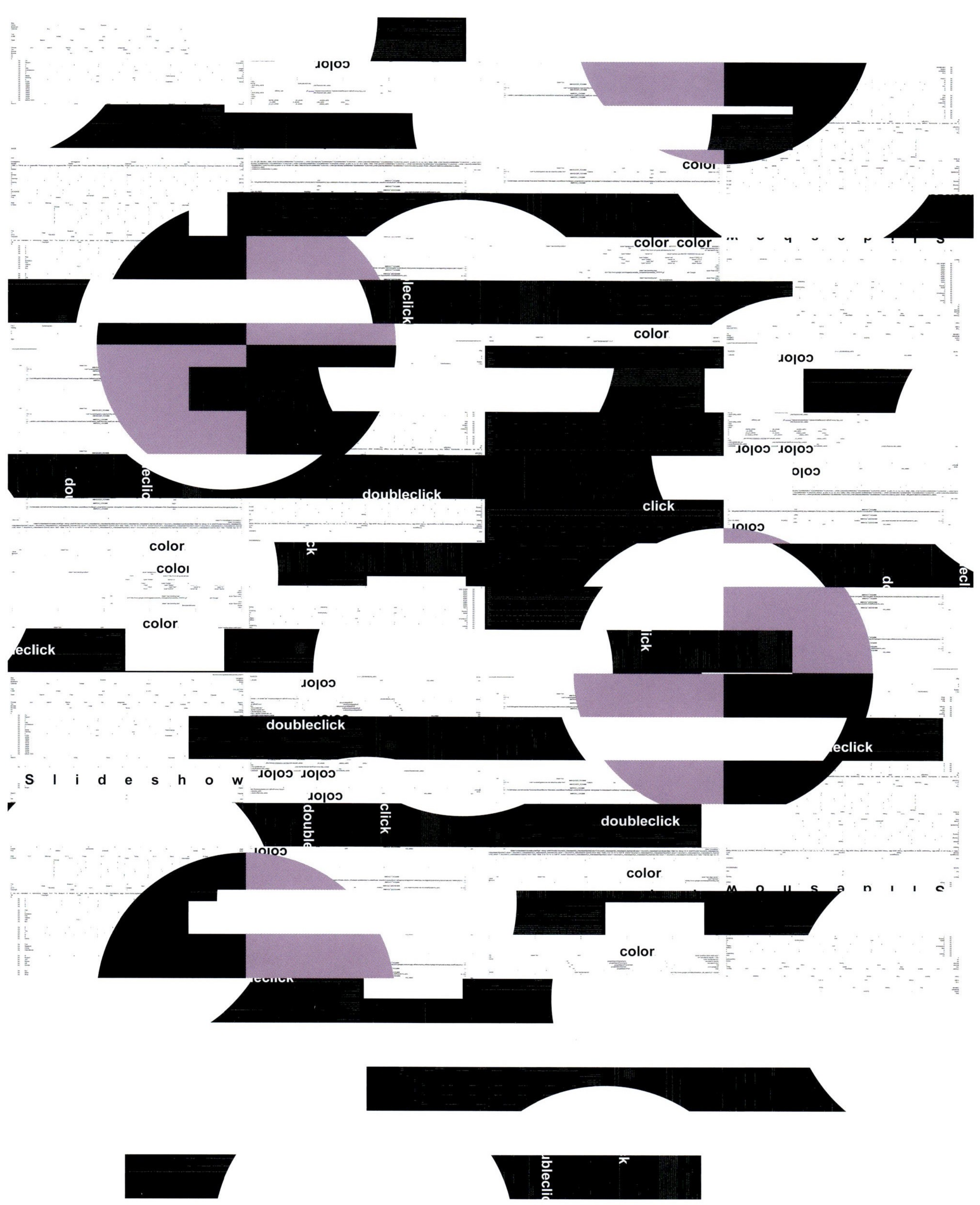

Untitled (Random Bars Horizontal), 2013
Silkscreen on linen
90 1/2 x 67 x 2 1/4 inches
(229.9 x 170.2 x 5.7 cm)

Following pages:
Installation view, *Michael Riedel: PowerPoint*
David Zwirner, New York, 2013

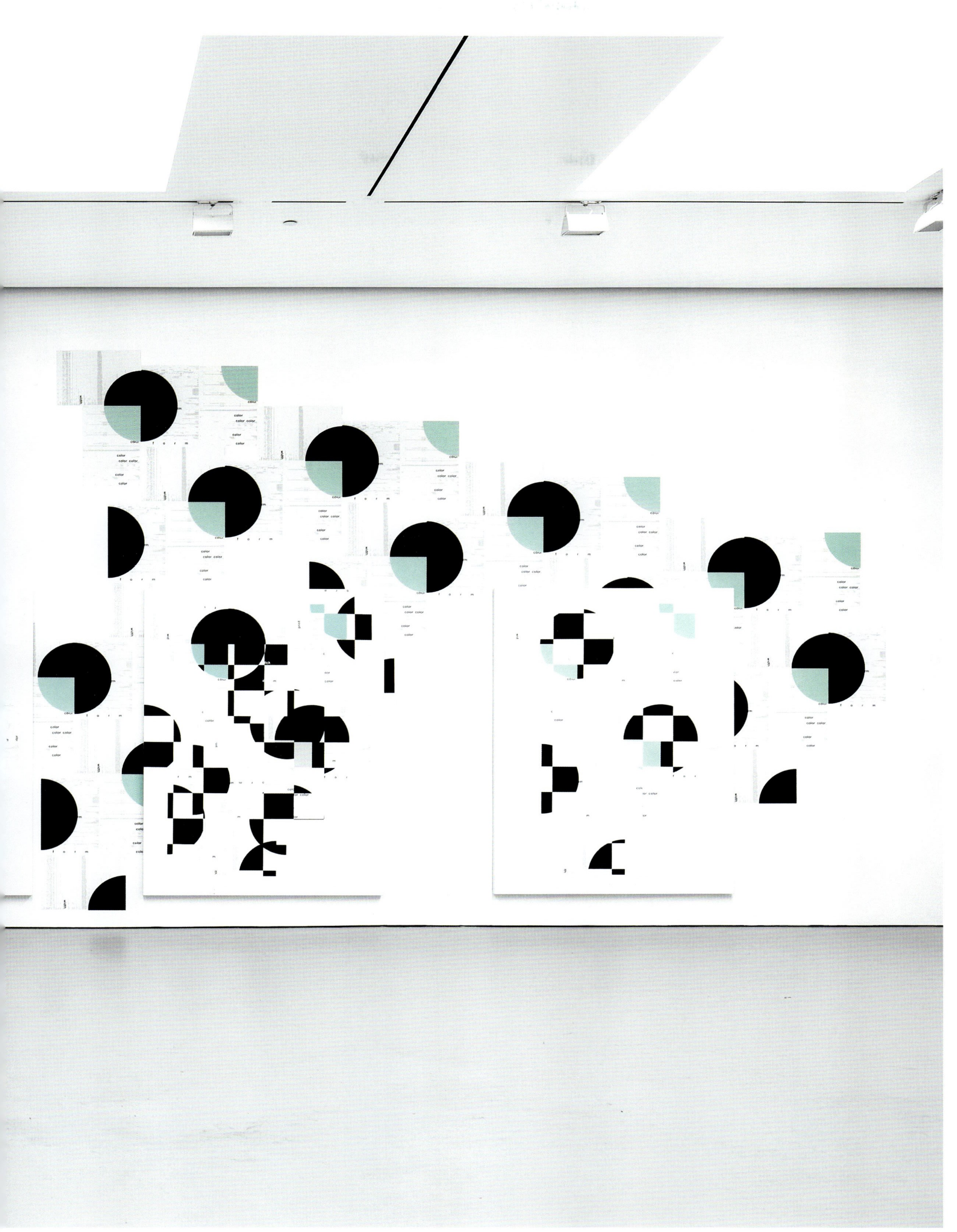

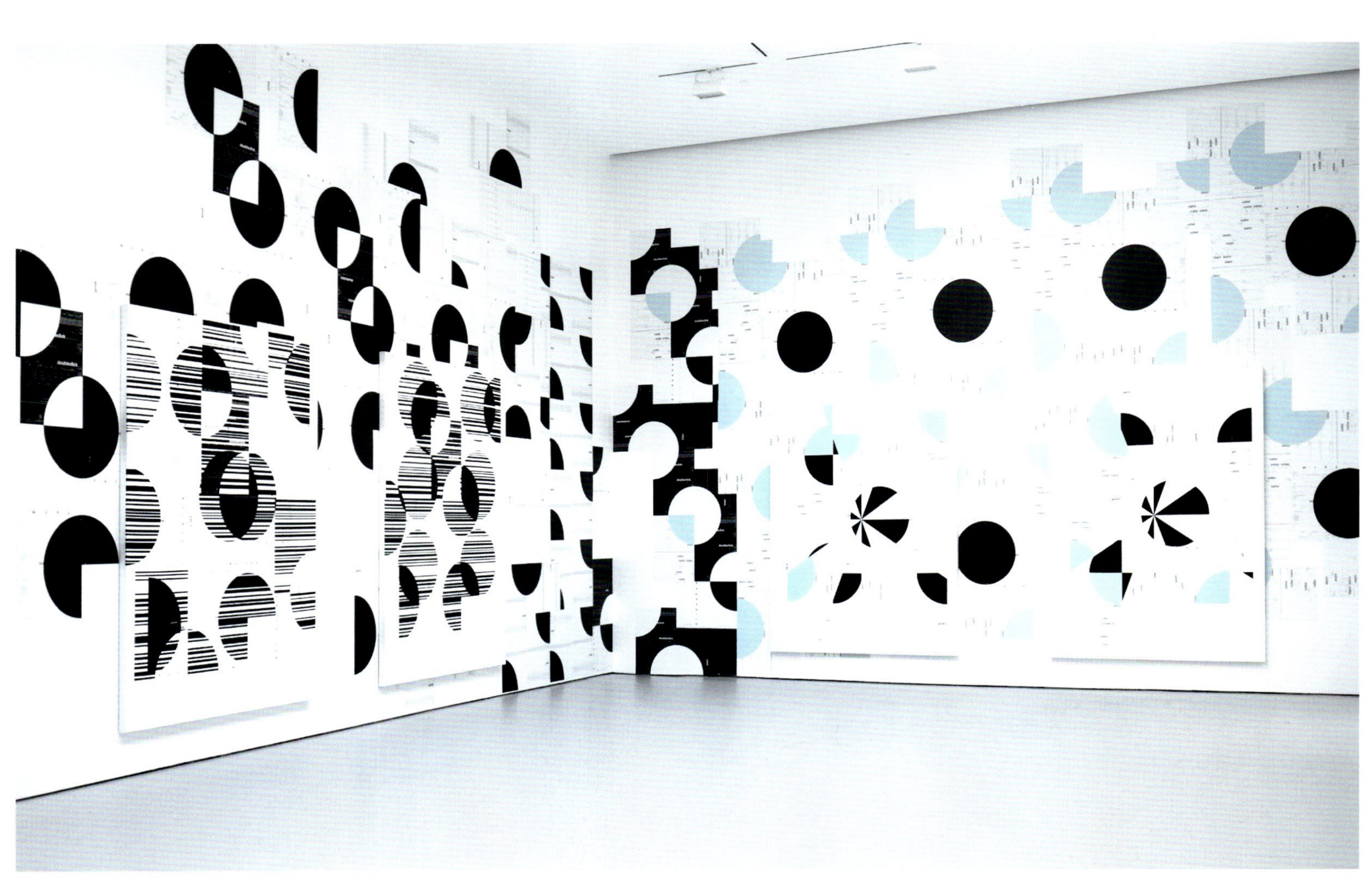

Installation view, *Michael Riedel: PowerPoint*
David Zwirner, New York, 2013

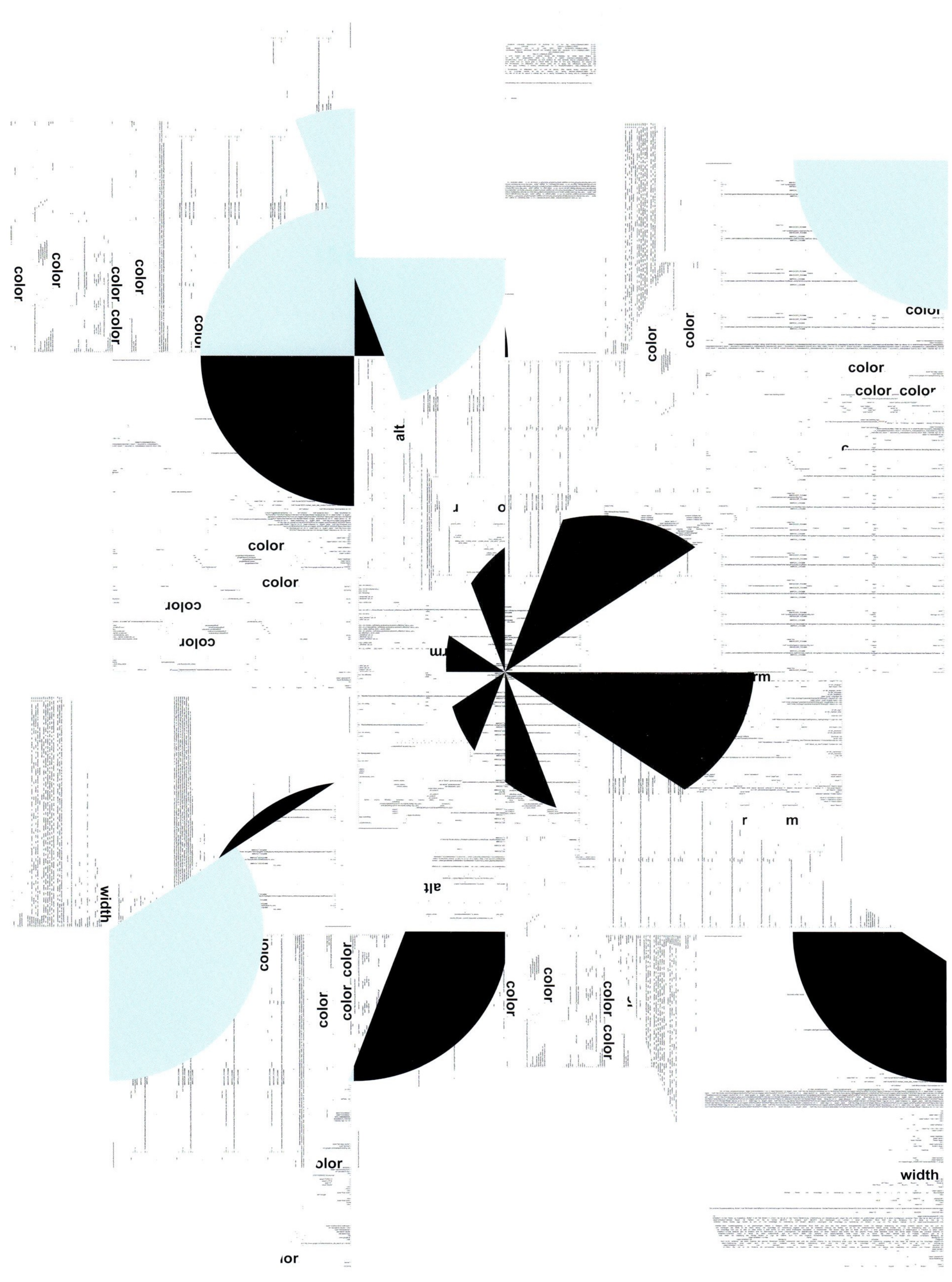

Untitled (Wheel, 6 Spoke), 2013
Silkscreen on linen
90 1/2 x 67 x 2 1/4 inches
(229.9 x 170.2 x 5.7 cm)

Following pages:
Installation view, *Michael Riedel: PowerPoint*
David Zwirner, New York, 2013

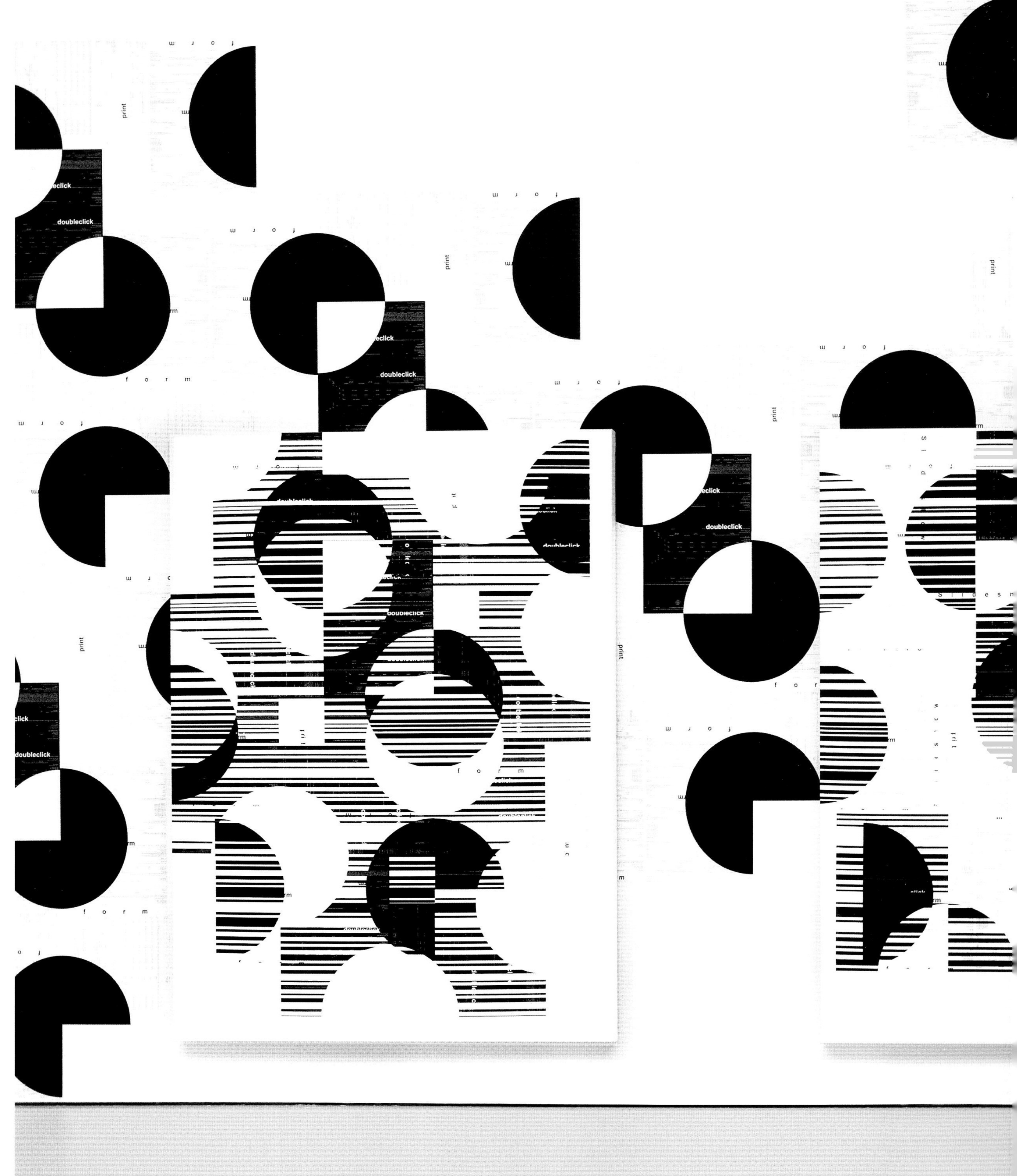
doubleclick
doubleclick
print
form
doubleclick
doubleclick
print
form
doubleclick
doubleclick
print
form

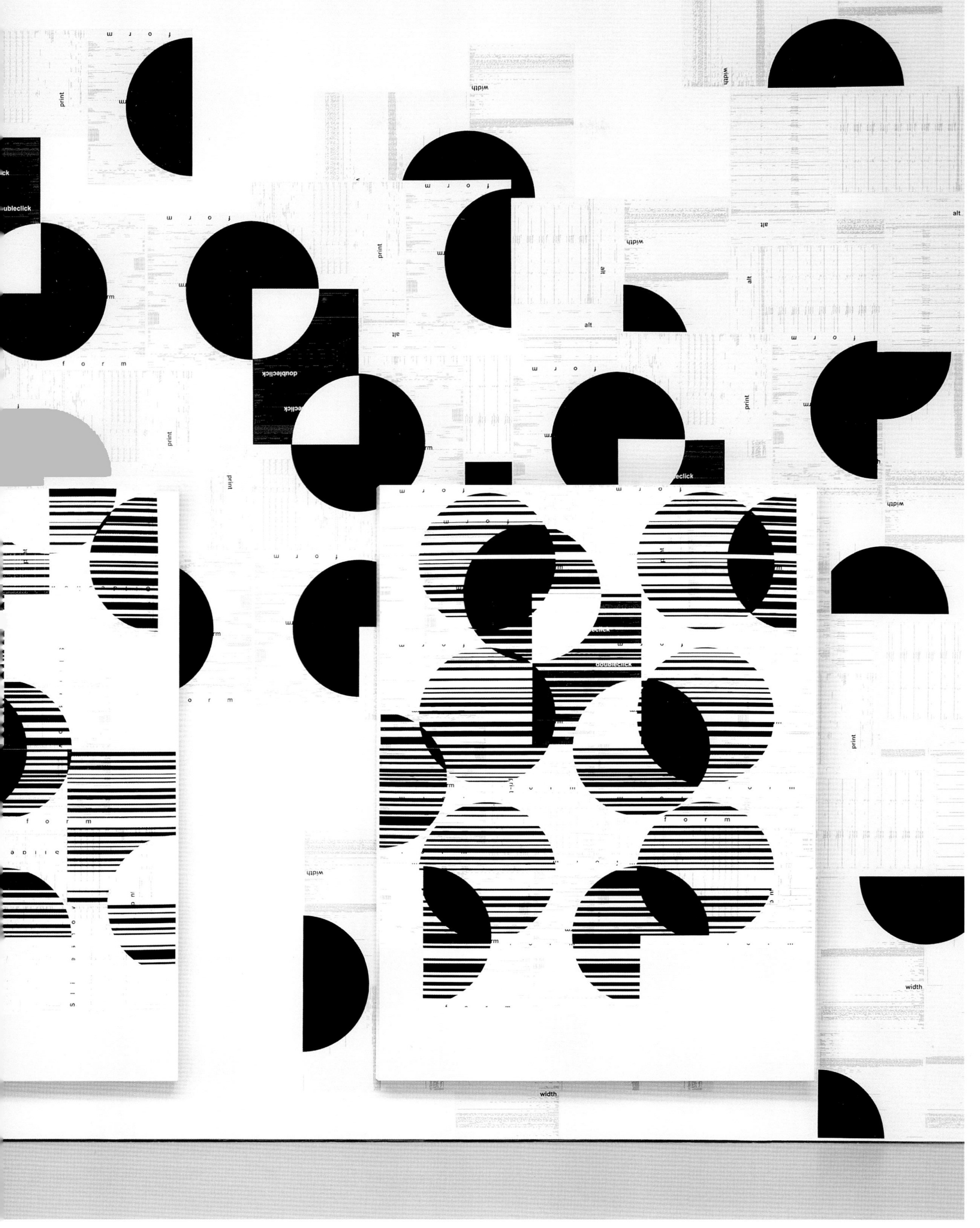
form
print
width
doubleclick
alt

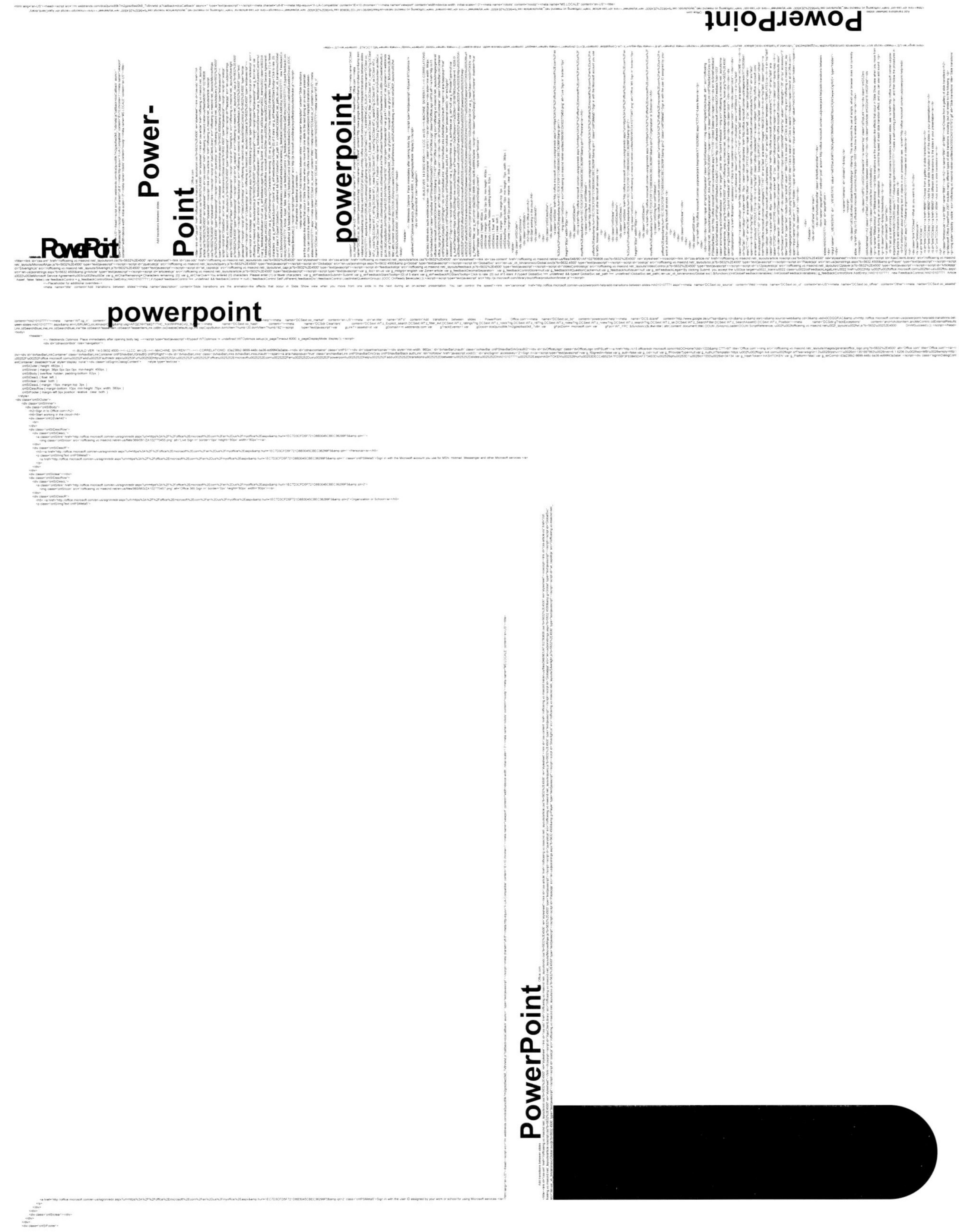

Untitled (PowerPoint), 2013
Offset print
46 1/2 x 33 inches
(118.1 x 83.8 cm)

Installation view, *Michael Riedel: PowerPoint*
David Zwirner, New York, 2013

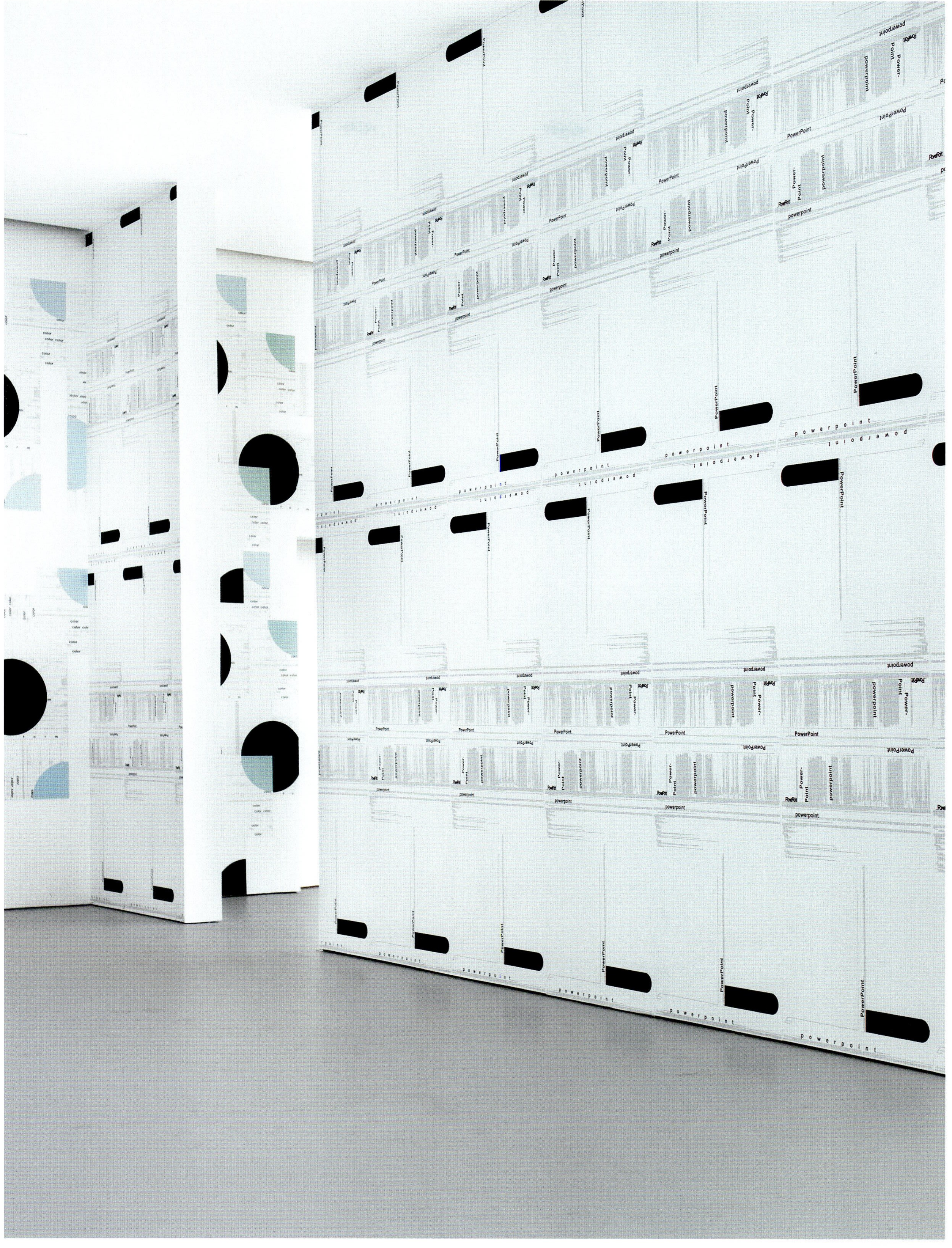
PowerPoint
powerpoint
Power-
Point
p o w e r p o i n t
color

Thanks to

David Zwirner, Veronique Ansorge, Todd Bradway, Julia Joern, Lucas Zwirner
Tina Kukielski
Florian Waldvogel
Gabriele Senn
Michel Rein, Angharad Williams
Larissa and Yigal Bischoff
Ales Ortuzar, Paul Pisoni
Silvana Battisti-Rudow and Marcus Herbert
Tony Chambers, Sarah Douglas, Marton Perlaki
Marie-Hélène and Marc Féraud

Michael Riedel

Born 1972.

SELECTED SOLO EXHIBITIONS, PRESENTATIONS AT ART FAIRS & ARTIST'S INTERVENTIONS

2015

Besuchte und nicht besuchte Ausstellungen [Einladungen 1997–2015], Kunstverein Braunschweig
fkk, Museum für Moderne Kunst, Frankfurt [permanent installation, freitagsküche im Museum für Moderne Kunst]
Michael Riedel, Le Box – Fonds M-ARCO, Marseille, France [catalogue]

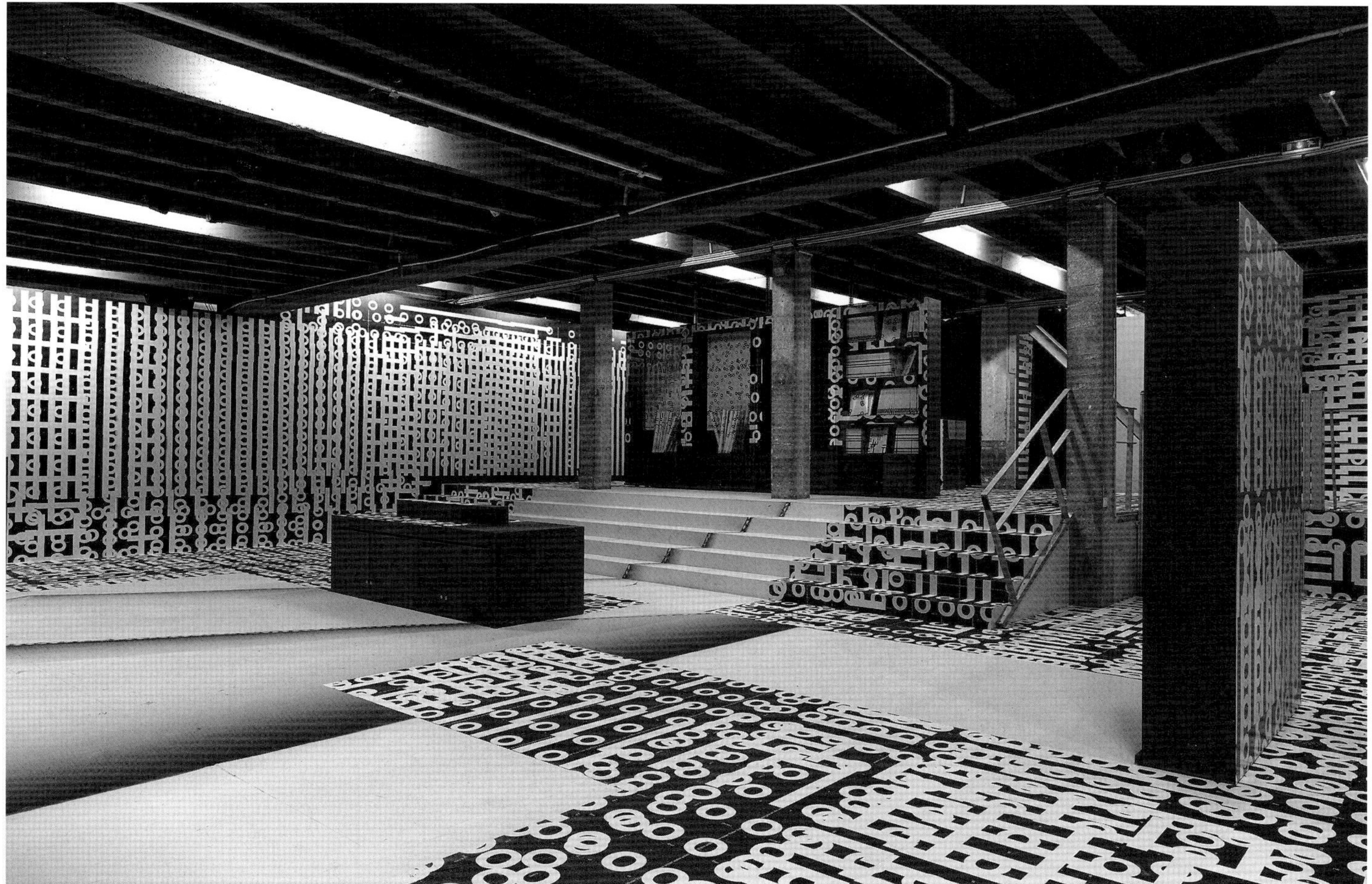

EFFJ KNOOS [JEFF KOONS], Palais de Tokyo, Paris [part three; site-specific installation] [catalogue]

'record, label, play back' (malentendu, ignorance, doubles flous), Galerie Michel Rein, Paris

2014

Michael Riedel liest Oskar, Österreichisches Museum für angewandte Kunst (MAK), Vienna

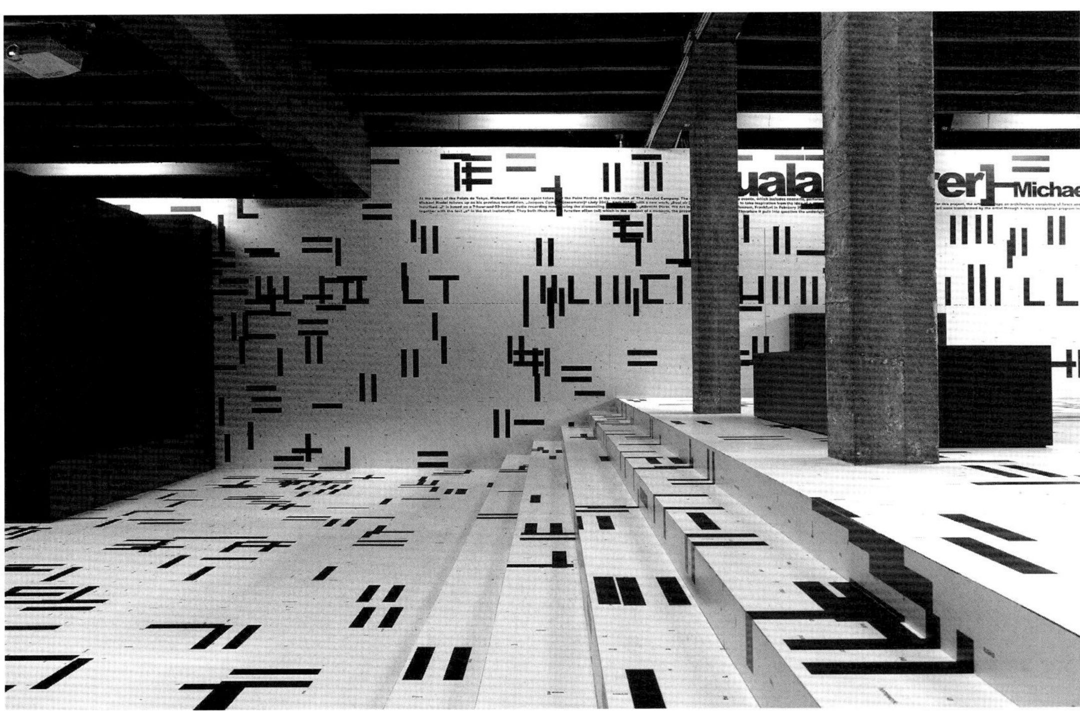

Dual air [Dürer], Palais de Tokyo, Paris
[part two; site-specific installation] [catalogue]

Interventions 03, Goethe-Institut, Amsterdam

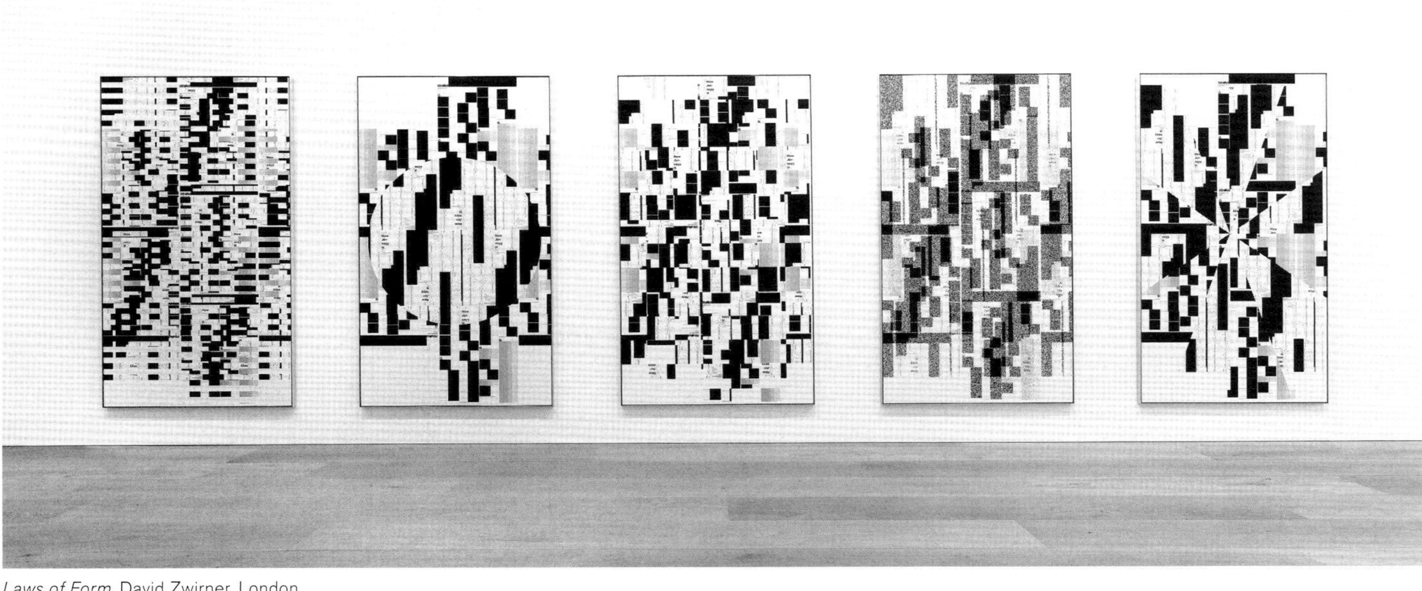

Laws of Form, David Zwirner, London

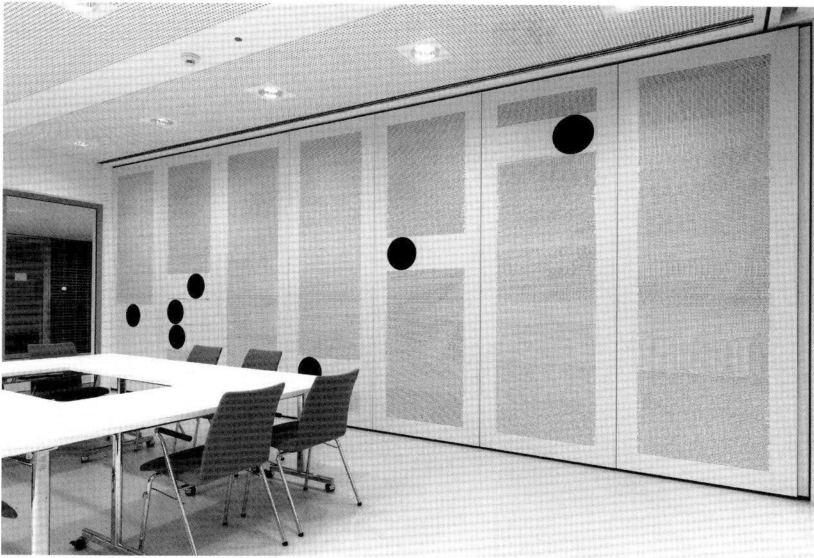

Ohne Titel (F-G / Die Traumdeutung), Sigmund Freud Institute, Frankfurt
[permanent installation] [limited edition set]
'record, label, play back' (Missverständnis, Ignoranz, doppelte Unschärfe), Gabriele Senn Galerie, Vienna

2013

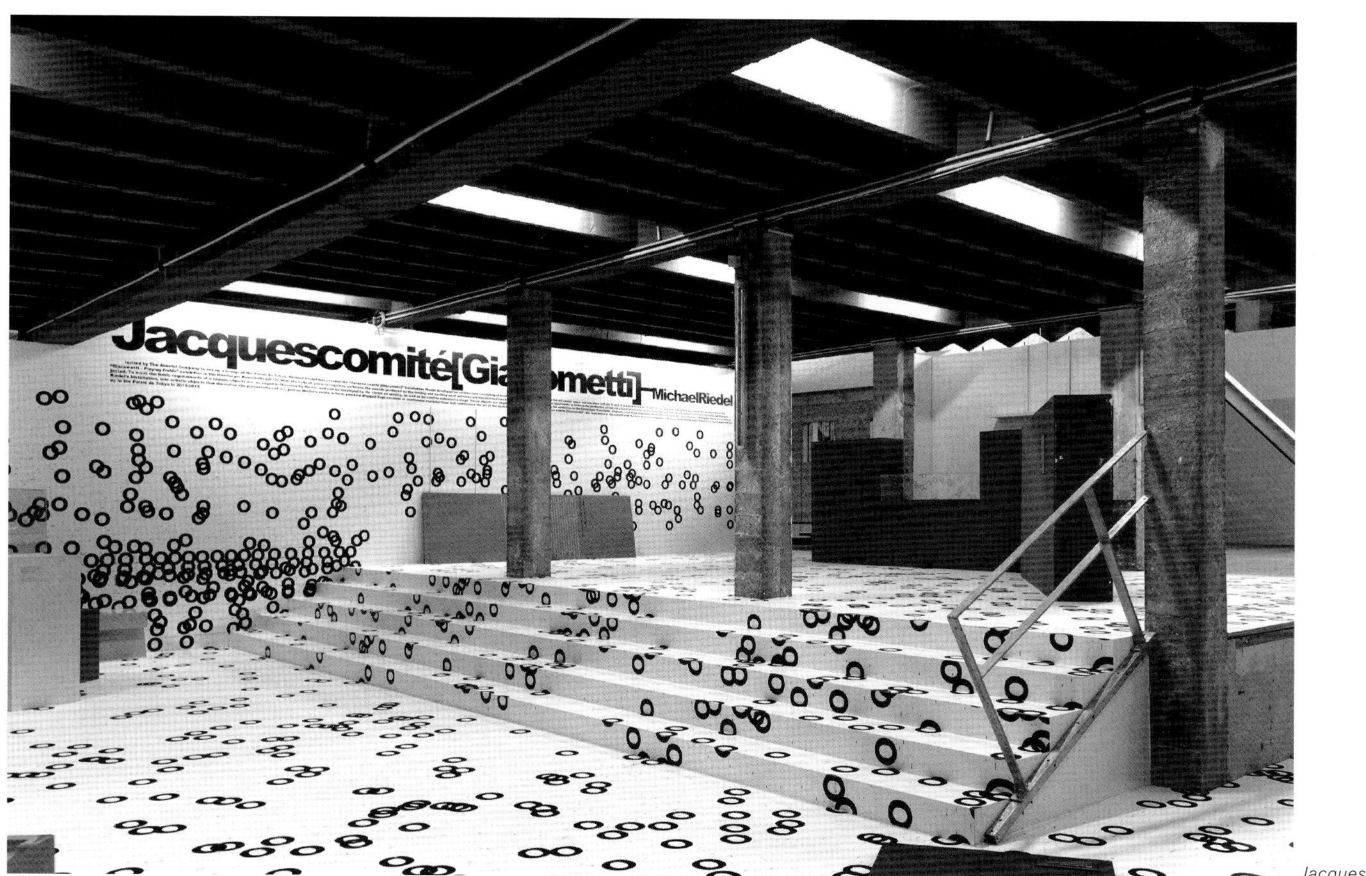

Jacques comité [Giacometti], Palais de Tokyo, Paris [part one; site-specific installation] [catalogue]
Michael Riedel, BWA SOKÓŁ Gallery, Nowy Sacz, Poland
Michael Riedel, Galerie Michel Rein, Brussels
Art material (Riesenalk), ABC Berlin [site-specific installation at Gabriele Senn Galerie booth]
Set design and limited edition cover for *Wallpaper* (Issue 180), London
Michael Riedel, Gabriele Senn Galerie, Vienna
PowerPoint, David Zwirner, New York

2012
Cinema curtain for *Double Feature*, Schirn Kunsthalle Frankfurt
Bar design for *Ricard*, Bal Jaune (Cirque en Chantier), Paris
Kunste zur Text, Schirn Kunsthalle Frankfurt [catalogue]
Kunste zur Text (Algorithmiques), Galerie Michel Rein, Paris

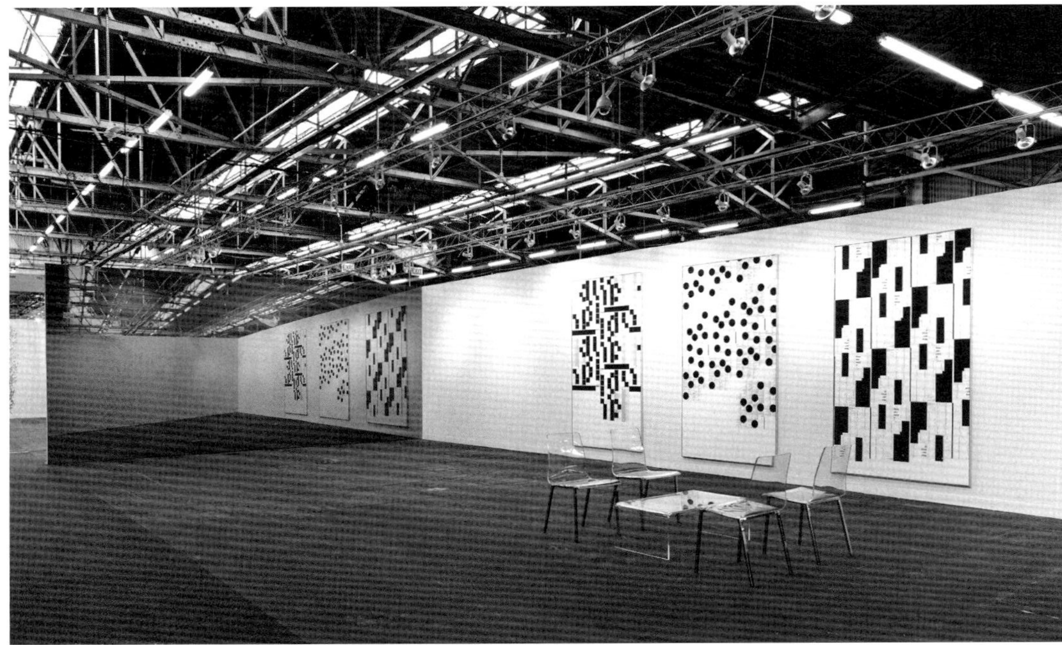
The Armory Show, New York [site-specific installation at David Zwirner booth]
Four Proposals for changing Bulletin 72, Christophe Daviet-Thery Bookshop / Gallery, Paris

2011
Club[b]ed Club, Zoo galerie, Nantes, France
Michael Riedel, Bischoff Projects, Frankfurt
The quick brown fox jumps over the lazy dog, David Zwirner, New York [limited edition set]
The quick brown fox jumps over the lazy dog, Gabriele Senn Galerie, Vienna
Time Bank Robbery, Portikus, Frankfurt [artist's intervention in *Time/Bank: Julieta Aranda and Anton Vidokle*]
Viennafair 2011 [site-specific installation at Gabriele Senn Galerie booth]

2010
Michael Riedel, Galerie Michel Rein, Paris
The quick brown fox jumps over the lazy dog, Kunstverein Hamburg [limited edition set]

2009
Michael Riedel, Galerie Francesca Pia, Zürich

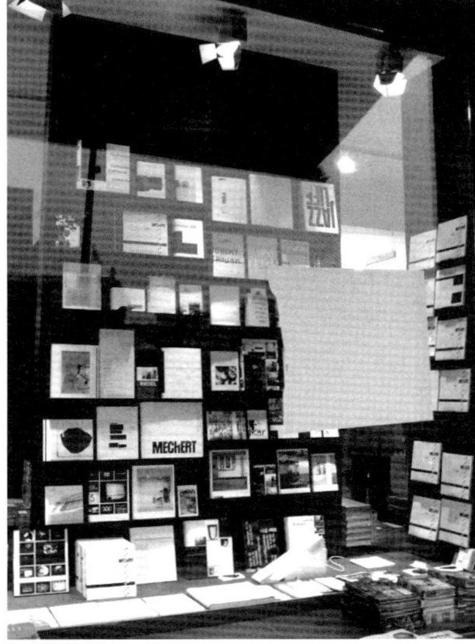
Shop window, Buchhandlung Walther König, Berlin

2008
Filmed Film David Zwirner, New York
Michael Riedel und die Ausstellung Der Meister von Flémalle und Rogier van der Weyden, Städel Museum, Frankfurt
The Inevitable Show (reproducing fame), Lewis Glucksman Gallery, Cork, Ireland [catalogue]
Vier Vorschläge zur Veränderung/Four Proposals for Change, Galerie Isabella Bortolozzi, Berlin

2007
Four Proposals for the change of David Zwirner in the logo of the gallery, México Arte Contemporáneo, Mexico City [site-specific installation at David Zwirner booth]
ARTIISSIIMA (II) ARTIIISSIIIMA (III), Artissima International Fair of Contemporary Art, Turin [site-specific installation at Galerie Isabella Bortolozzi booth]
Michael Riedel, Gabriele Senn Galerie, Vienna

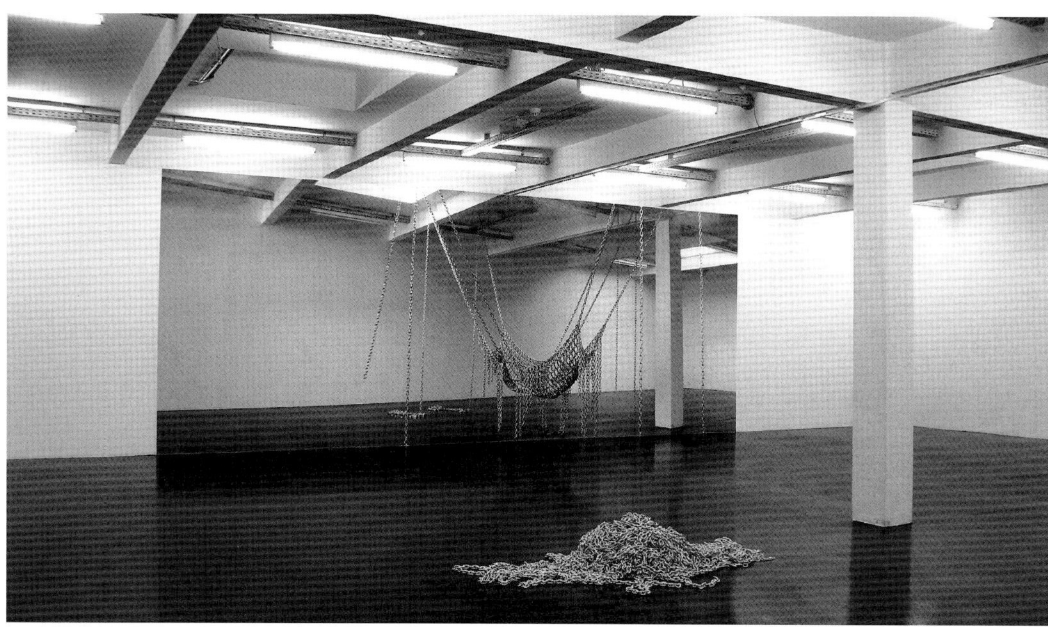

vicini ~~Michael S. Riedel~~ John Bo, Kunstraum Innsbruck, Austria [catalogue *Gedruckte und nicht gedruckte Poster (2003–08)/Printed and Unprinted Posters (2003–08)* published in 2008]
Frieze Art Fair, London [site-specific installation at David Zwirner booth]

2006
24.04.2001 – 16.03.2006, Galerie Michael Neff, Frankfurt [two-person exhibition with Achim Lengerer]
Oskar-von-Miller Strasse 16 (Textil), High & Low: Fine Art Fair Frankfurt [catalogue]
Tirala, Art Statements, Art 37 Basel [catalogue]

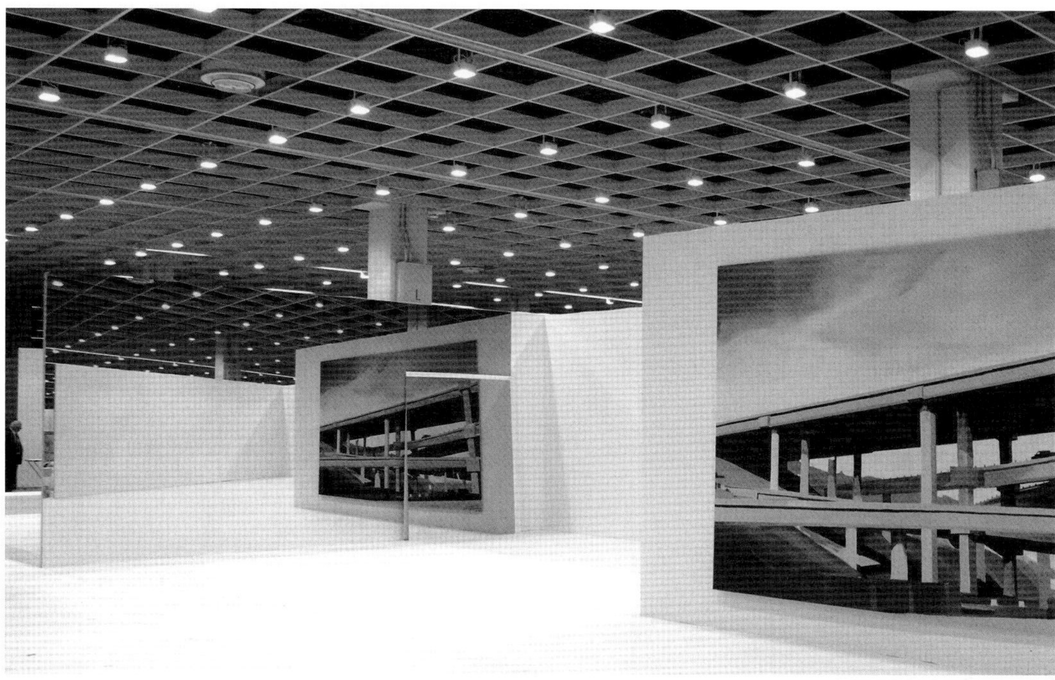

Open Space 2006, Art Cologne [site-specific installation at David Zwirner booth]

2000

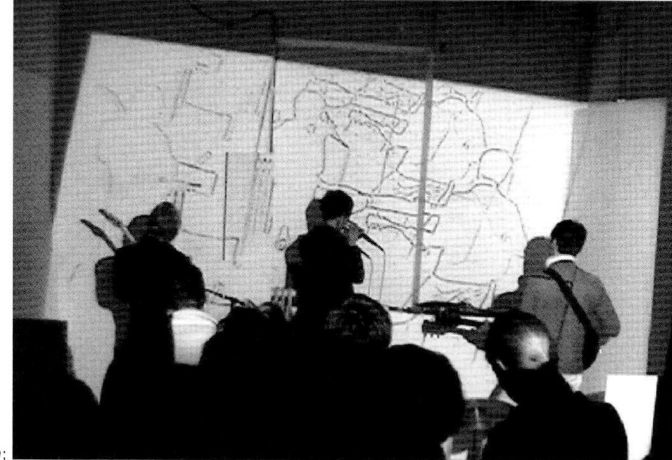

Benjamin v. Stuckrad-Barre – Blackbox; Guy Debord; Jim Isermann; Legendary Orgasm; Oppenheimer Bar; Recuperata Libertate

SELECTED GROUP EXHIBITIONS

2015

They printed it!, Kunsthalle Zürich
FAMED – Privileg der Umstände, Gabriele Senn Galerie, Vienna [part of curated by_vienna 2015: Tomorrow Today]
All Watched Over, James Cohan Gallery, New York
Individual Stories. Sammeln als Porträt und Methodologie, Kunsthalle Wien, Vienna [exhibition publication]
Une Saison Graphique 15, Gare du Havre, France [organized by Fonds regional d'art contemporain Haute-Normandie, Sotteville-lès-Rouen, France]

2014

Give Love Back, Museum für angewandte Kunst, Frankfurt
Infinite Jest, Schirn Kunsthalle Frankfurt [catalogue]
Wo ist hier? #1: Malerei und Gegenwart, Kunstverein Reutlingen, Germany

2013

I knOw yoU, Irish Museum of Modern Art, Earlsfort Terrace, Dublin [catalogue]

2012

Ändere dich, Situation!, Stadtgalerie Schwaz, Austria
Context Message, Zach Feuer, New York
Fremde überall / Foreigners everywhere: Contemporary Art from the Pomeranz Collection, Jewish Museum, Vienna [catalogue]
L'Institut des archives sauvages, Villa Arson, Nice, France
Made in Germany Zwei, Sprengel Museum Hannover, Kunstverein Hannover, and Kestnergesellschaft, Hanover [catalogue]
No Desaster. Sammlung Haubrok bei Falckenberg, Deichtorhallen Hamburg [catalogue]
Thomas Bayrle, Jürgen Krause, Michael Riedel, Jens Risch, Peter Roehr, Bischoff Projects, Frankfurt

2011

Books on Books, Swiss Institute, New York
Multiples & co, Villa du Parc, Centre d'art contemporain, Annemasse, France
So machen wir es. Techniken und Ästhetik der Aneignung / That's the way we do it: The Techniques and Aesthetic of Appropriation, Kunsthaus Bregenz, Austria [catalogue]

2010

And so on, and so on, and so on…, Harris Lieberman Gallery, New York
Die Blumen, COCO (Contemporary Concerns), Vienna
Funktionen der Zeichnung, Museum für Moderne Kunst, Frankfurt
Miroirs Noirs / Black Mirrors, Fondation d'entreprise Ricard, Paris
New Frankfurt Internationals: Stories and Stages, Frankfurter Kunstverein and Museum für Moderne Kunst, Frankfurt [catalogue]
Paradise Lost – Holidays in Hell, Centro Cultural Andratx, Andratx/Mallorca, Spain
Permanent Mimesis: An exhibition about Realism and Simulation, Galleria Civica d'Arte Moderna e Contemporanea, Turin [catalogue]
Von A Nach B, Von B Nach P/From A to B, From B to P, Bielefelder Kunstverein, Bielefeld, Germany [itinerary: *De A à B, de B à P/From A to B, From B to P*, Le Confort Moderne, Poitiers, France] [exhibition brochure]

2009

Best of Kunstraum Innsbruck 2004–2009, Kunstraum Innsbruck, Austria
Bridges and Tunnels, New Jerseyy at Hard Hat, Geneva

2014

Michael Riedel: Ohne Titel (A-Z / Die Traumdeutung)/Untitled (A-Z / The Interpretation of Dreams). Sigmund Freud Institute, Frankfurt [limited edition set of 50 portfolios]

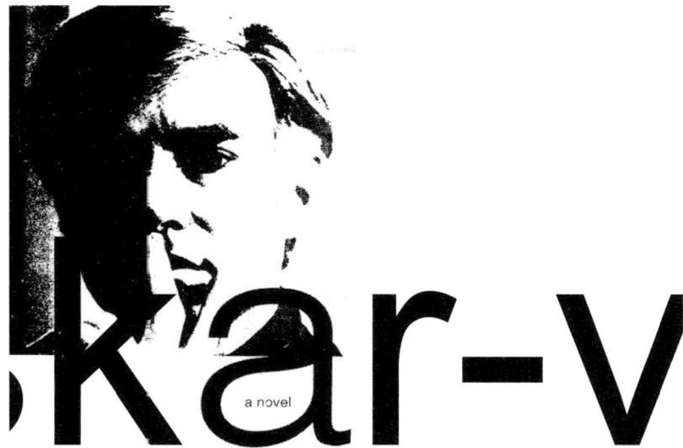

Michael Riedel: Oskar. Texts by Daniel Baumann, Michael Riedel, and Roberto Ohrt. David Zwirner, New York/London [revised and expanded edition; originally published in 2003]

"Michael Riedel." *Les Cahiers du Musée National d'Art Moderne* (Autumn 2014): cover; 4–23 [ill.]

2013

Riedel, Michael. "---- - - - - - - 'Goofiness' 'Production 'Things' 'Un 'Work' 'Yellow & (A (And (And (As (Buildings, (Chairs, (From (Or (You / 'With 'You 'Bob' 'Do 'Ending 'Fettered' 'Gino 'Grand I 'I 'In 'No 'The 'You' ' + 1. 11.5 14 18 1918 1928 1945, 1960s–1970s 1970's, 1978: 1979, 1979: 20,000 2010, 2010, 2012 20th 32." *ANNUAL* no. 5 (2013): 52–53

Riedel, Michael. "Linke Seiten Nr. 22." *Quart* no. 22 (2013)

Art Brut – Top of the Pops [cover artwork for Art Brut]

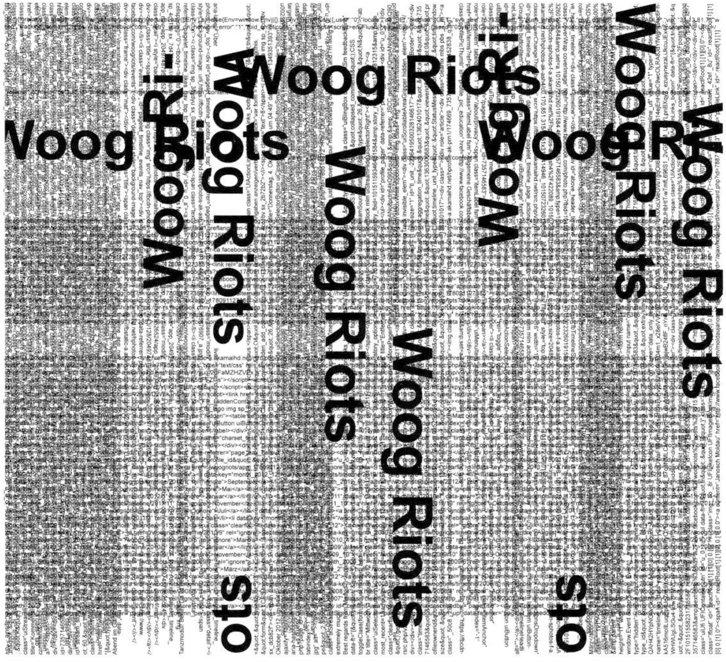

Woog Riots – From Lo-Fi to Disco [cover artwork for Woog Riot]

2012

Michael Riedel. Kunste zur Text. Edited by Max Hollein and Matthias Ulrich. Texts by Marcel Bugiel and Matthias Ulrich. Schirn Kunsthalle Frankfurt (exh. cat.)

Riedel, Michael. "Künstlerprojekt: Michael Riedel." *frieze d/e* (Summer 2012): 95–99 [ill.]

2011

Michael Riedel: The quick brown fox jumps over the lazy dog. Text by Michael Riedel. David Zwirner, New York [limited edition set of 17 booklets and 17 postcards]

Perlstein. Text by Michael Riedel. Koenig Books, London

2010

The quick brown fox jumps over the lazy dog. Edited by Michael Riedel and Florian Waldvogel. Text by Michael Riedel. Kunstverein Hamburg [limited edition set of poster, 10 booklets, and 10 postcards]

ZéroDeux (CMYK). Text by Michael Riedel. [limited edition set of 4 bound and printed magazines]

2009

Meckert. Text by Michael Riedel. Verlag der Buchhandlung Walther König, Cologne

2008

Der Meister von Flémalle und Rogier van der Weyden (CMYK). Text by Michael Riedel. [limited edition set of 4 bound and printed catalogues]

Gedruckte und nicht gedruckte Poster (2003–08)/Printed and Unprinted Posters (2003–08). Edited by Stefan Bidner. Text by Michael Riedel. Verlag der Buchhandlung Walther König, Cologne (exh. cat.) [two volumes] [published on the occasion of the solo exhibition *vicini ~~Michael S. Riedel~~ John Bo* at Kunstraum Innsbruck, Austria in 2007]

Spike (CMYK). Text by Michael Riedel. [limited edition set of 4 bound and printed magazines]

2007

Frieze (CMYK). [limited edition of 4 bound and printed magazines]

Sinnmachen beenden: Saab 95. / Stop Making Sense: Saab 95. Texts by Michael Riedel and Marcel Bugiel. Monobuch, Rüsselsheim, Germany

SK N E ST SSE . Text by Michael Riedel. Berlin (exh. cat.) [self-published]

2006

Tirala. Texts by Michael S. Riedel and Marcel Bugiel. Schlebrügge. Editor, Vienna (exh. cat.)

2005

Kühn Malvezzi. Text by Michael S. Riedel. Revolver, Frankfurt (exh. cat.) [published on the occasion of the solo exhibition *Momentane Monumente* at Aedes West, Berlin]

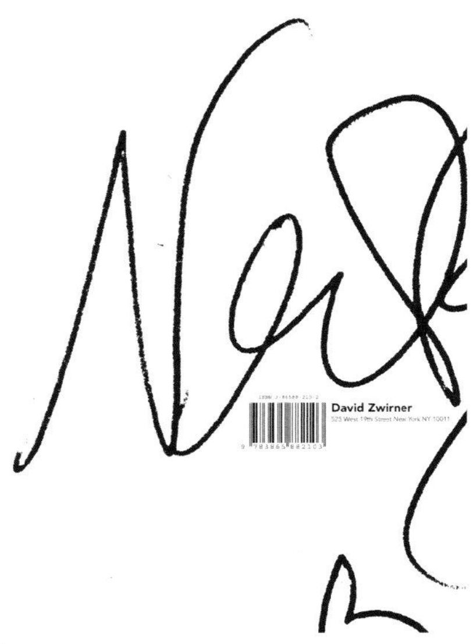

Neo. Text by Michael S. Riedel. David Zwirner, New York and Revolver, Frankfurt (exh. cat.)

2004

5. Teil (In a Glass Darkly). Text by Michael S. Riedel. Frankfurt [self-published]

Johnson Robert. Texts by Michael S. Riedel and Tobias Rehberger. Revolver, Frankfurt (exh. cat.) [published on the occasion of the exhibition *NOSNHO.-...... (ROBERT-JOHNSON)* at Galerie Michael Neff, Frankfurt]

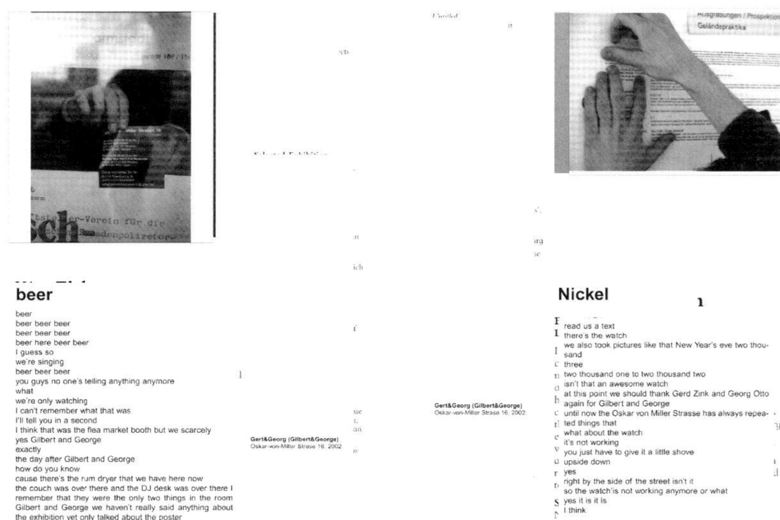

Quasi Portikus (False Frieze Art Fair Catalogue). Texts by Michael S. Riedel, Dennis Loesch, and Daniel Birnbaum. Revolver, Frankfurt (exh. cat.)

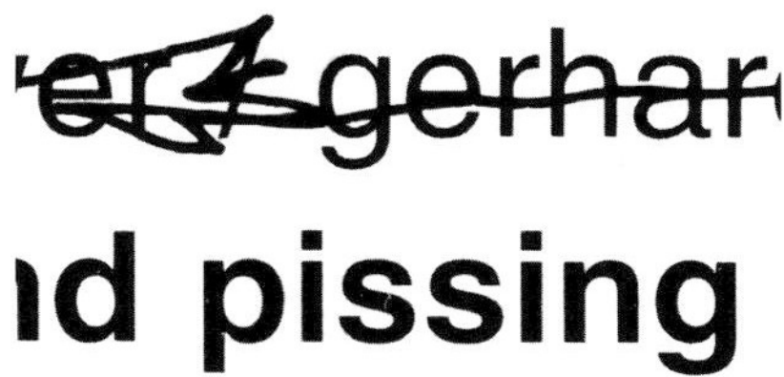

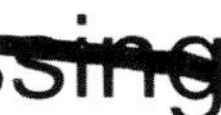

Scheissen und Brunzen (Shitting and Pissing). Text by Michael S. Riedel. Revolver, Frankfurt

2003

ABC Detroit. Text by Michael S. Riedel. x-15 Verlag [reprinted in 2008 by Monobuch, Rüsselsheim, Germany]
Dandy. Text by Michael S. Riedel. Frankfurt [self-published]
Oskar. Texts by Michael S. Riedel, Roberto Ohrt, and Daniel Baumann. Silverbridge, Paris

2002

Deutsch-Tedesco. Texts by Michael S. Riedel and Marcus Hurttig. x-15 Verlag [reprinted in 2007 by Monobuch, Rüsselsheim, Germany]

2001

Christopher Wool. Text by Michael S. Riedel. Frankfurt [self-published]
Riedel, Michael S. "1777,26 DM." *Subtropen* no. 5/09 (2001)
Riedel, Michael S. "Automatenstimmen." *Frankfurter Rundschau* (August-September 2001) [eight part series]
Riedel, Michael S. "Tausendsiebenhundertsiebenundsiebzig Mark." *Jungle World* no. 37/2001 (September 5, 2001)

2000

Blackbox. Text by Michael S. Riedel. Frankfurt [self-published]
Heldenplatz I. Text by Michael S. Riedel. Frankfurt [self-published]
Heldenplatz II. Text by Michael S. Riedel. Frankfurt [self-published]
Riedel, Michael S. "Abschriften." *Büchner* no. 8/10/11 2000; 1/3/4/5/6/7/8/9/10/12 2001 [one year column published monthly]

1999

Artforum. [self-published]
Velvet Years. Text by Michael S. Riedel. Frankfurt [self-published]

SELECTED ARTIST TALKS, LECTURES, PERFORMANCES & FILM SCREENINGS

2015

"Michael Riedel in conversation with Daniel Baumann," artist talk, Kunsthalle Zürich

2014

"8 Kunst & Publikation," artist talk, Hochschule für Grafik und Buchkunst, Leipzig; Akademie für Darstellende Kunst, Ludwigsburg, Germany
"Buchpräsentation Oskar," artist talk, Österreichisches Museum für angewandte Kunst (MAK), Vienna; Schirn Kunsthalle Frankfurt
"Michael Riedel in conversation with Bart Rutten" artist talk, Goethe-Institut, Amsterdam
"Michael Riedel in conversation with Gregor Muir," artist talk, David Zwirner, London

2013

"8 Kunst & Publikation," artist talk, Centre Georges Pompidou, Paris

2012

"8 Kunst & Publikation," artist talk, Bauhaus-Universität Weimar, Germany; Schirn Kunsthalle Frankfurt; Städelschule, Frankfurt
"Antrittsrede als neuer Leiter des Frankfurter Kunstvereins und des Künstlerhauses Wien/Speech as New Director of Frankfurter Kunstverein and Künstlerhaus Vienna," artist talk, Künstlerhaus Kino, Vienna [with Matthias Ulrich]
"Die Situationistischen Internationalen," artist talk, Freitagsküche, Frankfurt [with Daniel Birnbaum, Roberto Ohrt, and Kim West]
"Kunste zur Text (Algorithmen)," artist talk, Akademie der bildenden Künste – IKL, Vienna

2011
"8 Kunst & Publikation," artist talk, Einstein Auditorium, New York University; Kunsthaus Bregenz, Austria; Gabriele Senn Galerie, Vienna

2010
"8 Kunst & Publikation," artist talk, Akademie der Bildenden Künste, Vienna; Buchhandlung Walther König, Berlin; Fondation d'entreprise Ricard, Paris; Galerie Michel Rein, Paris; Sautter & Lackmann Bookstore, Hamburg; The Kitchen, New York
"Filmed Film Trailer," film screening, Metropolis Kino, Hamburg [organized in conjunction with the solo exhibition *The quick brown fox jumps over the lazy dog* at Kunstverein Hamburg]

2009
"Conversation between Michael Riedel and Dr. Eva Mongi-Vollmer," Städel Museum, Frankfurt
"Wie ihr wollt/As You Will," play reading, Kulturzentrum Mainz, Germany

2008
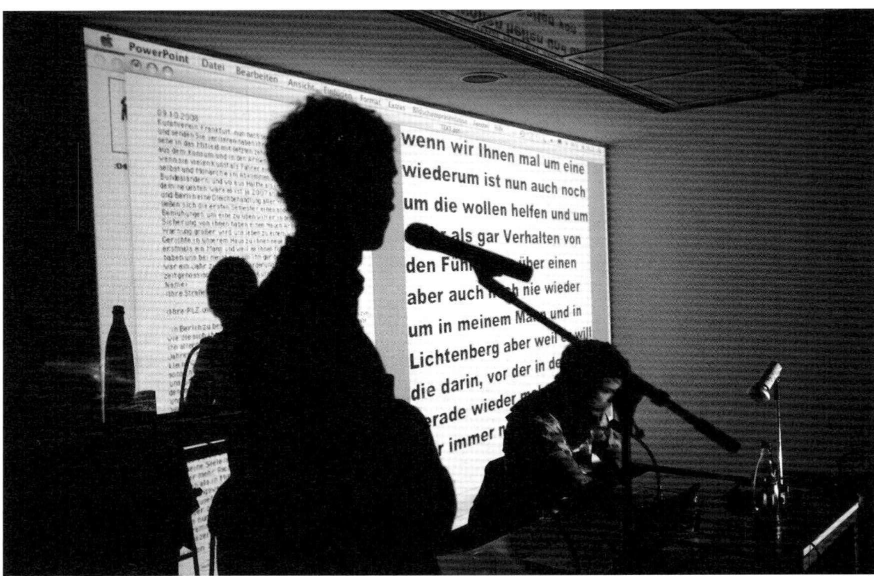

"Antrittsrede als neuer Direktor des Frankfurter Kunstvereins/Speech as New Director of Frankfurter Kunstverein," artist talk, Frankfurter Kunstverein, Frankfurt [with Daniel Baumann]
"Filmed Film," film screening, Shift Festival, Basel; Städel Museum, Frankfurt
"The Merry Nothing," Spike Talk, Kunsthaus Graz, Austria [with Daniel Baumann]
"Shift Talk with Michael Riedel," Shift Festival, Basel

2007
"Bruce Nauman," lecture, Akademie Nürnberg, Nuremberg, Germany
"Dandy," lecture, Kunstverein Braunschweig, Germany

2006
"Conferenced Conference of Anecdotes," recorded panel discussion from 2003 at Oskar-von-Miller Strasse 16, Hotel Blauer Bock, Munich
"Internationaler Frühschoppen," panel discussion, Virchowsaal, Berlin [with Jeppe Hein, Wilfried Kühn, Achim Lengerer, Gerhard Merz, and Brian O'Doherty; organized and filmed for video presentation part of the solo exhibition *24.04.2001 – 16.03.2006* at Galerie Michael Neff]

2004
"Buchpräsentation Oskar," artist talk, Deutsches Filmmuseum, Frankfurt; Kunstverein Hamburg; Neuer Aachener Kunstverein, Aachen, Germany

2003
"Buchpräsentation Oskar," artist talk, Gabriele Senn Galerie, Vienna

2002
"Dandy," recorded lecture of Michael Krebber and Fritz Heubach presented at the class of Michael Krebber, Städelschule, Frankfurt

2001
"Blackbox," recorded reading by Benjamin von Stuckrad-Barre, Stadttheater, Aachen, Germany
"Michal S. Riel," artist talk, class of Heimo Zobernig, Akademie der Bildenden Künste, Vienna

1997

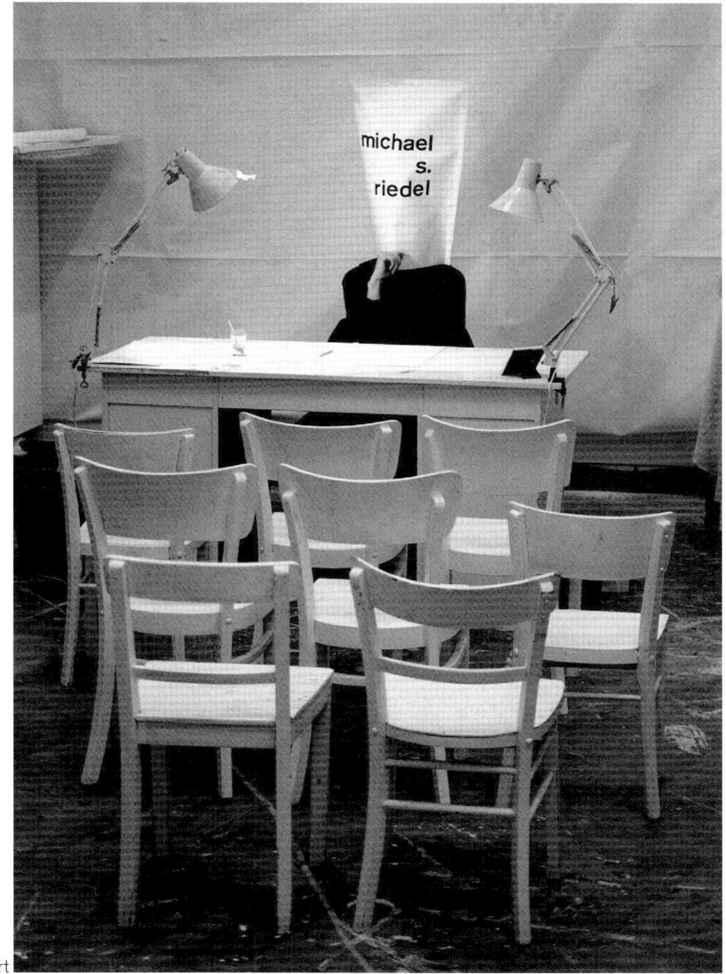

“Signetismus,” lecture, Städelschule, Frankfurt

Michael Riedel: Poster–Painting–Presentation

Published by
David Zwirner Books
529 West 20th Street, 2nd Floor
New York, New York 10011
+1 212 727 2070
davidzwirnerbooks.com

Editors: Michael Riedel, Lucas Zwirner
Project Manager: Todd Bradway
Copy Editor: Anna Drozda

Graphic Design & Color Separations: Büro für Gestaltung | Christian Bredl, Frankfurt
Printing: Benedict Press, Münsterschwarzach, Germany
Binding: Schaumann GmbH, Darmstadt, Germany

Typefaces: Akzidenz Grotesk, Arial
Paper: Inapa Infinity Gloss, Condat Matt Périgord

Photography Credits: Alex Delfanne, Fred Dott, Wolfgang Günzel, Florian Kleinefenn, Karl Kühn, Jason Mandella, Aurélien Mole, Marton Perlaki, Denis Prisset, Adam Reich, Jonathan Smith

Distributed in the United States and Canada by
ARTBOOK | D.A.P.
155 6th Avenue, 2nd Floor
New York, New York 10013
artbook.com

Distributed outside the United States and Canada by
Thames & Hudson, Ltd.
181A High Holborn
London WC1V 7QX
thamesandhudson.com

ISBN 978-1-941701-32-4
Library of Congress Control Number: 2016930350
Printed in Germany

Jacket: Details of *Untitled (update)*, *Untitled (drop)*, *Untitled (Slideshow)*, *Untitled (Link)*, *Untitled (method)*, *Untitled (poster)*, *Untitled (click 2)*, *Untitled (display 3)*, *Untitled (return)*, *Untitled (form)*, *Untitled (scroll)*, *Untitled (visible)*, 2010–2013

Cover: Detail of *Untitled (Correctable film ribbon for AX10/20/30)*, 2010